JESUS CHRIST
Is the
EASY and ONLY
Way to
HEAVEN

Published by Heaven Is Easy Ministries, Inc.
PO Box 540864
Lake Worth, Florida 33454
www.jesuschististheonlyway.org
www.heaveniseasy.org

ISBN-10: 0-615-52115-0
ISBN-13: 978-0-615-52115-2

Neither the publisher nor the author is engaged in rendering advice or services to the individual reader. Neither the author nor the publisher shall be liable or responsible for any loss, injury, or damage allegedly arising from any information or suggestion in this book. The options expressed in this book represent the personal views of the author and not of the publisher and are for information purposes only.

Unless otherwise indicated, all Scripture quotations are taken from the Holy Bible, New Living Translation, copyright © 1996, 2004, 2007 by Tyndale Foundation. Used by permission of Tyndale House Publishers, Inc., Carol Stream, Illinois 60188. All rights reserved.

FIRST EDITION 2011

JESUS CHRIST
Is the
EASY and ONLY
Way to
HEAVEN

By Tim Finley, sinner

Christianity, if false, is of no importance, and if true, of infinite importance. The only thing it cannot be is moderately important.
— C. S. Lewis (1898-1963)

Salvation = Faith + Nothing

This book includes more than 300 words in a detailed glossary, plus a timeline of important Christian events.

GIFT PAGE

"For God loved the world so much that he gave his one and only Son, so that everyone who believes in him will not perish but have eternal life. God sent his Son into the world not to judge the world, but to save the world through him."
John 3:16-17, Jesus' words

Date _____

To _____

From _____

I know for certain that I am going to Heaven and I want all my loved-ones and friends to spend eternity there too. You are one of them.

My eternal life in Heaven will not be the result of anything I have done, but what Jesus Christ did for me.

If you have not accepted Jesus Christ as your Savior, please read this book. If you are already a Christian, then this book will help you to become more knowledgeable.

DEDICATION

It is an honor to dedicate this book to my lovely wife, who –
like Jesus – forgets my many, many, many transgressions.

Ernest Hemingway once said, "There is nothing to writing.
All you do is sit down at a typewriter and bleed."

While writing this book I found out exactly what Mr.
Hemingway meant. Loveda spent hundreds of hours proofing
my book, putting on the final touches, and cleaning up my blood.
She was devoted enough to bleed with me. I honestly don't know
how to thank her except to tell her how much I love her.

I LOVE YOU!

Thank you Steve and David

COMMENTS REGARDING THIS BOOK FROM BOTH SIDES OF THE FENCE

EXCERPTS FROM STEVE BROWN'S LETTER

Hi Tim,

And I like your book, too…a lot. And it's not just because you said some nice things
about me.

Your book is theologically right on. Doesn't mean I agree with everything, but
everything is well within the bounds of orthodox theology. (I might have some
small quibbles with things like your view of the law – e.g., that it's not for Gentiles
– but even that is just a small disagreement and Christians differ on that. You
might be right because I'm wrong 50% of the time.)

But as I said, this is one of the most complete books I've read on these subjects. You've dealt with every question, every objection, every wrong road, every place where a pagan or believer would have a question about salvation and the Christian walk I can think of, and have done it with grace, clarity, and a crisp and readable style.

Bless,

Steve

Steve Brown is a radio broadcaster, seminary professor, and author. He served as a pastor for over twenty-five years, and now devotes much of his time to the radio broadcast Key Life.

A Professor of Preaching at Reformed Theological Seminary in Orlando, Florida, Steve also sits on the board of the National Religious Broadcasters. Traveling extensively, he is a much-in-demand speaker.

Steve is author of several books, including Follow the Wind, Approaching God, How to Talk So People Will Listen, *and* When Your Rope Breaks. *His articles appear in such magazines and journals as* Leadership, Decision, *and* Today's Christian Woman.

****

EXCERPTS FROM DAVID BERKOWITZ'S LETTER

Hi Tim,

Concerning your book, I appreciate the way you keep salvation and serving the Lord very simple. Even in here (in the prison church) there is a big emphasis on things like church attendance, prayer and Christian service - to a point where the line becomes blurred and men mistakenly get the impression that these things are needed to "stay saved." Legalism is unbelievably powerful because it's a concept that's entrenched in one's flesh. While these things are important and while every Christian should be involved in church and Christian service, and have an active prayer life too, we know these things do not mean salvation. They have nothing to do with the eternal security of the believer. So thanks for bringing all this out in your writings. God bless!

Yours in Christ,

David

David Berkowitz - AKA "Son of Sam," AKA "Son of Hope" - is currently serving 365 consecutive years in prison as punishment and repayment to society for his 13-month killing spree in the New York metropolitan area from late 1975 through 1977. In his book <u>Son of Hope</u>, <u>The Prison Journals of David Berkowitz, Volume 1</u>, *David states, "By God's grace I am living proof that anyone can be forgiven, if they want to be." Although still repaying his societal debt, David's sins were forgiven on Jesus' Cross 2,000 years ago.*

Notes:

CONTENTS

Your family tree may need pruning[1]

Throughout the world, billions of religious individuals are performing all sorts of rituals, hoping to earn their way to eternal life. You may be one of them.

Some folks dress in black, others in white. Some wear cute little caps, some shave their heads, others grow their hair long. Some kneel, some roll, others extend their hands toward the heavens and many fold them on their laps. Some sing, some chant, others holler, and some remain silent. A few sacrifice animals, yet some refuse to kill anything. Crazies blow up buildings, and gentle ones won't fight to defend themselves.

Most people's beliefs are inherited from their family, right or wrong. Many people's perception of what is right exists simply because that is what they were told to believe. Many children and young soldiers in the world today are being taught to kill, and that is how they will spend their lives, because that is what they were taught. There are also many moral people in the world who deserve Heaven, but who won't make it because they followed incorrect teachings, refusing or not bothering to seek the truth.

CHRISTIANITY IS THE ONLY MAJOR WORLD FAITH IN WHICH THE INDIVIDUAL RECEIVES ETERNAL LIFE IN HEAVEN AS A *FREE GIFT* SIMPLY BY BELIEVING. THERE IS ONLY ONE PATH TO HEAVEN!

JESUS CHRIST

---

1. This book will provide you with further information regarding pruning your family tree. Refer to Chapters 3 and 32 for more information.

 **Notes:**

Foreward

Tim Finley is at his best here!

I was raised Jewish, but accepted Jesus Christ as my Savior in 1991, at which time I understood the truth regarding the Messiah. My life was changed instantly and forever and I now consider myself a born-again Christian, while proudly retaining my Jewish heritage.

Tim Finley's book may anger some people, but it will also lead many others into the Kingdom of Heaven. I love it! It is direct, forthright, pulls no punches, and provides the reader with the opportunity to understand and accept the wonderful love of Jesus Christ. Tim's evangelistic heart is poured out with no filters in this book.

I've known Tim for over 10 years and I know him to be passionate about the truth and stubborn as a mule. Here he combines the best of both as he shares the truth of Jesus Christ, boiled down to its simplest form – just the way God intended it to be. Tim is honest, intelligent, and has a mission to make sure the religious entities of the world do not stop people from accepting the simple, beautiful truth of Jesus. Tim's genuine love of the Lord is reflected with hammering honesty and candor.

I do not know of another book like this! Read it – it will change and save your life! If you are already sure you know Jesus as Lord, then give it as a gift to every unsaved family member and friend. They will be thanking you in Heaven.

Jack Alan Levine
Pastor, Great Hope Church
Author of *Don't Blow It With God* and *Where the Rubber Meets the Road with God.*
Founding director of Voice of God Ministry, Inc.

 **Notes:**

Author's Note

When you sell a man a book, you don't sell him 12 ounces of paper and ink and glue – you sell him a whole new life.
Christopher Morley (1890-1957)

Are you really happy? I didn't think so. Most people in this world today are not truly happy; they are content at best. Seldom can we watch TV without seeing a commercial promoting an anti-depressant drug. Unhappiness is an epidemic, but this book will reveal a unique way that unhappiness can be cured forever. It is called Spirituality, and it is the only way to peace.

The most important question anyone should ask themselves is, "Am I sure I will go to Heaven when I die?" Our life on Earth is but a flicker in time, though eternity is forever. God wants all of his children to spend eternity with him in Heaven. Therefore, 2,000 years ago God made a simple plan achievable by everyone, everywhere.

Unfortunately, throughout the centuries religious leaders have complicated this simple plan into something called "religion." Before Jesus, God's people had a covenant (agreement) with God. But because of man's weakness, they were unable to abide by this *Old Covenant*, so God made a promise to make a *New Covenant*.

This *New Covenant* (I will use that term repeatedly throughout this book) is a gift of Spiritual birth that is receivable just by having faith, and it lasts forever. This book will answer all of your questions, and it will also explain how you can find peace and happiness today and forever.

You may be thinking, "If salvation is so easy, why does it take an entire book for me to understand it?" The answer is that salvation is easy, but undoing the false teachings and beliefs propagated throughout the centuries is difficult. God so loved the world that he made salvation simple; mankind made it complicated.

This book is not a manual that teaches how a person can become guilt-ridden by religion. It is about the amazing, miraculous, and abundant freedom from religion, and the infectious peace one inherits by accepting Jesus Christ as Savior.

There are many contributing factors to our gloom: unhappy childhoods, failed marriages, financial dilemmas, lack of (or excessive) education, physical appearance, poor health, family problems, guilt, boredom, addictions – the list goes on! Most of us would give anything to lead rich, full lives. Unfortunately, many individuals have no idea how to do that, don't have the time, or fear they will be ridiculed if they buck the trend of popularity.

We live in an era when everyone in the world is scrambling to keep up with the Joneses by acquiring as much *stuff* as they can. This comes with a price: failed marriages, kids on drugs, single-parent families, and all of those other things that accompany the fast life. We have become a society of "me, me, me," and "take, take, take." The world is moving quickly, and we are all trying desperately to keep up with it. The *accumulation of stuff* never has, and never will provide us with the ingredients necessary for tranquility. Materialism and self-centeredness isn't working, and faith in a Creator has taken a back seat.

There is another very serious problem in this country – we treat one another horribly. Self-centeredness has become so ravaging that it makes me wish I were a part of another species, a kinder one. We have always bragged that we are the most sophisticated of all the species, yet dogs get along better with cats than humans get along with each other. At least dogs and cats have a mutual respect for one another, which is more than I can say for humans. Yes, we humans have risen to the top intellectually, but our sophistication has not advanced the species. Instead, it has become a weapon of mass destruction – not only between nations, but also within families. Now is the time for you to take the leap of faith, and begin your everlasting Spiritual journey, and it begins by learning the basics and purpose of the Bible.

Throughout my years as a Christian evangelist, thousands of seeking people have told me they have picked up the Bible in an effort to read it, but put it down again because of its complexity. The problem is that the average person has very little idea what is between the covers of the Old and New Testament Bibles. Many have heard some of the intriguing stories, like Adam and Eve, Noah and the Ark, David and his slingshot, the baby in the manger, the crucifixion, and so forth. Sadly, that is the extent of the average individual's knowledge of where we came from, why we are here, and where we are going after we die. Even many lifelong Christians have very little knowledge about their faith; they claim to be Christians, but aren't sure what that really means.

I chose the epigraph, "When you sell a man a book, you don't sell him 12 ounces of paper and ink and glue – you sell him a whole new life," because I believe this book will change your life by clarifying the subject of Christian salvation once and for all. Not only does this book put Christians on the path of truth, it also provides all of the information to remain on that path. Often Christians have questions they are embarrassed to ask their pastors or other Christians, so this book was created to provide accessible and understandable answers to most questions.

 **Notes:**

About the Author (Testimony)

*But my life is worth nothing to me unless I use it for finishing the
work assigned me by the Lord Jesus — the work of telling others
the Good News about the wonderful grace of God.*

Acts 20:24

My name is Tim Finley, and I want to thank you for reading my book. I honestly
believe I am called by God to pursue this project just for you. He chose me
because, throughout my more than 60 years, I have been somewhat of a maverick.
Plus, I am probably not considered the typical Christian. But what is fantastic about
Christianity is that one does not have to be typical to fit in.

Even though I have always danced to the beat of a different drummer, I know that I
will spend eternity in Heaven. The best part is, it is not because of anything I have or
have not done, but what was done for me by a Jewish carpenter 2,000 years ago. That
revelation is what I am going to share with you.

My Beginnings

I was born in Canton, Ohio, and my parents moved eight miles away to Massillon,
Ohio, when I was four. I came out of the womb with ADHD, so I have been very
hyperactive throughout my life. I learned to control my hyper-activity 30 years ago
without medication. But in my younger days, the ADHD caused me to be very mis-
chievous. I did not do anything criminal, but I was extremely ornery.

As a very lively youngster, I attended a mainline church in Massillon where I bounced
off the walls, so I was looked upon as being less than a Christian. Although I learned
the basic stories of a Creator God, the Garden of Eden, Noah's Ark, and a guy named
Jesus, this church incorrectly taught that only well-behaved people go to Heaven,
and that all bad people go to Hell. They also taught that we would not know for certain where we would go until we got there.

The church leaders also spoke of the Ten Commandments as the way of measuring our standing with God. I knew that I could obey a few of the commandments, but obeying all of them was impossible. I had already broken several of the commandments without even trying. Feeling overwhelmed by religious laws, I turned my back on the demanding God who set up that unachievable system. Instead, I chose to go through life thinking I might end up in Hell. Because God's demands were so unattainable, I threw my hands up and just sinned more. My thought was, "Why not?"

Periodically, I heard the term *salvation*, but I chose not to listen because I was sure it would instill more religious guilt. By the time I reached my mid-20s, I was fairly certain that if I died I would go to Hell, even though I was not a bad person. I knew I could never be good enough.

My midlife crisis

By 1980, at the age of 34, I had become a successful stockbroker. As a big shot, my private office was located in a prestigious bank building overlooking the state capitol in downtown Columbus, Ohio, where I had relocated after a failed first marriage. I had an intercom on my telephone so I could give directives to a secretary, drove a new Cadillac that I parked in a valet-parking garage, wore expensive suits, and had about 20 pairs of fine leather executive-styled shoes that a shoeshine boy kept looking spiffy. All this, plus my new home in the country and a couple racehorses proved that I had arrived. Although I appeared to have it all, a midlife crisis took me to my knees.

Occasionally I read about Christianity and thought that maybe someday I could become good enough to live by God's rules but I was not convinced that Christianity was the true faith. There were so many religions from which to choose that I was very confused. I spent about a year studying all of the world religions and they all sounded reliable and moral. However, the more I studied, the more I was convinced that Jesus was God.

Jesus was the only religious leader who claimed to be God, was born of a virgin, and performed dozens of miracles. In addition to all of the other miracles, Jesus was crucified on a cross to pay for all of my sins, and then he rose after being dead for three days. That was really cool! All of the other religious leaders had died and remained dead, but Jesus came back from being dead and is still alive today.

I couldn't believe that we evolved from monkeys, as advocated by evolutionists, and that our life had no purpose. I was convinced there had to be more. I began an enthusiastic search for answers. In my quest, I desperately needed to find out three things:

1. From where did mankind come?

2. Why are we here?

3. Where do we go after we die?

Next, I purchased an easy-to-read New Testament Bible and attempted to comprehend what was between the covers. At first, it was confusing. But the more I read, the more I began to understand why it was the best-selling book ever. Little by little, with the help of my wife and the Holy Spirit, I started to understand. The more I understood, the more enthusiastic I became.

I found answers to my perplexing questions:

1. We were created by the God of Abraham, Isaac, and Jacob. He is the Creator God.

2. We have a purpose.

3. When our hearts make their last beat, we immediately go to a place called Heaven if we simply trust in the life, death, and resurrection of a carpenter named Jesus, who lived on this Earth 2,000 years ago as the incarnate representation of God.

I felt very good about the progress I was making, but there was still a void. A good client of mine suggested I attend a Cursillo retreat. He explained that it was a weekend sponsored by the Catholic Church, and he assured me that it would be worth my time. That weekend had a dramatic, life-changing, personality-altering effect on me. I had not yet accepted Jesus as my Savior, but the Holy Spirit had me in his grip.

I was still avoiding this Holy Spirit thing, until one day shortly following the Cursillo experience. A very pleasant-looking young female walked into my office pretending to seek investment advice. Although I had never met her before that day, I instantly felt very comfortable with her. Someway, the conversation very quickly switched from investments to Christianity.

She informed me that she was a Christian, and I was very proud to tell her that I was also. She said, "But have you been born again?" I cringed and told her I was born once and that was good enough. She replied, "That may be good enough for you, but it is not good enough for God, and it is not good enough to get you into Heaven." She insisted that in order for me to be a Christian, I had to accept Jesus as my Savior and be born Spiritually. In my heart, I knew she was right.

I listened very closely and thoughtfully, but the *born again* phrase really scared me. I was very honest with her regarding my apprehension. Still not being in a position of absolute peace and having the desire to be more knowledgeable, I continued to let her talk – knowing in my heart that her words were the truth.

Two hours later, after the stock market closed and our offices were being locked for the day, our conversation was moved to the alley behind the building. I was ready and she knew it. I also began to realize she did not walk into my office seeking investment advice, she was sent by God. I never saw her again after that day.

This young woman's message nagged at me for several days. A few mornings later, I got on my knees and said a prayer, accepting Jesus Christ as my Savior.

There were no fireworks, no instant changes. But I immediately knew that all of my past, all of my present, and all of my future sins were forgiven. It was not my imagination playing tricks on me. It was real. At that exact moment, I knew I was going to Heaven, not because of anything I had done, but because of what Jesus did for me.

No fanfare

On my knees, I nervously waited for my old nature to die and for a new creature to appear within my carcass. I was told that I would become a new creation, and I wondered if this new creation would remember me. I fully expected to begin speaking unrecognizable words and phrases and presumably experience an uncontrollable urge to roll around on the floor. None of it happened.

I got off my knees and walked into the kitchen, where the same bills laid on the table – still unpaid. Looking out the window, I was surprised to see the grass still needed mowing. Nothing had changed dramatically. No bells and whistles. I had no desire to shave my head, or to exchange my expensive business suits for a robe and sandals.

However, I will admit that a huge weight was lifted from my soul, because I had finally done what had been nagging me for years. I finally felt the peace and contentment of having tackled what I had run from for years. What I had anticipated to be a gigantic mountain was nothing more than a molehill. Yes, I finally knew that I was a full-fledged *born again Christian*. The most difficult part had been the many years of fear.

I took a shower, got dressed, and walked outside. The well-built 20-year-old neighbor girl was washing her car, and she looked as attractive as she did the day before. I had anticipated that my appreciation for the female gender was going to breathe its last breath when I was reborn, but obviously, it did not.

I am not going to bore you with details of my day-to-day activities, or with my month-to-month modifications, but my persona did gradually change.

> *He must become greater and greater, and I must become less and less.*
> John 3:30

The things that changed over the next year were as follows:

- I started to study the Bible vigorously and finally understood what I was reading. I still continue to research the Scriptures regularly, and I have also read dozens of additional theology books. The Bible is still my favorite.

- My horrible temper lessened dramatically, but I still have to count to 10 occasionally.

- I started to feel guilty for my tactics as a stockbroker, and eventually left the profession.

- I became more compassionate and understanding of others and their short-comings. In the words of George W. Bush, "Jesus softened my heart."

- My greed diminished, and then vanished.

- My pride diminished, and then vanished.

- I drove my car more slowly, so I wouldn't hurt anyone. I have had a perfect driving record for 30 years.

- I am not ashamed to tell someone I was *born again*, and to talk to them about Jesus.

Now I am cool because of the Spirit

Today, more than 30 years after my conversion, I can honestly say that I am still a normal red-blooded American man. I had really feared losing my masculinity and identity, but today I am more of a man because I am more like Jesus. I know he has a plan for my life that is different from your life's plan, or that guy's life plan, or that guy's life plan, or that guy's life plan. I still maintain my individuality; however, he has called upon me to participate in some very exciting and rewarding endeavors, including writing this book.

I believe the primary reason I was called to write this book was that I fully understand the enormity of God's overflowing goodness, verified by the death of his Son on the Cross. It was God who sent him to the Cross so that we may spend eternity in Heaven simply by our trusting in him as our Savior.

There have been many books written regarding evolution versus creation and many written regarding our life's purpose, but very few have been written regarding our eternal destination. Having been prompted by the Holy Spirit, who is stronger than I am, I decided to follow his instructions to write a book specifically regarding salvation.

I honestly believe the one true God of Abraham, Isaac, and Jacob is using me to change the way the world perceives him. I also believe that God is using me to present his simple plan of salvation the way it was designed from eternity past – not the way in which many of the churches and their religious leaders have misrepresented God's plan to suit their own agenda.

As a Christian evangelist

A Christian evangelist is someone who teaches that, according to the Bible, the carpenter named Jesus was God incarnate, and that Jesus is the only way to Heaven. By believing and trusting in Jesus' finished work on the Cross, an individual is born Spiritually – which ultimately results in receiving the gift of eternal life in Heaven.

A Christian evangelist also teaches that, according to the Bible, a person's good deeds are the Christian's way of thanking Jesus. But, a Christian's good deeds have no effect on his or her eternal destiny.

Being a Christian evangelist does not mean I live a sinless life, but it does mean I believe my sins were all paid for on the Cross. However, because of what Jesus Christ did for me, I attempt to live my life according to how I am instructed by the Holy Spirit who lives in me. I will be the first to admit that sometimes, although my spirit is willing, my flesh is weak. That is where amazing grace comes into play. I am going to teach you all about grace.

My deepest desire is to convince you that being a Christian does not make you a wimp, a weirdo, boring, or anything else that is sometimes attributed to people of faith. In my 30 years of being an evangelist, I have never met one person who regretted accepting Jesus as their Savior. You will not either.

In 2001, I moved to Lake Worth, Florida, where I felt the call to write this book. I have spent almost a decade making notes and studying the Scriptures because I am extremely dedicated to ensuring that you are taught the truth and not a denominational version, or a version that your neighbor or co-worker made up.

Yes, there are denominations that teach the truth, but it is my job to give you the foundation so that, when choosing a church, you will choose one that has sound doctrine. Basic Christianity is fairly simple, but theology can become very complicated. Consequently, it is vital that you start out on the right foot.

This book

This book provides you with all of the basics and then some. When an individual becomes a Christian, he or she is usually so excited that he or she charges forward recklessly. Recklessness can turn people off. Slow down and get it right. Look before you leap, and thoroughly investigate the terrain around where you might land. There is quicksand out there. Your mission as a Christian is to turn people toward Christ – not to scare them from him.

Notes:

About the Author's Wife (Testimony)

My name is Loveda Ruth Knore Finley, and I am the mother of three children – Tom Finley (step), Melissa (Finley) Nino (step), and Daveda Lynn Edgar-Smith and three grandchildren (step). I have always been very proud of our children, and we are a family.

I was born and raised in the hills of southern Ohio, the daughter of Calvin Waite Knore and Mabel Louise (Rapp) Knore. My mother was a stay-at-home mom, and my father worked in a steel mill. Mom and Dad had four children who shared one bedroom in the family's very modest home, which we fondly referred to as "our four-room shack with a path." The path led to the two-seater outhouse, which was periodically moved and backfilled.

According to most folk's standards, we were poor, but we didn't see it that way. A home overflowing with love doesn't need *things* to keep the family together. We were devoted Baptists, and I give credit to our moral Christian environment that kept us out of trouble. Sixty years have gone by, and I am still very proud of my siblings and their offspring for their good morals and accomplishments. All of us have attended college and/or have excelled in our careers. I am proud to say that both of my brothers have college degrees, one a master's and the other a doctorate.

At the age of 13, I accepted Jesus Christ as my Lord and Savior and displayed my proclamation by being water baptized in the Rocky Fork Creek in Ohio on a very cold March morning. I believed as strongly then as I do today; I have never lost my faith.

It was difficult being a Christian teenager, but fortunately I had many wise Christian friends and role models who encouraged me. There were also a few Christians who turned out to be not such good role models. I placed too much faith in church elders and pastors from time to time, and found they were only human with feet made of clay, and should never have been put on a pedestal. As I matured, and as a Christian, I realized that all Christians have transgressions and none of us deserves the gift of Christ's forgiveness, although we receive it anyway.

The love of one's family, plus the devotion to Jesus Christ as Lord, is what families and this country need today more than anything.

I truly believe that Tim and I were meant to present the forgiveness and the redeeming power of Jesus Christ to the world via this book.

Note from the author: *Although I am listed as the author, the credit for the finishing of the book goes to the woman who kept me going. I cannot tell you how many times I wanted to give up, but thanks to both my wife, Loveda, and the Holy Spirit of Jesus Christ – I got the job done. I asked her to write a little biography.*

This is important information that *must* be understood before you read this book.
Please, please, please!

Orthodox Evangelical

What is presented to you in this book is from an *orthodox evangelical* perspective.

Orthodox with a capital "O" refers to Eastern Orthodox Christians, a division within the early Christian Church that still exists today. The term *orthodox*, when in lowercase, as is the case for describing this book, refers to the traditional/historical Christian belief that the Bible is the Word of God, written by men, but inspired by the Holy Spirit. An orthodox Christian believes the original manuscripts of the Bible are without error or contradiction and that the Bible is the complete and sufficient revelation of God.

> *All Scripture is inspired by God and is useful to teach us what is true and to make us realize what is wrong in our lives. It corrects us when we are wrong and teaches us to do what is right. God uses it to prepare and equip his people to do every good work.* 2 Timothy 3:16-17

Evangelical is the word used to describe those Christians who believe we are saved (worthy of eternal life in Heaven) only by grace through faith. An evangelical believes that good deeds are a person's way of thanking God for the Blood of Jesus, but have no effect on one's salvation. This is referred to as the *Good News* or *Gospel of Jesus Christ.* In other words, this book has been written using the Old and New Testament Bibles as the authority for teaching that mankind is saved only by grace through faith.

Jesus was/is God

The book you are about to read was written by an American Christian, who believes it is my responsibility to proclaim and educate the world that Jesus Christ was, is, and always will be the one and only Creator God. I believe it is also the responsibility of the millions of others who believe that the God of Abraham, Isaac, and Jacob came to this Earth in the form of a man and died on the Cross to pay for the sins of all mankind to proclaim that Jesus is God. Also, to prove his divinity and his authority over death, Jesus arose from death, so that those who believe in him will have eternal life.

> *"For God loved the world so much that he gave his one and only Son, so that everyone who believes in him will not perish but have eternal life. God sent his Son into the world not to judge the world, but to save the world through him."* John 3:16-17, Jesus' words

This book is about Jesus Christ, but please don't be afraid

Many people become anxious when hearing or thinking about Jesus because the simple mention of his name reminds them of their sins. That is very sad because the name of Jesus should be a reminder of God's overwhelming love for us and his *forgiveness* of our sins, not a reminder of how bad we are, or how guilty we should feel. The New Testament refers to the *forgiveness of sin* more than it does *sin* itself, and that is the reason you should not be anxious or afraid.

Christianity is not a crutch

Let's make it perfectly clear that a man can become Spiritual (indwelled with the Holy Spirit) without being made weak. Contrary to what the boys down at the bowling alley may think, a decision to believe in something factual is not a weakness. It is generally the weak people who are afraid of the truth – courageous people face it.

This book's primary mission

The primary mission of this book is to powerfully teach the distinct difference between *salvation* and *discipleship*. Salvation has nothing to do with a person's behavior as is commonly taught. Simply trusting in Jesus Christ as one's Savior attains salvation, at which time the believer is born Spiritually.

Tragically, the colossal error of combining salvation (a gift) with discipleship (behavior) has been fabricated by organized religions to maintain control over their parishioners. This occurs in all world religions, including within many Christian denominations.

Combining salvation, which is a gift, with discipleship has caused many would-be Christians to reject learning about Jesus because they think salvation necessitates an impossible change of behavior and includes a lifestyle that is almost impossible for the normal person to live. Because of this, they think salvation is much too guilt-provoking. Many believe they are too flawed or too weak to be saved. This has been a dilemma since the ministry of Jesus began.

The *Good News* is that God came to Earth in the form of a man named Jesus to be a sacrifice for the sins of the entire world.

The intent of this book is not to diminish the benefits of good works and behavior, but to educate the individual. It is not *faith* plus *works* that saves a person; it is *faith* alone. However, if one's faith is real, it will be demonstrated by deeds.

The book's secondary mission

Although it is the primary purpose of this book to explain God's simple plan of salvation, the secondary mission is of equal importance: to humbly and lovingly introduce the newly-saved individual to God via the Holy Spirit, which is a wonderful experience that accompanies the gift of salvation. The moment a person is saved, the Holy Spirit becomes the *Counselor* of the Christian, enabling him or her to live the life God has planned. This is commonly called *discipleship.*

> *But the Holy Spirit produces this kind of fruit in our lives: love, joy, peace, patience, kindness, goodness, faithfulness, gentleness, and self-control. There is no law against these things!* Galatians 5:22-23

It is also not the intent of this book to teach individuals morality and proper behavior, as behavioral changes are the purpose of the Holy Spirit and the written Word of God.

Once saved – always saved

This book teaches that once a person is saved, they are saved forever. This means that salvation cannot be lost. If you are a saved person, and you are under the impression you can lose your salvation, then I ask you, "Which of your sins did Jesus *not* die for?"

Understanding the meanings of *atonement, justification, reconciliation, regeneration,* and *santification* and their differences can be as important as understanding the difference between salvation and damnation. Below are the definitions of these terms, which you must examine and understand to appreciate God's simple plan.

Atonement means compensation for a loss. In Christianity the term **atonement,** when used to describe Christ's death on the Cross, means that his shed Blood was the propitiation (a gesture of reconciliation to gain or regain the favor of someone or something) for the sin of mankind. God offers the invitation to all, but it is only those who respond in faith that receive Spiritual birth.

Justification is what saves. When we are **justified**, it means that we are made righteous through **grace** because of the Blood of Christ. God imputes the Christian's righteousness because of his love for us. It is a gift and it is not earned.

Reconciliation is used to describe what was accomplished when Christ died on the Cross, and the fact that his shed Blood satisfied God's judgment. Christ's Blood reconciled us to God.

Regeneration is the term used to identify the act of being **born again** and the internal change in which the Christian receives Spiritual life in addition to the physical (carnal) life.

Sanctification is the growth process of the believer by lessening sinful behavior and yielding one's life to the guidance of the Holy Spirit. This adaptation takes place after a person has been justified, and is not instantaneous as is justification. It is a combination of the saved person's efforts combined with the counseling of the Holy Spirit. Sanctification is the result of a Christian becoming a **disciple** (follower) of Christ subsequent to being Spiritually born.

It is important for you to realize there are many disciples of Christ, who have not accepted him as Savior, and thus have not been born Spiritually. Following the moral teachings of Jesus Christ is not the method for being born Spiritually. A person must actually agree that the death and resurrection of Jesus is their only means of receiving eternal life. Salvation is by faith and not by works.

Sanctification, or lack thereof, has no effect on justification. In other words, if a person fails to follow the guidance of the Holy Spirit and lives a life that lacks Christian deeds, that person continues to be justified. If you think you can lose your salvation, or that obtaining salvation is difficult, you are going to love this eye-opening book.

Here is something to think about: If you could lose your salvation, how would you get it back? The answer is good behavior, right? But that would make *you* the savior, *not* Jesus. If you are the savior, then Jesus died for nothing, right?

No, you cannot lose your salvation. Jesus is your Savior. His death on the Cross paid your penalty for sinning from the time you were born until the time you die.

Redundancy versus repetition

This is the perfect point to address the matter of *redundancy* versus *repetition.* The term *redundant* is defined as something unnecessary. Every effort has been made in this book to not be redundant.

However, *repetition* is how we learn. The trick is to teach by utilizing repetition without being redundant. God's plan of salvation is so simple, and so permanent, that many people find it difficult to comprehend. In order for you to totally grasp this simplicity, it will be repeated many times. Please excuse this if it offends you.

When I taught my children to look both ways before crossing a street, I didn't tell them just once and hope they remembered. I repeated it hundreds of times so they would understand and remember. I am sure they got tired of hearing it, but a car never hit them.

This book addresses many who know very little about Christianity. Therefore, I took the liberty of repeating the most important doctrines multiple times to be certain the new Christian does not forget. My editors warned me this may offend some readers, but I was led by the Holy Spirit to follow his supervision.

The Holy Bible contains approximately 30,000 verses on many topics, and the same message is repeated multiple times, so I believe the Lord advocates repetition. An example of this is the first four books of the New Testament (Matthew, Mark, Luke, and John) are very similar. The great Apostle Paul also repeats the same message throughout his letters.

Plurality

This book has two primary authors – Tim Finley and the Holy Spirit. When you see the word "we" used in reference to the compilation of the book, it is usually referring to these two authors. In addition to the assistance of the Holy Spirit, I also received input from theologians, my wife, family members, friends, editors, and proofreaders. I was criticized by a very highly respected pastor/scholar who was kind enough to edit my book for theological accuracy prior to publication. He was critical of my including the Holy Spirit as functioning through me as I wrote. I immediately asked him if he ever gives credit to the Holy Spirit for assisting him in his ministry, and his answer was, "Of course." So, I asked this pastor why the Holy Spirit could work through him when delivering a sermon, but not work through me as I write. That quickly ended his censure.

Capitalization

Certain words not usually capitalized were shown respect throughout this book by being capitalized, such as: *God, Cross, Spiritual, Heaven* and *Hell* when they refer to specifics.

> **God**: The term *god* has become pluralistic with many people conjuring up their own idea of a god. When referring to the God of Abraham, Isaac, and Jacob – the term **God** was revered with a capital "G."

> **Cross**: *Cross* was capitalized when referring to the specific Cross upon which Jesus was crucified.

> **Spiritual**: In today's cultures, the term **spiritual** has become very popular, having multiple meanings. Many non-Christians describe themselves as **spiritual** when referring to their **emotions** or **moods**. In this book, when referring to the indwelling of the Holy Spirit, the terms **Spiritual** and **Spirituality** were capitalized to differentiate between the indwelling of the Holy Spirit and a person's spiritual emotions or moods.

> The following passage makes it clear that Satan is a spirit, so beware:

> *You used to live in sin, just like the rest of the world, obeying the devil—the commander of the powers in the unseen world. He is the spirit at work in the hearts of those who refuse to obey God.*   Ephesians 2:2

> **Heaven and Hell**: These are literal places, such as Miami and Florida so they deserve capitalization.

Dead or alive

You will see the terms *dead* and *alive* frequently in this book, but they have a different meaning in Christianity than when used in everyday life. People usually define the word *dead* as meaning that a person's organs are lifeless, and *alive* as meaning that one's organs are functioning. However, in Christendom, the terms *dead* and *alive* refer to a person's Spiritual condition, which ultimately refers to a person's eternal destination. The following passage is an example of how the terms are used Biblically.

"I tell you the truth, those who listen to my message and believe in God who sent me have eternal life. They will never be condemned for their sins, but they have already passed from death into life." John 5:24, Jesus' words

In order for a person to go to Heaven, a person must be *alive* Spiritually. If a person is not alive Spiritually, he is referred to as *dead*, and that means he will go to Hell. One becomes Spiritually alive when the Holy Spirit comes to live in him, which takes place at the instant of salvation.

The Triune nature of God

Throughout this book, you will read the names God, Lord, Creator, Jesus, Christ, Jesus Christ, and the Holy Spirit used hundreds of times. Please be advised they are all referring to the same person, as you will learn by reading this book.

No coincidence

Your reading this book is not a coincidence. You are reading this book because it is in God's plan. The God we discuss in this book is the God of Abraham, Isaac, and Jacob – the Creator of all things. He is also the first person of the Godhead, as Jesus is the second, and the Holy Spirit is the third.

The Holy Bible is the source

This book is based on the teachings of the Old and New Testaments of the Holy Bible, although the New Testament was its primary source. I am utilizing these historical recordings because I have never found anything that is more authoritative, nor have I ever encountered any conclusions written by anyone, anywhere or anytime that delivers so much wisdom. If you can provide me with something that has more historical or practical data, I may change my mind. In the meantime, I believe the Bible to be the infallible, inspired Word of God.

> *For the word of God is alive and powerful. It is sharper than the sharpest two-edged sword, cutting between soul and spirit, between joint and marrow. It exposes our innermost thoughts and desires.* Hebrews 4:12

> *All Scripture is inspired by God and is useful to teach us what is true and to make us realize what is wrong in our lives. It corrects us when we are wrong and teaches us to do what is right. God uses it to prepare and equip his people to do every good work.* 2 Timothy 3:16-17

Know what it means

The author was careful not to pick one lone verse of Scripture regarding a subject, and then overworking it in order to win the reader to one way of thinking. This is a common mistake. When utilizing the Bible to establish doctrine, the Christian must consider God's *entire* message and not just a few select verses. Knowing what the Bible says and knowing what it means are two different things. It requires the Spirit of God living in the reader to understand its meaning.

Church

The words *Church* and *church* are used frequently. When capitalized, it means the entire body of Christ's believers. When lowercased, it refers to a building with attendees who profess to be Christians. The term *church* means: group of people who are called together.

Straight from the Bible

It is the intent of this book to present Christianity in its original form, as the Apostles knew it and taught it. Throughout the years, theologians, pastors, church leaders, and other Christians have formed unwavering opinions that they insist should be accepted by everyone else. Christianity can become a very complex atmosphere, even though its formation was very basic. The problem is that people have fashioned it into a complicated system. Hopefully, this book will help to simplify it.

The term *religion*

The word *religion* is derived from the Latin *religare*, meaning "to tie or bind." *Religious* means: devout, pious, and concerned with religion. Religion usually requires "work," which is not in the plan of salvation. You must remember salvation is a gift that does not require work. Therefore, we have tried to refrain from using the word *religion*, or any derivative, when discussing Christianity. There are instances in which those terms were used to make a description more clear. Keep in mind that it was religious people who wanted Jesus crucified because he was not religious.

Glossary

In the back of this book, you will find a glossary of Christian terms, many of which I did not use because they pertain to a more in-depth study of theology. However, this glossary has been included in anticipation of your continued study of the New and Old Testaments and the history of Judaism and Christianity. I hope that you will keep this book nearby as a tool for your growth.

Dates

Scholars differ regarding many dates in Biblical records. Therefore, it was impossible to be precise regarding the dates presented. Those that are listed should be used only as a guide regarding the period of time in which an event occurred.

Faith without fanaticism

Often people are afraid of studying Christianity because they fear they might become a religious fanatic and their friends will laugh at them. Yes, there are people who are fanatical about their faith, but they represent a small percentage. Chances are that you will not become a fanatic. But even if you do, so what? Quit worrying about what other people think!

Disclaimer

I, the author of this book, am neither a theologian nor a scholar. I am a humble sinner saved by grace through faith who daily, for 30 years, has studied the Scriptures and the interpretations by theologians and scholars.

Throughout this book, you will see many quotations. This is not a textbook and is only designed to provide the reader with information I obtained from my experiences, my research, my interpretations, my thoughts and impressions. If a quote is incorrect or misrepresented in any way, it was strictly unintentional.

For instance, I cannot give a citation regarding my source for the definition of *Heaven*. I have defined Heaven as I understand it through reading the Scriptures and as interpreted and described by many other authors. This method of interpretation applies throughout this book.

I have done my utmost to provide the reader with accurate and concise information but, like me, this book is imperfect in many ways. I sincerely apologize for any errors, omissions, etc.

 **Notes:**

PART ONE

Your Eternal Evaluation

 **Notes:**

1

Where will you spend eternity?

Faith is the confidence that what we hope for will actually happen, it gives us assurance about things we cannot see.

Hebrews 11:1

Most people spend more time planning a two-week vacation than they do thinking about where they will spend eternity. Yet we should all face reality and ask ourselves where we go following our last heartbeat. This is the most important question one must ask oneself. There are only three plausible answers: Heaven, Hell, or just plain dead. The latter is a possibility, but I believe in Heaven and Hell. But how does one get to Heaven?

Sadly, during the last 2,000 years many religious leaders in all levels of Christianity, from small churches right through large denominations, have convoluted the Holy Scriptures to suit their own agendas, causing many of their followers to be misled about various truths. The most serious of these convolutions is how one receives eternal life in Heaven.

Furthermore, most Christian authors devote their pages to informing the reader what they have done, and are doing, to please God. While this may be good, very few Christian books and articles inform readers what God has done for them. What we do for God is miniscule compared to what he has done for us.

The most important thing God has done for humankind is to make getting into Heaven very easy. Because so many preachers, authors, and teachers spend an abundance of time emphasizing their good deeds toward God, most people believe we must add to what God has done so we may *earn* an eternal place where the streets are lined with gold and there is no sickness or pain. Not so. God wants everyone to enjoy this paradise so much that he made it an *easy reach*. This *easy reach* is one of the results of a phenomenon called *salvation*, an immediate Spiritual birth that saves a person from eternal punishment and allows him to live in a daily personal relationship with God from this life into the next, which is known as Heaven.

This overview explains what God did for humankind when he sent his Son to die on the Cross, and how his Son's resurrection gives believers eternal life in Heaven. When you are finished reading this, you may find God's simple method for salvation too easy to believe, but you will not be confused.

A wager worth placing

Pascal's Wager is an inspiration proposed by French mathematician, physicist, and religious philosopher Blaise Pascal (1623-1662), which can be found on the Internet. Pascal suggested that even though the existence of God cannot be determined through reason, a person should wager as though God exists. In other words, it makes more sense to believe in God than not to believe. If you believe, and God exists, you will be rewarded in the afterlife. If you do not believe, and he exists, you will be punished for your disbelief. If God does not exist, you have lost nothing. The wager is this:

> God either exists or He doesn't. Based on the testimony, both general revelation (nature) and special revelation (Scriptures/Bible), it is safe to assume that God does in fact exist. It is abundantly fair to conceive, that there is at least a 50% chance that the Christian Creator God does in fact exist. Therefore, since we stand to gain eternity, and thus infinity, the wise and safe choice is to live as though God does exist. If we are right, we gain everything, and lose nothing. If we are wrong, we lose nothing and gain nothing. Therefore, based on simple mathematics, only the fool would choose to live a Godless life. Let us see. Since you must choose, let us see which interests you least. You have nothing to lose. Let us estimate these two chances. If you gain, you gain all; if you lose, you lose nothing. Wager, then, without hesitation that He is.

That sounds like a wager worth placing. This principle demonstrates that it is sensible to seek God.

The following is an outline of how one receives eternal life in Heaven, according to the Christian belief. Remember that the term *believe* means "to accept as true, have faith, and trust." Believing does not mean that you will never have doubts. Belief and faith require a trust that does not depend on proof. Sometimes believing in God is difficult, but when most people lay their head on the pillow at the end of the day, I believe they know the truth.

Heaven

Heaven is the dwelling place of God, and it is where those who accept Jesus Christ as Savior will spend eternity. The word *Heaven* is used almost 300 times in the New Testament Bible. It is beyond the region of the air and clouds, and of the planets and stars. It is called "the third Heaven" because it is above the visible heavens.

The Scriptures tell us that there is no sin, evil, tears, pain, or sorrow in Heaven.

Most major religions believe in a heaven, but Christianity is the only major religion that believes a person can go there based strictly on faith in Jesus as the Savior. Most religions believe entrance into their heaven is conditional on having lived a "moral life," or by their continually making sacrifices.

Christianity teaches that from the time of original sin God required sacrifices from his people. This sacrificial ritual lasted only until the Savior Jesus made the ultimate and final sacrifice on the Cross. Cain and Abel brought sacrifices to the Lord, but Cain's was offensive because he brought fruit. Abel's was acceptable because it was the firstborn of his animal flock.

Judaism, as illustrated in the Old Testament, is a perfect example of a religion that demanded sacrifices as payment for sin. God commanded the nation of Israel to perform numerous sacrifices according to specific procedures prescribed by God. God commanded animal sacrifices so that the human being could receive temporary forgiveness of sin. The animal served as a substitute, which died in place of the sinner. But the sacrifice was merely temporary and had to be offered continuously. These Old Testament sacrifices were a foreshadowing of Christ's sacrifice on our behalf.

Heaven is a place for only perfect people. Unfortunately, no one is perfect. But wait! There is *Good News*. What continuous animal sacrifices represented in the Old Testament, Jesus accomplished once and for all in the New Testament. We are made perfect in God's eyes simply by accepting the Jewish carpenter named Jesus, who took our sins to the Cross as Savior. His Blood was the ultimate and final sacrifice for all of humankind. Isn't that amazing!

The remainder of this book will discuss this in detail, plus you will learn that Jesus' resurrection proved that he had the power to overcome death, which gives believers the same power over death.

Of special note: As a Christian evangelist, one of the most frequent questions that I am asked is if people's pets will go to Heaven. I have read several books on the subject and the commentaries of more than 60 pastors from many denominations, all of whom emphatically state they believe the Bible is clear that our pets will be in Heaven.

Hell

Christians believe that people who do not accept Jesus Christ as their Savior must spend eternity in Hell. Most major religions believe those who do not go to their heaven will spend eternity in a hell.

Many people prefer to not believe there is a place of suffering to which a loving God would send them eternally, especially if they have not done something horrible. However, if you believe in Heaven, it makes sense that there must be a Hell. The misconception throughout the world is that God will allow only "good" people to go to Heaven, and that he sends all "bad" people to Hell. That is not how it works, according to the Word of God.

The misery of Hell will consist of: the deprivation of the vision and love of God, exclusion from every source of happiness, perpetual sin, remorse of conscience in view of the past, malevolent passions, the sense of the just anger of God, and all other sufferings of body and soul that are the natural results of sin, or that the law of God requires as penal inflictions. There is a Hell, and I choose Heaven.

2

Millions will love this book, but many will hate it

There are no easy steps to witnessing! No painless, unembarrassing methods! You must bring men to see that they are filthy sinners under the wrath of God who must flee to Christ for mercy. That is offensive. And there is no way to coat it with honey.

Walter J. Chantry (born 1938)

This book is not a manual that teaches how a person can become religious. Religion is an undertaking people around the world practice in a feeble attempt to reach up to God. Christianity is God gently reaching down to us.

This book is about freedom *from* religion – the freedom that one receives by accepting Jesus Christ as Savior. Christianity is a freedom in which Jesus came down to us, eliminating the need for religion.

> *"For God loved the world so much that he gave his one and only Son, so that everyone who believes in him will not perish but have eternal life. God sent his Son into the world not to judge the world, but to save the world through him."* John 3:16-17, Jesus' words

There is just one God and his name is Jesus!

Many will hate this book because it is all about the one true God, the Creator of all things, who came to Earth in the form of a Jewish carpenter named Jesus, who was crucified on the Cross to forgive the world of its sins, and who rose from death to demonstrate his ability to overcome death.

Jesus Christ was an actual person recognized by respected historians to have done what is recorded in the New Testament Bible. Many love him, but many hate him – usually because their ancestors told them to hate him, or because he reminds people of their sins.

Who was Jesus?

In the past decade several fictional books have been published concerning Jesus and his life that have left many people perplexed about the truth. Sadly, most of those who have read these tales have never read the best-selling book ever published – the Holy Bible. Their lack of research has caused them to be confused.

To further complicate this "Who was Jesus?" dilemma, there are many false world religions that proclaim individuals other than Jesus to be God. These well-meaning but false beliefs cause many people to become *pluralists*, believing there may be many paths to eternal life. Pluralism sounds good, but in reality, it is ludicrous. Pluralism causes many would-be Christians to remain on the fence. My friend, it is time to get off that fence and make a commitment based on *facts*. Remaining on the fence is not the place to be if it affects your eternal life. Your indecision may have sizzling consequences.

There is a Hell

This book also discusses the realities of Heaven and Hell and briefly describes their differences. Many do not want to believe that a loving God would allow someone to spend eternity in Hell. However, those who have studied the history of God's retribution understand that while he is loving (that is why he died on the Cross), he can be merciless to those who disobey him. This is his world and he calls the shots, whether you like it or not.

The truth about Heaven

Several years ago, Barbara Walters anchored a TV show titled, *Heaven – Where is it? How do we get there?* Ms. Walters traveled the world seeking answers from many theologians. Nine out of 10 theologians who were polled admitted they believe in Heaven. Unfortunately, Ms. Walters' search had so many varied opinions that it left the audience hanging.

This book leaves nobody hanging. It presents overwhelming historical and Spiritual evidence that enables the reader to have an opinion based on facts rather than fiction. Unlike Ms. Walters, this book answers those questions regarding where Heaven is and how to get there. By reading this book, you will know more about Christian salvation than most Christians, including some pastors.

The Good News is that getting to Heaven is easy

You may be asking why you should accept Jesus Christ rather than one of those other guys. There are three great reasons to accept Jesus Christ. The first is because Jesus Christ was, is, and always will be the Creator God. You will learn more about him later in this book, and it will convince you. Second, his gift of eternal life in Heaven (unlike the other guys' plans to get there) is free to all who believe. Nothing is better or easier than that. Third, although eternal life should be the primary concern of all humans, not only does Jesus Christ offer eternity in Heaven, he also provides believers with a peaceful and joyful life while on Earth. Jesus is the Prince of Peace.

Satan is the father of the big lie that salvation is obtained by good behavior!

> *"Why can't you understand what I am saying? It's because you can't even hear me! For you are the children of your father the devil, and you love to do the evil things he does. He was a murderer from the beginning. He has always hated the truth, because there is no truth in him. When he lies, it is consistent with his character; for he is a liar and the father of lies."*
> John 8:43-44, Jesus' words

Satan is referred to by several names in the Scriptures. The following are a few of his many names: Lucifer, the prince of the world, the prince of darkness, the devil, the liar, the father of lies, the accuser, the deceiver, the old serpent, the god of this world, the tempter, the enemy, the wicked one, the dragon, the piercing serpent, the angel of light, the adversary, the murderer, the roaring lion, the oppressor, the son of the morning, the dragon that is in the sea, the angel of the bottomless pit, the prince of the power of the air, the prince of the demons, the thief.

Satan is a key personality throughout the Scriptures. He is introduced in the beginning of the Book of Genesis, but his fate is sealed in the Book of Revelation.

The origin of Satan/Lucifer

Satan did not begin as a devil. He began as an angel named Lucifer, but because he was given free will he rebelled against God, and so was cast from Heaven to the Earth, where he can disguise himself as an angel of light. The word *Lucifer* means "the light bringer."

These people are false apostles. They are deceitful workers who disguise themselves as apostles of Christ. But I am not surprised! Even Satan disguises himself as an angel of light. So it is no wonder that his servants also disguise themselves as servants of righteousness. In the end they will get the punishment their wicked deeds deserve. 2 Corinthians 11:13-15

Therefore, God didn't create a devil, but with the power of free choice, Lucifer transformed himself into a devil by his own free choice of rebellion against God.

Facts about Satan

> ➢ Satan instigates false doctrine.
> ➢ Satan influences misinterpretation of Scripture.
> ➢ Satan cannot be two places at one time, but dispatches demons.
> ➢ Satan cannot tempt a believer without God's permission.
> ➢ Satan is the author of confusion.
> ➢ Satan wants people to think salvation is difficult.

For centuries, religious leaders have lied to their followers; insisting that Heaven is a reward for good deeds. Tragically, most folks think that good people go to Heaven and bad people go to Hell.

This book drives home what the Great Apostle Paul stated in Romans:

And if by grace, then it is no more of works, otherwise grace is no more grace. But if it be of works, then it is no more grace; otherwise work is no more work. Romans 11:6 (KJV)

Eternal life in Heaven is a gift to all who will accept it. A gift is free!

Contrary to man's belief, it is harder to stay out of Heaven than it is to get in. Most people believe we gain entrance into Heaven by trying to follow the Ten Commandments or by being a good person. The Ten Commandments were given only to the Jews. When God came to Earth in the form of a man named Jesus, the Ten Commandments were fulfilled by his death on the Cross. We are not bound by laws written on stone, but by the love of Jesus Christ, while his Holy Spirit guides and counsels us.

Sadly, many Christian churches incorrectly teach that one receives eternal life in Heaven by obeying God's laws. This is not Biblically correct.

I was a doubter

Most of my life I had a difficult time believing in a devil. That concept seemed a little too much like an evil comic book personality. Even after I accepted Jesus as my Lord and Savior, I had trouble accepting the reality of such an evil character. One day I asked a friend what he thought, and he simply replied, "If you believe in God, you must believe in the Satan."

Soon after my conversion, I ran across a short yet powerful Bible verse that has freed me from the overwhelming anxiety caused by feeling the two opposite forces of good and evil. Whenever I feel the presence of Satan, I just repeat this two or three times and he is gone:

> So humble yourselves before God. **Resist the devil**, and he will flee from you.
> James 4:7

I put the words *resist the devil* in bold type because that is the most important part of this verse. I believe that if you constantly resist him, he will eventually leave you alone. I simply refuse to accept him into my presence. When I feel him getting near, I just boldly say, "Get out of here, Satan," and he goes away. This really works, so I am going to abide by my own rule and resist him by not giving him much recognition in this book.

You have been forgiven

Jesus Christ's death on the Cross paid for the sins of the entire world. If you are a saved person, and you are under the impression you can lose your salvation, then I ask you: Which of your sins did Jesus *not* die for?

> For God made Christ, who never sinned, to be the offering for our sin, so that we could be made right with God through Christ. 2 Corinthians 5:21

> He canceled the record of the charges against us and took it away by nailing it to the cross. Colossians 2:14

God loves us so much that he came up with a method by which we can become righteous in his eyes, even though we continue to sin. This means that no matter what you have done, what you are doing, or what you will ever do, you have already been forgiven. Hard to believe? It is true! The only sin that has not been forgiven is the rejection of Jesus Christ as God, who is the Savior for all who will accept him.

Take a firm stand against legalism

Satan confuses would-be Christians.

> *Stay alert! Watch out for your great enemy, the devil. He prowls around like a roaring lion, looking for someone to devour. Stand firm against him, and be strong in your faith. Remember that your Christian brothers and sisters all over the world are going through the same kind of suffering you are.*
> 1 Peter 5:8-9

Satan has a huge agenda, but his primary objective is to keep as many good people from going to Heaven as possible. To succeed, he has continuously urged many Christian religious leaders to teach and preach a very false and dangerous doctrine – works. Consequently, throughout the ages humankind has been duped into believing salvation is a reward for the righteous. The deceiver loves to see people become religious rather than saved. Paul recognized this 2,000 years ago, and we are still being warned of it today via God's Word.

> *But I fear that somehow your pure and undivided devotion to Christ will be corrupted, just as Eve was deceived by the cunning ways of the serpent. You happily put up with whatever anyone tells you, even if they preach a different Jesus than the one we preach, or a different kind of Spirit than the one you received, or a different kind of gospel than the one you believed.*
>
> *But I don't consider myself inferior in any way to these "super apostles" who teach such things. I may be unskilled as a speaker, but I'm not lacking in knowledge. We have made this clear to you in every possible way.*
> 2 Corinthians 11:3-6

The defeat of Satan

> *Then I saw an angel coming down from heaven with the key to the bottomless pit and a heavy chain in his hand. He seized the dragon—that old serpent, who is the devil, Satan—and bound him in chains for a thousand years. The angel threw him into the bottomless pit, which he then shut and locked so Satan could not deceive the nations anymore until the thousand years were finished. Afterward he must be released for a little while.*
> Revelation 20:1-3
>
> *When the thousand years come to an end, Satan will be let out of his prison. He will go out to deceive the nations—called Gog and Magog—in every*

corner of the earth. He will gather them together for battle—a mighty army, as numberless as sand along the seashore. And I saw them as they went up on the broad plain of the earth and surrounded God's people and the beloved city. But fire from heaven came down on the attacking armies and consumed them.

Then the devil, who had deceived them, was thrown into the fiery lake of burning sulfur, joining the beast and the false prophet. There they will be tormented day and night forever and ever.   Revelation 20:7-10

Throughout this book, I have emphasized the simplicity of salvation, just as I have verbally emphasized the same simplicity of the Gospel to thousands. Many get it, but unfortunately, many do not. The most common objection I receive is: It sounds too simple. The fact is, salvation is very simple.

Making sense of it all

The Holy Bible is a compilation of many stories, and each may contain more than one verse or passage that is applicable to Christian doctrine. This book assembles hundreds of passages that are scattered throughout the Scriptures regarding the doctrine of salvation and presents them in easy-to-understand paragraphs and chapters. The reader has all of the pertinent salvation passages in this one book, accompanied by explanations and commentaries. Rather than spending years attempting to understand the issue, the student will learn it quickly and without confusion.

A personal relationship with our Creator is very easy, extremely gratifying, and will provide you with strength and wisdom to find peace on Earth, as well as offering you eternal life. You will be lifted to heights not reachable by non-Christians, and will face challenges not enjoyed by them either. The most rewarding part of your journey is not learning about Jesus, but getting to know him personally. That is called *Spirituality* – not *religion*.

You may be offended by what is presented in this book, but it is not my intention to win friends and influence people. My purpose is to provide a truth that may have been overlooked due to a person's heritage, laziness, lack of education, lack of common sense, or stubbornness.

Notes:

3

Prune the family tree!

*We pray that the Lord would open their eyes and hearts
to 'the Way, the Truth and the Life.'*

Reverend Majed El Shaie (see story below)

Your family tree may need trimming

Most people's beliefs are inherited from their kinfolk. We tend to tag along with what our parents and grandparents believed, whether we truly think it is right or wrong. Usually we think it is right because it is what we were told. But there is only one way to get to Heaven.

I am not the type of person who is an easy sell. Before I accepted Christianity as the true faith, I explored other faiths. Now that I have been a Christian for 30 years, I enjoy learning about those of other faiths who convert to Christianity because they come to realize it is the truth.

One individual who I consider to be a tremendous witness for Christ is Reverend El Shafie, who was raised in another faith. His story is publicized on his website, as follows:

> Born in Cairo, Egypt into a prominent Moslem family of lawyers and following in the footsteps of his father and uncles, Majed too chose to become a lawyer. Through the witness of his best friend, Tamir, he experienced the love of Christ and made the decision to give his life and service to the LORD.
>
> He began the mission to bring the Christian community all of the same legal rights as the Moslem community in Egypt. He began a ministry which in just two years grew to 24,000 Christians. His ministry built 2 churches inside mountains,

a bible school and medical clinic. He established a newspaper to request from the Egyptian government the same equal rights to the Christian community. The Egyptian government did not tolerate this and Majed was arrested and taken to the torture section of the Abu Zaabel prison in Cairo.

During his time in prison, Majed underwent severe torture for seven days in the underground prison. He experienced everything from having his head shaved and placed under hot and cold water, being hung upside down, being burned with cigarettes. He experienced a miracle when the attack dogs were silenced and did not attack him. He was crucified during the last two and a half days with a mixture of salt and lemon to anoint his wounds. He went through all of this because of his new faith in the LORD Jesus Christ. He eventually escaped through a whirlwind journey, fleeing to Israel, where he was jailed for over a year because the Israeli government did not know what to do in his circumstance. Legally he could not stay in Israel, but if they sent him back to Egypt, he would be executed.

Through the intervention of Amnesty International and the United Nations, Majed was released from prison and became a free man in Jerusalem, Israel. Since then he has relocated to Toronto, Ontario, where he has actively started his own ministry and is now the President and Founder of One Free World International. Rev. El Shafie became a Canadian citizen on May 29, 2006.

Along with One Free World International, Majed also has a Christian Arabic radio program, "River of Love" reaching the Middle East and North Africa. He has started a second Arabic radio program called, "Encourage Iraq" to help encourage the Iraqi people in this time of unrest and to introduce them to the Prince of Peace, Jesus Christ.

Majed has visited and spoken in many churches and congregations in both Canada and the United States. He has also been interviewed by several magazines, television and radio programs both Christian and secular.

Majed's passion is to help the persecuted Christians around the world and be their voice when their voices are not heard.

The story of Majed is not only a story of violence and persecution but a story of Glory and Victory. It's a story about fighting the darkness by the light of Christ.

I was so impressed with Reverend El Shafie's story that I contacted him for approval to quote him. He said, "We pray that the Lord would open their eyes and hearts to 'the Way, the Truth, and the Life,'" and promptly gave me permission.

Chances are if you are Catholic, it is because your family is Catholic. If you are Jewish, it is probably because your family is Jewish. If Muslim, it is also probably an inherited belief. If you fit into the category of a family *hanger-on*, have you ever stopped to think that perhaps your family is wrong? Your belief, if erroneous, could cause you eternal punishment.

Our ancestors did not have access to the educational resources we are privileged to enjoy today. Thanks to modern communications and vast educational resources at our fingertips, no one should live in ignorance.

If you are one of those whose beliefs are fruits of your family tree, perhaps you may discover the tree needs pruning, or it may be so diseased that the family roots should be pull up. Please keep in mind that becoming aware of truths that are in opposition to what you were told as a child does not mean that you are deserting your heritage. It simply indicates you are progressing, and that is what life is all about.

What is the truth?

We humans are often afraid of the truth because it can be very convicting. It is much easier to bury our heads in the sand than to face reality.

When I began to study all world religions, each one sounded credible and moral. But I kept coming back to this Jesus fellow, for he has characteristics that all historic major religious leaders lack.

- ✓ He claimed to be God incarnate.
- ✓ He performed multiple miracles, including raising the dead.
- ✓ Many people witnessed his miracles.
- ✓ He rose from being dead.
- ✓ Many people saw him alive and well after he had died.
- ✓ He said I could go to Heaven just by believing in him.
- ✓ When I prayed to accept him as my Savior, the Holy Spirit came to live in me.

Although I did not witness what happened 2,000 years ago, I can assure you that Jesus' Spirit lives in me. That happened in 1980, exactly at the moment I accepted Jesus as my Savior. The Holy Spirit is the key to truth, and also the only way a person can be a Christian.

> *But you are not controlled by your sinful nature. You are controlled by the Spirit if you have the Spirit of God living in you. (And remember that those who do not have the Spirit of Christ living in them do not belong to him at*

all.) And Christ lives within you, so even though your body will die because of sin, the Spirit gives you life because you have been made right with God. The Spirit of God, who raised Jesus from the dead, lives in you. And just as God rasied Christ Jesus from the dead, he will give life to your mortal bodies by this same Spirit living within you. Romans 8:9-11

Jesus was God incarnate

Christ is the visible image of the invisible God.
He existed before anything was created and is supreme over all creation,
for through him God created everything
in the heavenly realms and on earth.
He made the things we can see
and the things we can't see—
such as thrones, kingdoms, rulers, and authorities in the unseen world.
Everything was created through him and for him.
He existed before anything else,
and he holds all creation together. Colossians 1:15-17

All honor and glory to God forever and ever! He is the eternal King, the unseen one who never dies; he alone is God. Amen. 1 Timothy 1:17

Jesus said it and I believe it

Jesus told him, "I am the way, the truth, and the life. No one can come to the Father except through me. If you had really known me, you would know who my Father is. From now on, you do know him and have seen him!" John 14:6-7

Jesus performed multiple miracles

Everyone tried to touch him, because healing power went out from him, and he healed everyone. Luke 6:19

The disciples saw Jesus do many other miraculous signs in addition to the ones recorded in this book. But these are written so that you may continue to believe that Jesus is the Messiah, the Son of God, and that by believing in him you will have life by the power of his name. John 20:30-31

Jesus rose from death – witnessed by hundreds

It was early on Sunday morning when Jesus rose from the dead, and the first person who saw him was Mary Magdalene, the woman from whom he had cast out seven demons. She went and found the disciples, who were grieving and weeping. But when she told them that Jesus was alive and she had seen him, they didn't believe her.

Afterward he appeared in a different form to two of his followers who were walking from Jerusalem into the country. They rushed back to tell the others, but no one believed them.

Still later he appeared to the eleven disciples as they were eating together. He rebuked them for their stubborn unbelief because they refused to believe those who had seen him after he had been raised from the dead. Mark 16:12-14

He said I could go to Heaven just by believing in him

"For God loved the world so much that he gave his one and only Son, so that everyone who believes in him will not perish but have eternal life. God sent his Son into the world not to judge the world, but to save the world through him." John 3:16-17, Jesus' words

He said if I don't believe in him I won't go to Heaven

"But everyone who denies me here on earth, I will also deny before my Father in heaven." Matthew 10:33, Jesus' words

"The world's sin is that it refuses to believe in me." John 16:9, Jesus' words

I prayed to accept him, and the Holy Spirit came to live in me

And now you Gentiles have also heard the truth, the Good News that God saves you. And when you believed in Christ, he identified you as his own by giving you the Holy Spirit, whom he promised long ago. The Spirit is God's guarantee that he will give us the inheritance he promised and that he has purchased us to be his own people. He did this so we would praise and glorify him. Ephesians 1:13-14

God saved you by his grace when you believed. And you can't take credit for this; it is a gift from God. Salvation is not a reward for the good things we have done, so none of us can boast about it. Ephesians 2:8-9

The Spirit of God, who raised Jesus from the dead, lives in you. And just as God raised Christ Jesus from the dead, he will give life to your mortal bodies by this same Spirit living within you. Romans 8:11

Jesus divides families

Although faith in Jesus Christ provides Christians with peace on Earth and eternal life in Heaven, one's faith may cause strains on friendships and within families. However, Jesus is very bold, stating that we must choose him.

> *"Don't imagine that I came to bring peace to the earth! I came not to bring peace, but a sword.*
>
> *'I have come to set a man against his father,*
>   *a daughter against her mother,*
> *and a daughter-in-law against her mother-in-law.*
>   *Your enemies will be right in your own household!'*
>
> *"If you love your father or mother more than you love me, you are not worthy of being mine; or if you love your son or daughter more than me, you are not worthy of being mine. If you refuse to take up your cross and follow me, you are not worthy of being mine. If you cling to your life, you will lose it; but if you give up your life for me, you will find it."* Matthew 10:34-39, Jesus' words

At the time Jesus made this proclamation, he knew there would be conflict between Jews who accepted Jesus as the Messiah, and their family members who would not accept his divinity. Although Jesus made this statement primarily to Jews, the same problem exists today within Jewish, Gentile, Muslim, atheist, and other families in which one person accepts Jesus as their personal Savior and others refuse.

You may be offended by Jesus' harsh statement, but because he is God he is entitled to make the rules. When he used the term *sword* in the passage above, it is not to be taken literally, but as a metaphor for conflict rather than violence. Jesus was not advocating that family members feud, but if it comes to choosing him or family members, he demands that we choose him regardless of the effect it has on our human relationships.

When a person becomes a Christian, it can strain relationships because those who are unsaved do not understand living in the Spirit.

> *But people who aren't spiritual can't receive these truths from God's Spirit. It all sounds foolish to them and they can't understand it, for only those who are spiritual can understand what the Spirit means. Those who are spiritual can evaluate all things, but they themselves cannot be evaluated by others. For,*

"Who can know the Lord's thoughts?
Who knows enough to teach him?"

But we understand these things, for we have the mind of Christ.
1 Corinthians 2:14-16

If we are to follow Jesus, many people will get angry with us, argue with us, hurt us, and mock us. Although this may be unpleasant, the eternal rewards are worth it for those of us who choose him.

When you are ostracized and want to pay back in kind, remember that the Apostle Paul tells us we must attempt to live peaceably with all men.

Never pay back evil with more evil. Do things in such a way that everyone
can see you are honorable. Do all that you can to live in peace with everyone.
Romans 12:17-18

If you value family and friendship more than a relationship with God, then Christianity may not be for you. But if you want to live eternally with our Creator in Heaven, then you may be forced to make a choice.

God created the world and everything in it. Then, he came to Earth in the form of a man, for the specific purpose of dying on the Cross, to forgive all of mankind for their sins. Then he arose from the dead so that all who believe in his divinity will live eternally with him. All that God requires is that you believe this. Following Jesus may cause you to generate enemies, but it can also provide you with the opportunity to be a light for those living in darkness.

Jesus is freedom from religion

All world faiths except Christianity involve good behavior to receive God's favor for eternal life. Unlike the others, Christianity is not a school to reform behavior and to make immoral men moral. Christianity is a way that immoral people can spend eternity in Heaven with the Creator God, clothed in the righteousness of Jesus Christ. Christianity demands nothing more than faith. Good behavior is desirable, but it is not mandatory.

You now have the opportunity to understand truth, receive eternal life in Heaven, and take as many people with you as possible to Heaven. Don't blow it!

Don't wait until you are dead to discover your family was wrong

Family heritage is important, but if it means choosing between eternity in Heaven or living somewhere else unpleasant, choose Heaven. Eternity is a long time. Don't put off making the decision until it is too late.

Saying a prayer works

Although we become Christians only by believing, the Bible tells us that we must confess with our mouth.

> *If you confess with your mouth that Jesus is Lord and believe in your heart that God raised him from the dead, you will be saved.* Romans 10:9

You don't need a degree in theology to become a Christian, nor do you have to quit any of your bad habits. Christ accepts you just the way you are. Then, believe it or not, when you become a Christian, you will be clothed in the righteousness of Jesus Christ. That is the *Good News* that we Christians praise.

The following prayer is similar to what you should say:

> God,
>
> I don't know very much about Christianity, but I want to accept your Son Jesus as my personal Savior and to be clothed in his righteousness, even though I do not deserve it. I am now taking this opportunity to become a Christian and am asking you to send the Holy Spirit to live in me and teach me all that you want me to know about you. I also ask that you help me to share my Christianity with those who I love who are not Christians. But allow me to present my faith to them gradually and gently as I grow. Thank you.
>
> Amen

The remainder of this book will elaborate on what you have just learned in this section, plus you will become more than just a Christian. You will be a knowledgeable Christian.

PART TWO

The Failure of the Church

The terms "church" and "Church" are used frequently throughout this book. When capitalized it means the entire body of Christ's believers. When lower case, it is referring to a building with attendees who profess to be Christians. The term church means "a group of people who are called together."

Notes:

4

Failure of the Church overview

*When a man unites with the church, he should not come saying,'
I am so holy that I think I must go in among the saints,' but, 'O
brethren, I find I am so weak and wicked that I cannot stand
alone; so, if you can help me, open the door and let me enter.'*

Henry Ward Beecher (1813-1887)

The intention of this section is not to attack all churches or all denominations, but to build up the Church by presenting areas that need improvement. Being critical is easy, but compassionate constructive criticism is necessary to inspire improvement and growth. It is only fair that if I criticize, I first begin by applauding the tremendous effect the Christian Church has had on the entire world.

The Christian Church began 2,000 years ago and has suffered tremendous persecution since, yet it has endured. Today, the Church is filled with people worldwide who love God and who celebrate the Savior Jesus.

Contrary to what many believe, the United States is a Christian nation. It is because we have always been a Christian nation that we enjoy freedom, prosperity, and morality. We have many faults, but we are the greatest nation in the world, thanks to Jesus Christ and the churches that minister him. Thank you, Jesus!

That's the *Good News*, but here is the bad news

Christianity can be very complex, particularly because there are so many varying interpretations of the Scriptures, which result in countless denominations. These disparities have led to splintering the body of Christ. These divisions are terrible, but more horrific is that our differences have been used as weapons by those insisting they are the authority. Since the beginning of Christ's Church, there have been personal disagreements that caused the Apostle Paul to write multiple letters to new believers encouraging unity. Our modern doctrinal differences are nothing new; however, harmony is possible.

I am very critical regarding the following four problems within Christ's Church that we all should consider for restoration:

1. Many churches, denominations, and Christian people insist on combining *deeds* with *grace.*
2. Many churches, denominations, and Christian people overlook the Holy Spirit.
3. Many churches, denominations, and Christian people fabricate *shall-nots.*
4. Many churches, denominations, and Christian people try to emasculate men.

Despite our denominational and interpretational differences, the Christian community should unite and wrap itself around the world as a blanket, and every thread (you are one of those threads) woven into that blanket must be part and parcel of its warmth and strength. However, to do that, we must recognize our differences and strive to adhere to the Word of God, rather than by changing Christianity to suit our personal agendas.

5

Many Christians erroneously combine deeds with grace

*Grace…means the full and free forgiveness of every sin,
without God demanding or expecting anything from the one
so forgiven—is a principle so opposed to all man's thoughts and
ways, so far above man, that he dislikes it. His own heart
often secretly calls it injustice. He does not deal in this
way and he does not like to think of God doing so.*

J.N. Darby (1800-1882)

If I could fault Christendom for just one thing, it would be that since the beginning of Jesus' ministry many Christians, Christian churches, and Christian denominations have felt the need to combine deeds with grace. Tragically, this colossal error of combining the two, generally fabricated by organized religion, has caused many would-be Christians to reject learning about Jesus because they think Christianity is a religion that is too difficult to attain or too guilt-provoking.

Combining deeds with grace also misleads people into believing they are gaining favor with God by their good deeds, rather than accepting what Jesus did on the Cross as their only means for eternal life in Heaven. Throughout the world there are millions who consider themselves Christians, yet they are constantly trying to work their way to Heaven, rather than trusting in Jesus Christ's finished work on the Cross. This blending of deeds with grace has been a dilemma since the ministry of Jesus, as evidenced by the words of the great Apostle Paul.

> *I am shocked that you are turning away so soon from God, who called you to himself through the loving mercy of Christ. You are following a different way that pretends to be the Good News but is not the Good News at all. You*

are being fooled by those who deliberately twist the truth concerning Christ.
Galatians 1:6-7

The *Good News* to which Paul is referring is that God came to Earth in the form of a man named Jesus to be a sacrifice for the sins of the entire world, and that by believing in his death, burial, and resurrection as the only means for eternal life in Heaven a person is *saved.*

As an evangelist and author, my primary mission is to powerfully teach God's extremely simple plan of salvation and to explain the distinct difference between salvation and discipleship.

Combining deeds with grace is called *Galatianism*

In the Christian vernacular, a person's *good deeds* are those things they do to please God.

A quick definition of *grace* is "receiving something that is undeserved." To understand the Biblical application of grace in the doctrine of salvation, further explanation is required. *Grace* is the formula for one's eternal destiny; it is a result of the undeserved favor from God, who justifies those who trust in the finished work of Jesus Christ as their only means for salvation.

Galatianism is discussed in detail in the chapter titled *The New Covenant.* The *Old Covenant,* which included obeying the Ten Commandments to merit God's favor, is, tragically, still being taught in many churches, although it changed 2,000 years ago.

> *If the first covenant had been faultless, there would have been no need for*
> *a second covenant to replace it. But when God found fault with the people,*
> *he said: "The day is coming, says the Lord, when I will make a new covenant*
> *with the people of Israel and Judah."* Hebrews 8:7-8

What you have just read makes it crystal clear that attempting to follow the Ten Commandments was unachievable, so God provided humankind with a new way – *grace.*

The intent of this book is not to diminish the benefits of good works and behavior, but to educate the reader to the fact that it is not faith plus works that saves a person; it is faith alone. However, if one's faith is real, it will be demonstrated by deeds.

The moment a person accepts Jesus Christ's finished work on the Cross as their only means of salvation, the Holy Spirit immediately indwells that person permanently. It is the guidance of the Holy Spirit that encourages the Christian to produce good deeds. Adhering to the guidance of the Holy Spirit is defined as *discipleship*.

> *But the Holy Spirit produces this kind of fruit in our lives: love, joy, peace, patience, kindness, goodness, faithfulness, gentleness, and self-control. There is no law against these things!* Galatians 5:22-23

> *Don't be selfish; don't try to impress others. Be humble, thinking of others as better than yourselves. Don't look out only for your own interests, but take an interest in others, too.* Philippians 2:3-4

Too much grace?

I am told frequently that I put too much emphasis on grace, which encourages people to sin more. That's ridiculous! People need no encouragement to sin. People need to accept Jesus Christ as their Savior. Rather than feebly attempting to live their lives for him, they should allow him to live through them via the Holy Spirit.

Instilling fear and guilt usually scares people from Jesus! It often takes away hope from an individual and causes would-be Christians to go the opposite direction believing they are hopeless. Hopelessness can lead to more sin, substance abuse, and even criminal behavior.

In order to quit sinning, people must enjoy something more. That something more is allowing the Spirit to be their personal counselor. The flesh is weak, but the Spirit is strong. The more a person allows the Holy Spirit to work through them, the less sin will be enjoyed. A Christian can sin more, but he will enjoy it less, thanks to the indwelling of the Holy Spirit.

Notes:

6

Churches overlook the Holy Spirit

You might as well try to hear without ears or breath
without lungs, as to try to live a Christian life
without the spirit of God in your heart.

Dwight L. Moody (1837-1899)

Countless churches, preachers, and teachers neglect giving equal opportunity to the Holy Spirit. They speak of God and Jesus, yet frequently leave out the third party of the Godhead from their teaching.

Churchgoers worship God and praise Jesus, but neglecting the Holy Spirit is common. Refraining from giving proper recognition to the person (the Holy Spirit is a person) who provides the conduit to Jesus is prevalent. When the Holy Spirit does not live within a person, that person is not a Christian.

> *But you are not controlled by your sinful nature. You are controlled by the Spirit if you have the Spirit of God living in you. (And remember that those who do not have the Spirit of Christ living in them do not belong to him at all.) And Christ lives within you, so even though your body will die because of sin, the Spirit gives you life because you have been made right with God. The Spirit of God, who raised Jesus from the dead, lives in you. And just as God raised Christ Jesus from the dead, he will give life to your mortal bodies by this same Spirit living within you.* Romans 8:9-11

Knowing *about* Jesus is not enough! A person must be baptized into his body to be a Christian.

The human body has many parts, but the many parts make up one whole body. So it is with the body of Christ. Some of us are Jews, some are Gentiles, some are slaves, and some are free. But we have all been baptized into one body by one Spirit, and we all share the same Spirit. 1 Corinthians 12:12-13

When we are baptized into Christ's body, we instantly and automatically inherit the *New Covenant*, which is referred to as being *born again* or *saved*. Please memorize the term *New Covenant*; it will be discussed in detail later in this book, because it is the soul of Christianity. To help you: *New Covenant, New Covenant, New Covenant!*

He has enabled us to be ministers of his new covenant. This is a covenant not of written laws, but of the Spirit. The old written covenant ends in death; but under the new covenant, the Spirit gives life. 2 Corinthians 3:6

Jesus replied, "I tell you the truth, unless you are born again, you cannot see the Kingdom of God." John 3:3

The *Old Covenant* included laws that must be followed to receive eternal life in Heaven. But because people were incapable of keeping laws, and because God wants us all in Heaven with him, he made a new way for us to get there, the New Covenant. That new way is via our baptism in the Holy Spirit, which takes place the instant one trusts in the finished work of Jesus.

This may sound scary to some, but the truth must be taught. I asked a Methodist pastor once why he did not talk to his congregation about being *born again*[2], and he told me that term had such an intimidating connotation that he was afraid everyone would walk out.

---

2. For futher information and for a more in-depth enlightenment of this topic, please refer to the chapter entitled *The Holy Spirit.*

7

Man-made shall-nots

In religion and politics, people's beliefs and convictions are in almost every case gotten at second-hand, and without examination.

Mark Twain (1835-1910)

I wish I had a dollar for every time someone told me I am not a Christian because I smoke an occasional cigar. A statement like that is utter nonsense! So are many other statements made within the Christian world regarding things that a person cannot do and still be a Christian. Christians love to formulate shall-nots for fellow Christians.

You will learn in this book that in order to be a Christian, a person must have a personal relationship with Jesus Christ via the Holy Spirit. It is the Holy Spirit living in and through a person that not only makes him or her a Christian, but also who convicts him or her individually of what is good and bad behavior. For me, an occasional cigar is apparently OK with the Holy Spirit, or I would not partake. But for someone else, this may not be appropriate behavior.

One of my favorite radio pastors is a very learned and wise Christian college professor named Steve Brown. Steve hosts the radio and Internet organization Key Life Ministries. I have listened to him daily for about five years and have the utmost respect for his ability to teach how to balance the Christian life. The following is an excerpt from the Key Life website.

> Key Life isn't for everyone. If you want the Bible to be a 'book of rules,' if you think there is something unspiritual about laughter and dangerous about freedom and

if you define faithfulness as conformity to Christian stereotypes, then Key Life probably isn't for you.

However, if you are interested in an honest, non-manipulative and thoughtful presentation of Biblical truth presented in the context of Christ's unconditional love, Key Life may be for you. If you need to hear the hopeful truth that God isn't mad at you, Key Life is for you.

Key Life is committed to the teaching of Biblical life principles – the whole counsel of God – to those who want to live an authentic, relevant and balanced Christian life.

During a recent program, a caller asked if playing poker is a sin. Steve said, "No, playing poker is not a sin," but he followed with a Bible passage:

> *You say, "I am allowed to do anything" – but not everything is good for you.*
> *You say, "I am allowed to do anything" – but not everything is beneficial.*
> *Don't be concerned for your own good but for the good of others.*
> 1 Corinthians 10:23-24

Steve admitted that he loves to play poker, but that he has not played for several years. He emphasized the fact that, although playing poker is not sinful, some consequences may be harmful to oneself or others. The point is that at one time playing poker was not a sin for Steve, but at the prompting of the Holy Spirit, playing poker became undesirable. What I love about Steve is that he teaches Biblical truths.

Painting with black or white

Many Christians insist on making everything black or white, right or wrong, good or bad, and so forth. Although many Christian doctrines are either black or white, radicalism that is not strongly Biblical presents hurdles that cause people who would like to know Jesus to turn away – defeated before they start. That is why it is so imperative that we present Christianity to the lost in its most common denominator, which is salvation by grace.

For instance, many pastors teach their flock that drinking alcoholic beverages is sinful. This is a boldfaced lie, according to the Scriptures. People drank wine regularly in Biblical times just as they do today. It was not a sin then, nor is it a sin today. However, the Bible warns us not to get drunk.

Don't be drunk with wine, because that will ruin your life. Instead, be filled with the Holy Spirit, singing psalms and hymns and spiritual songs among yourselves, and making music to the Lord in your hearts. Ephesians 5:18-19

The notion that Christians cannot enjoy alcoholic beverages is man-made. It simply is not Biblical. Yes, there are many verses that warn us not to get drunk, but it certainly does not say not to drink.

Known until this day as the wisest man who ever lived, King Solomon suggests we enjoy the nectar of the grape.

Even so, I have noticed one thing, at least, that is good. It is good for people to eat well, drink a good glass of wine, and enjoy their work—whatever they do under the sun—for however long God lets them live. Ecclesiastes 5:18 (NLT 1996)

So go ahead. Eat your food with joy, and drink your wine with a happy heart, for God approves of this! Ecclesiastes 9:7

In the great Apostle Paul's letter to Timothy, Paul recommends that Timothy drink wine for his health.

Don't drink only water. You ought to drink a little wine for the sake of your stomach because you are sick so often. 1 Timothy 5:23

I believe Jesus drank wine, as evidenced by the following verse.

"The Son of Man, on the other hand, feasts and drinks, and you say, 'He's a glutton and a drunkard, and a friend of tax collectors and other sinners!' But wisdom is shown to be right by its results." Matthew 11:19, Jesus' words

You see; even Jesus Christ couldn't satisfy people, so don't be surprised when you are put through the wringer.

Notes:

8

Many churches emasculate men[3]

To hear many religious people talk, one would
think God created the torso, head, legs and arms,
but the devil slapped on the genitals.

Don Schrader

Why is it that many church buildings are designed primarily for women and children, but very little space is set apart for high-testosterone guys like me? I am serious! Give me a good reason – please. I get nervous when I am in a church because it is so solemn, and I am not wired for serenity. There is nothing in the Bible that says a place of gathering and worship must be solemn.

I am not suggesting that all churches redesign their interiors to look like a sports bar, but a little modification might make them more accommodating to those guys who feel like they do not belong. I have never yet been in a church that has a sports room. They have arts & crafts rooms, Bible study rooms, libraries, and kitchens – but no special place for rugged guys.

A lot of men do not want anything to do with Jesus because historically most churches have tried to feminize the male gender. Pitifully, the clergy cannot figure out why so many men stay at home while their wives bring the kids.

Jesus Christ was a carpenter, not a florist (not that there is anything wrong with being a florist). Jesus' very first miracle was turning water into wine at a party. Yes, Jesus was at a party. Jesus' disciples and apostles were fishermen and businessmen, not harpists. Yet the inside of most churches are feminine in nature. Most churches

---

3.   Admittedly, this is a sexist chapter—and it is meant to be.

teach that the man in the family is to be the faith leader, yet they create an atmo-sphere more accommodating to women.

By God's design, men have needs that are more adventurous and exciting than those of women. When it comes to movies, men like shoot-em-up bang-bangs and women like warm & cozy. Men like flowers, but they prefer guns and fishing rods. Pastors warn men not to drink, smoke, cuss, gamble, or look at women lustfully. That is like telling a fish not to swim. Let us talk about reality and moderation – not guilt.

Wild at Heart

The most revealing book I have read regarding the Church attempting to feminize men is *Wild at Heart* by John Eldredge.

An author, counselor, and lecturer, Eldredge was a writer and speaker for *Focus on the Family* for 12 years. He is now director of Ransomed Heart Ministries, a teach-ing, counseling, and discipling fellowship devoted to helping people live from deep within their hearts.

Wild at Heart is a book for guys just like you and me. Eldredge is adamant that men need adventure more than we need security, big houses, fancy clothes, and even our politely reserved church pews. He insists that most men have become civilized to the point of over-domestication and because of this they are merely existing rather than pursuing the adventure and excitement that was planted in their hearts by God. John blames part of this problem on the established church, reminding us that church leaders have traditionally focused only on promoting morality and niceness. He also blames the fear of failure for our obvious lethargy. He is emphatic that spiritual ful-fillment is more than just becoming religious.

Wild at Heart bulges with Biblical passages reinforcing Eldredge's convictions that we are given permission and even expected to be all that we can be, while utilizing our Creator's divine guidance. He also makes it very clear that we can be simultane-ously moral and responsible while being bold and daring. I chuckled when I read C.S. Lewis' quote, "We castrate the gelding and bid him to be fruitful." As a reader, I was pleased that Eldredge calls a spade a spade. What I enjoyed most is the humorous way Eldredge shares his own failures, indecisions, fears, weaknesses, and wimpiness. He is a man with whom I can definitely identify.

Male hormones

Churches insist that the men change their hormones, rather than admitting that churches must change.

I have read several books on biopsychology, and James McBride Dabbs and Mary Godwin Dabbs' *Heroes Rogues and Lovers* was the most compelling. This comprehensive book presents thorough and conclusive studies:

> Social psychologists explain people's behavior by their backgrounds, surroundings, and personalities. Over the past decade I have done this, but I have added testosterone and other hormones to the usual social variables. My students and I have studied testosterone measures from more than eight thousand men, women and children, and I am convinced that what we and others are learning will fill a gap in our understanding of social behavior. **Prologue xvi**

> It is clear that testosterone affects our bodies in many ways, but some people reject the idea that testosterone has important effects on how we think and act. This latter view arises in part from the political philosophy that all people are created equal, at least in the eyes of God and the law. If we are created equal, it is said, then important differences among us must come from education and experience. In this view, biology and testosterone do not matter much, and studying them will only distract us from more important issues of human justice. I have a different view. I agree that education and experience are important, but I think biology is important, too. It is obvious to me that we are biological creatures who live and die according to the rules of nature. Illness wears us down. Bad food shortens our lives. Genetic disorders cloud our judgment. Chemicals affect our moods. When people say testosterone is unimportant in the study of human affairs, I think they are speaking more from bias than from evidence. **Page 19**

Research establishes that high-testosterone men are more likely to have misbehaved in school as children, get into more trouble with the law as adults, use drugs and alcohol more frequently, and have more sex partners than men with low testosterone.

In their research, Dabbs found that trial lawyers had more testosterone than all other lawyers. Construction workers and prison inmates had high levels of testosterone. Ministers and farmers had low levels of testosterone.

As Christians we should learn more about the chemical makeup of the body and its contribution to our behavior, rather than pounding on the lectern instilling guilt for being human. Of course, environment and circumstances have a major effect on one's desires and behavior, but hormones are an important contributor. The church is pushing good men from Jesus!

It is time for a change. I do not feel it is the purpose of this book to determine what changes should be made, but I suggest that all Christians pray for divine guidance as to what improvements should be implemented to attract more men into Jesus' Church.

Notes:

PART THREE

The Basics of Christianity

Notes:

9

A basic belief in one God is a good place to begin

By reading the scriptures I am so renewed that all nature seems renewed around me and with me. The sky seems to be a pure, a cooler blue, the trees a deeper green. The whole world is charged with the glory of God and I feel fire and music under my feet.

Thomas Merton (1915-1968)

The first thing a person does to receive eternal life in Heaven is to believe in the one God (with a capital "G") as described in the Bible. The God we discuss in this book is the God of Abraham, Isaac, and Jacob – the Creator of all things. He is also the first person of the Godhead, as Jesus is the second, and the Holy Spirit is the third.

No, it cannot be a "god" that you personally invent. Many people form an image in their own minds using the characteristics they believe a god should have, and reject those of the God described in the Bible. For instance, many believe a loving god would not allow good people to spend eternity in Hell, which is a distortion, or rejection, of the God of the Bible. You cannot make God into what you want him to be. Yes, he does allow people to go to Hell, but he allows them to make the choice.

> *In the beginning God created the heavens and the earth. The earth was formless and empty, and darkness covered the deep waters. And the Spirit of God was hovering over the surface of the waters.*
>
> *Then God said, "Let there be light," and there was light. And God saw that the light was good. Then he separated the light from the darkness. God called the light "day" and the darkness "night."*
> *And evening passed and morning came, marking the first day.*

Then God said, "Let there be a space between the waters, to separate the waters of the heavens from the waters of the earth." And that is what happened. God made this space to separate the waters of the earth from the waters of the heavens. God called the space "sky."
And evening passed and morning came, marking the second day.

Then God said, "Let the waters beneath the sky flow together into one place, so dry ground may appear." And that is what happened. God called the dry ground "land" and the waters "seas." And God saw that it was good. Then God said, "Let the land sprout with vegetation – every sort of seed-bearing plant, and trees that grow seed-bearing fruit. These seeds will then produce the kinds of plants and trees from which they came." And that is wat happened. The land produced vegetation – all sorts of seed-bearing plants, and trees with seed-bearing fruit. Their seeds produced plants and trees of the same kind. And God saw that it was good.
And evening passed and morning came, marking the third day.

Then God said, "Let lights appear in the sky to separate the day from the night. Let them be signs to mark the seasons, days, and years. Let these lights in the sky shine down on the earth." And that is what happened. God made two great lights – the larger one to govern the day, and the smaller one to govern the night. He also made the stars. God set these lights in the sky to light the earth, to govern the day and night, and to separate the light from the darkness. And God saw that it was good.
And evening passed and morning came, marking the fourth day.

Then God said, "Let the waters swarm with fish and other life. Let the skies be filled with birds of every kind." So God created great sea creatures and every living thing that scurries and swarms in the water, and every sort of bird – each producing offspring of the same kind. And God saw that it was good. Then God blessed them, saying, "Be fruitfull and multiply. Let the fish fill the seas, and let the birds multiply on the earth."
And evening passed and morning came, marking the fifth day.

Then God said, "Let the earth produce every sort of animal, each producing offspring of the same kind – livestock, small animals that scurry along the ground, and wild animals." And that is what happened. God made all sorts of wild animals, livestock, and small animals, each able to produce offspring of the same kind. And God saw that it was good.
Genesis 1:1-25

NOTE: I am interrupting the Scripture verses that describe creation to interject that the term *us* and *our* used in the following passage is interpreted by most Christians to describe the *Triune nature of God* – God the Father, Jesus Christ the Son, and the Holy Spirit – all of whom are God. This explains why Chrisians believe that Jesus Christ has been in existence from eternity past.

> *Then God said, "Let us make human beings in our image, to be like us. They will reign over the fish in the sea, the birds in the sky, the livestock, all the wild animals on the earth, and the small animals that scurry along the ground."*
>
> *So God created human beings in his own image. In the image of God he created them; male and female he created them.*
>
> *Then God blessed them and said, "Be fruitful and multiply. Fill the earth and govern it. Reign over the fish in the sea, the birds in the sky, and all the animals that scurry along the ground."*
>
> *Then God said, "Look! I have given you every seed-bearing plant throughout the earth and all the fruit trees for your food. And I have given every green plant as food for all the wild animals, the birds in the sky, and the small animals that scurry along the ground – everything that has life." And that is what happened. Then God looked over all he had made, and he saw that it was very good!*
> *And evening passed and morning came, marking the sixth day.* Genesis 1:26-31
>
> *So the creation of the heavens and the earth and everything in them was completed. On the seventh day God had finished his work of creation, so he rested from all his work. And God blessed the seventh day and declared it holy, because it was the day when he rested from all his work of creation.*
>
> *This is the account of the creation of the heavens and the earth.* Genesis 2:1-4

Doubting is normal

Please do not beat yourself up for doubting. Most people have doubts about God from time to time, but faith is a leap of acceptance without facts.

Faith

> *Faith is the confidence that what we hope for will actually happen; it gives us assurance about things we cannot see. Through their faith, the people in days of old earned a good reputation.*

By faith we understand that the entire universe was formed at God's command, that what we now see did not come from anything that can be seen. Hebrews 11:1-3

Faith without fanaticism

I mentioned faith without fanaticism in the beginning of this book, but I must mention it again. As a Christian evangelist, I have found that many would-be Christians are afraid to make the commitment because they fear they may become extremely zealous, as some new Christians do. Yes, there are people who are fanatical about their faith, but they represent a small percentage. Chances are that you will not become a fanatic – but even if you do, so what? Quit worrying about what other people think!

You don't have to like God

As an evangelist for 30 years, I have talked with thousands of unsaved people regarding their beliefs about a supreme being. Many reject the God of the Bible because they are mad at him. Many reject the existence of the Biblical God and Jesus because they cannot fathom the Creator God allowing the bad things that happen in the world. I readily share with them my similar sentiments. When I look around at all of the pain and suffering in the world, and my own pain and suffering, it is difficult for me to agree with everything on God's agenda. But that does not mean I deny his existence.

God's Son, Jesus, cried out to God when he was dying on the Cross, asking why he had forsaken him. God had a reason, and now we know why. Many times, I have cried out to God asking him why he let something happen to me. I usually find the answer within a year or two. Sometimes it takes longer, and sometimes I never understand, but I still believe.

Although you may not be pleased with everything God does, and although God may not be pleased with everything you do, he loves you so much that he sent his Son to die on the Cross so all your sins would be never remembered.

I doubt anyone who is being honest would admit that sometimes they question why God allows bad things to happen. For now I ask you to accept the fact that there is a Creator God, whether you agree with him or not. Please understand that no one is capable of thinking like God, so let us move on.

God loves the imperfect

If you believe you are not worthy of God's love, you are right. Yet he loves you anyway. Many people unfamiliar with the Bible believe the pages are filled with the stories of saintly people and that studying the Bible would just make them feel terrible about their own flaws. Wrong! The Bible tells the stories of everyday people, just like you and me. In fact, many of God's favorites were very imperfect. The following are a few examples of some people whom God loved dearly, yet were far from perfect:

- Abraham sacrificed Sarah's safety to save his own neck.
- David, although Godly, had an adulterous affair and was a murderer.
- Jacob was cunning and deceptive.
- Moses was a murderer.
- Noah got drunk.
- Peter denied Jesus three times.
- Rahab was a prostitute.
- Samson was a womanizer.

This list of sinners could go on indefinitely, pointing out the sinfulness of us all, but hopefully, you have gotten the point. Instead of hiding human weaknesses, the Bible records them faithfully to show that there are no perfect human beings on Earth. This certainly does not imply that God approves of sinful behavior, but it does prove that God loves and uses imperfect people. The lesson here is that every saint has a past and every sinner has a future. You are not as unworthy as you think you are. God loves you regardless of what you have done.

Notes:

10

Why most people reject God

When I was a kid I used to pray every night for a new bicycle.
Then I realized that the Lord doesn't work that way
so I stole one and asked Him to forgive me.
Comedian Emo Phillips (born 1956)

Those folks who reject a belief in or a relationship with our Creator do so for one or more of these reasons:

1. They want to advocate a contemporary speculative belief system that makes them appear intellectual, rather than agreeing with the time-honored Judeo-Christian faith. This is sometimes the case with those who receive a college degree. They believe their degree makes them an intellectual and that by rejecting faith they appear even smarter.
2. They are afraid that an affiliation with God will inspire them to give up what is pleasing to their flesh. This is called *guilt*.
3. Here is a big one: They don't like God because they have experienced personal tragedies or the world's unpleasant circumstances. They are of the opinion that a good God would not allow bad things to happen to good people, so they make an effort to deny his existence.
4. They are afraid they might become religious fanatics and their peers will laugh at them.
5. Historically, many denominations have presented God as the father of vengeance, rather than as a man named Jesus who is the supplier of grace.

I can identify with all of these reasons and excuses. But once I faced my apprehensions, the truth allowed me to understand and respect God and his system. I am a Christian evangelist even though I have suffered from all of the reservations listed above. It is my hope to help others who are lost by setting the example of a person who has average intelligence, is educated, has suffered from life's problems, and is a sinner. I believe God called me to tell others about him because I am typical.

I have had heart-to-heart conversations with many, many professing atheists, who have admitted to me that they know the truth when they lay their heads on the pillow at night. What about you?

11

Assume the Bible is Trustworthy

I believe the Bible is the best gift God has ever given to man.
All the good from The Savior of the
world is communicated to us through this Book .

Abraham Lincoln (1809-1865)

A thorough understanding of the Bible is
better than a college education.

Theodore Roosevelt (1858-1919)

Of the many influences that have shaped the United States into a
distinctive nation and people, none may be said to be
more fundamental and enduring than the Bible.

Ronald Reagan (1911-2004)

The Holy Bible of the Christian faith is both the most criticized and most loved book in history. The criticism results from a lack of knowledge regarding its contents. The Bible can also be construed as confrontational because it reminds readers of their sins, and can cause them to question their beliefs.

The Bible is the inspired word of God

I get tired of hearing non-Christian people say, "I don't believe the Bible was divinely inspired because it was written by mortal men." Yes, mortals wrote the Bible, but God inspired it. Do these self-styled intellects actually think an all-powerful God would allow a book that was not holy to circulate the world using his name? That's ludicrous.

All Scripture is inspired by God and is useful to teach us what is true and to make us realize what is wrong in our lives. It corrects us when we are wrong and teaches us to do what is right. God uses it to prepare and equip his people to do every good work. 2 Timothy 3:16-17

The Bible was composed and compiled by individuals who were chosen by God, then inspired and instructed by the Holy Spirit what to write. The Spirit uses it to reveal the purpose, vision, love, and power of God.

For the word of God is alive and powerful. It is sharper than the sharpest two-edged sword, cutting between soul and spirit, between joint and marrow. It exposes our innermost thoughts and desires. Hebrews 4:12

The Word of God has the power to reach the deepest parts of our spirit and soul, and serves as the roadmap for developing strength of character and morals. With the assistance of the Holy Spirit, the Bible instructs us how to live in the world, but not be of the world.

History of the Bible

The Bible has been translated into more than 2,000 languages. John Wycliffe completed the very first translation of the complete Bible from the Latin Vulgate into English in 1382. Today there are more versions available in English than any other language.

The original Bible was written in Hebrew, Aramaic, and Greek. However, in January of 1604 the King of Scotland – James Charles Stuart – called the Hampton Court Conference in order to hear of things "pretended to be amiss" in the church. At this conference, Dr. John Reynolds, a Puritan, requested of the king a new translation of the Bible because those Bibles that were allowed during the reigns of Henry the VIII and Edward VI were corrupt.

In July 1604 the king appointed 54 men to the translation committee. These men were considered to be the best linguists and scholars in the world. Much of their work on the King James Bible formed the basis for our linguistic studies today. These men were not only world-class scholars; they were Christians who lived holy lives as deans and presidents of major universities such as Oxford, Cambridge, and Westminster.

In 1611, the Authorized King James Version of the Bible was published, and it has become the best selling book of all time.

Sadly, many people criticize the Bible, without any basis for such criticism. The proof of the Bible's accuracy involves intellectual analysis, not feeble guesswork. Two very compelling tests demonstrate that the Bible is trustworthy.

The first test

The first test is the reliability of the Holy Scriptures in predicting future events. The Old Testament contains hundreds of prophecies that have already come true, and dozens that are being revealed today. The Bible's ability to prophesize is the irrefutable evidence that differentiates it from all other books. The most important Old Testament prophecies, numbering about 200, are those of the coming Jewish Messiah, revealed in the New Testament to be Jesus. Specific details regarding Jesus' birth, life, death, and resurrection were prophesized centuries prior to his birth.

The second and most revealing test

The second and most revealing test of the reliability of the Bible is the amazing power it has to affect a person's life. Following the Bible's teaching is what demonstrates that it is alive, and proves its integrity.

The Bible is the greatest book on psychology ever written. I have read dozens of psychology books and have benefited from most. But the greatest book I have ever read for peace of mind is the New Testament. It reveals the origin of mankind, why we are here, and where we will go following death. If studied correctly it eliminates all guilt, assists us in handling the difficult times, and teaches us how to treat others. Millions and millions of people agree with me. Do you?

However, it is not a book for those who cannot handle truth or confrontation.

 **Notes:**

12

What is Christianity?

The church is the great lost and found department.
Robert Short (1932-2009)

Before I tell you what Christianity is, allow me to tell you what Christianity is not. Christianity is not a religion. *Religion* is the term used to describe a belief system that requires an individual to behave in a certain way or adhere to certain rituals and laws to gain approval by their god or gods. Religion forces people into bondage.

All world religions require human performance to get to their heaven, but Christianity requires only belief and faith to receive eternal life in Heaven. That is what separates Christianity from the rest.

> *"For God loved the world so much that he gave his one and only Son, so that everyone who believes in him will not perish but have eternal life."* John 3:16, Jesus' words

> *And since it is through God's kindness, then it is not by their good works. For in that case, God's grace would not be what it really is—free and underserved.* Romans 11:6

Christianity sets people free from the bondage of religion. Christianity is *anti-religion* because it affirms that humans cannot do anything to be approved by God except trust and believe in his Son, Jesus Christ, as Savior. The Christian Bible declares that Jesus died to set those who believe free from the bondage of religion.

> *So Christ has truly set us free. Now make sure that you stay free, and don't get tied up again in slavery to the law.* Galatians 5:1

Christianity is a faith that believes God came to Earth in the form of a man named Jesus, who was crucified on a cross to pay for the sins of all mankind. Jesus then was resurrected so all who believe in him and trust in him as their Savior will have eternal life. Christian's also believe there is no condemnation in Christ Jesus.

> *So now there is no condemnation for those who belong to Christ Jesus.*
> Romans 8:1

Unlike most religions, Christianity is not a set of rules to follow. It is a faith in which an individual can place his trust in Jesus Christ as his only means to eternal life in Heaven. Jesus' purpose was not to make immoral people moral, but to give immoral people eternal life in Heaven.

> *"There is salvation in no one else! God has given no other name under heaven by which we must be saved."* Acts 4:12

Moral behavior was practiced in the Jewish religion, the predecessor to Christianity. In fact, the Jews were given 603 commandments and laws in addition to the Ten Commandments given to Moses. Rules for morality were plentiful when Jesus lived, so his reason for existence in human form was not to enforce laws. The purpose of Jesus' life, death, and resurrection was to make it possible for all mankind to receive eternal life simply by believing.

> *The law of Moses was unable to save us because of the weakness of our sinful nature. So God did what the law could not do. He sent his own Son in a body like the bodies we sinners have. And in that body God declared an end to sin's control over us by giving his Son as a sacrifice for our sins. He did this so that the just requirement of the law would be fully satisfied for us, who no longer follow our sinful nature but instead follow the Spirit.* Romans 8:3-4

In the Jewish religion, God demanded blood sacrifices, often by killing a lamb. However, the need for blood sacrifices ended when Jesus became the Sacrificial Lamb on the Cross. His shed Blood paid for all of mankind's sins (including yours and mine).

On the third day following Jesus' death, he arose from the dead. His resurrection is what proved his deity, including his power over death. Belief in Jesus' resurrection gives a person eternal life.

> *And this is what God has testified: He has given us eternal life, and this life is in his Son. Whoever has the Son has life; whoever does not have God's Son does not have life.*

I have written this to you who believe in the name of the Son of God, so that you may know you have eternal life. 1 John 5:11-13

The moment we accept Jesus Christ as our Savior, we are indwelled with the Holy Spirit, which sets us apart as sacred. It is this indwelling that gives us eternal life in Heaven. The Bible tells us that when a person acknowledges Jesus as Savior, the Holy Spirit comes to live in that person, and seals the deal. It is only when the Spirit lives in an individual that he or she is born Spiritually. It is only this second birth (the first birth is that of flesh, and the second birth is Spiritual) that provides us with eternal life.

And now you Gentiles have also heard the truth, the Good News that God saves you. And when you believed in Christ, he identified you as his own by giving you the Holy Spirit, whom he promised long ago. The Spirit is God's guarantee that he will give us the inheritance he promised and that he has purchased us to be his own people. He did this so we would praise and glorify him. Ephesians 1:13-14

Although Christianity is not a set of rules, when the Holy Spirit comes to live in a Christian he or she may desire to make behavioral changes, as prompted by the Spirit. Many have reported immediate delivery from such vices as drugs and alcohol addiction, addiction to pornography, homosexuality, and many other behaviors that were unwanted or considered immoral. Whatever changes may take place, they will be welcomed and rewarded both while on Earth and in Heaven.

Christians believe that if we accept Jesus as Savior, we will go to Heaven. If we reject him, we will go to Hell. It is that simple.

Jesus told him, "I am the way, the truth, and the life. No one can come to the Father except through me." John 14:6

"But everyone who denies me here on earth, I will also deny before my Father in heaven." Matthew 10:33, Jesus' words

Notes:

13

What is a Christian?

*I would rather a thousand times be five minutes at the feet of
Christ than listen a lifetime to all the wise men in the world.*

Dwight L. Moody (1837-1899)

It's not by being religious

The term *Christian* is so broadly used that oftentimes people think they are Christians merely because they live in America, which is considered by most to be a Christian country.

Throughout the years, the term Christian has lost its accurate Biblical meaning and evolved to erroneously mean a person who has high moral values and is religiously observant. This colossal error has probably caused millions of would-be Christians to reject learning about Jesus because they had the false idea that Christianity is a strict religion, which it is not.

A gold cross necklace, faithful church attendance, weekly Bible study, and a fish symbol on your trunk lid are nice, but they do not move you close enough to the baby in the manger. Kneeling, singing, and raising your hands toward the heavens look good, but these outward acts do not give you an inward relationship with Jesus. Delivering hot meals to shut-ins may bring you closer to your fellow man, but kind acts will not provide you with a personal relationship with the One who paid the price for your sins.

Adhering to strict religious rules, attending church, singing in a church choir, tithing, and all of those other behaviors falsely associated with being a Christian are actually not what makes a person a Christian. Christians generally practice these good deeds, but a Christian's soul is not saved by good deeds.

It's by having faith

The Bible teaches that the good works we do cannot make us acceptable to God, and it is only our belief and faith in Jesus Christ as our Savior that makes us a Christian.

> *He is so rich in kindness and grace that he purchased our freedom with the blood of his Son and forgave our sins.* Ephesians 1:7

> *But—"When God our Savior revealed his kindness and love, he saved us, not because of the righteous things we had done, but because of his mercy. He washed away our sins, giving us a new birth and new life through the Holy Spirit. He generously poured out the Spirit upon us through Jesus Christ our Savior."* Titus 3:4-6

We become Christians when we accept Jesus Christ as our Savior, at which time the Holy Spirit comes to live in us. It is only when the Holy Spirit lives in us that we are Christians.

> *But you are not controlled by your sinful nature. You are controlled by the Spirit if you have the Spirit of God living in you. (And remember that those who do not have the Spirit of Christ living in them do not belong to him at all.) And Christ lives within you, so even though your body will die because of sin, the Spirit gives you life because you have been made right with God. The Spirit of God, who raised Jesus from the dead, lives in you. And just as God raised Christ Jesus from the dead, he will give life to your mortal bodies by this same Spirit living within you.* Romans 8:9-11

A Christian is someone who has been born again

Although the term *born again* has a scary connotation, it describes how we receive Spiritual eternal life.

> *Jesus replied, "I tell you the truth, unless you are born again, you cannot see the Kingdom of God."* John 3:3

> *But to all who believed him and accepted him, he gave the right to become children of God. They are reborn – not with a physical birth resulting from human passion or plan, but a birth that comes from God.* John 1:12-13

For you have been born again, but not to a life that will quickly end. Your new life will last forever because it comes from the eternal, living word of God. 1 Peter 1:23

Because Christians have the Holy Spirit living in them, they know for certain they are going to Heaven.

I have written this to you who believe in the name of the Son of God, so that you may know you have eternal life. 1 John 5:13

A Christian also lives in Christ's body

Simultaneously, when the Holy Spirit comes to live in us, we become a part of Christ's body.

The human body has many parts, but the many parts make up one whole body. So it is with the body of Christ. Some of us are Jews, some are Gentiles, some are slaves, and some are free. But we have all been baptized into one body by one Spirit, and we all share the same Spirit. 1 Corinthians 12:12-13

There is no longer Jew or Gentile, slave or free, male or female. For you are all one in Christ Jesus. Galatians 3:28

A Christian believes Christ paid for mankind's sins once and for all

"I tell you the truth, those who listen to my message and believe in God who sent me have eternal life. They will never be condemned for their sins, but they have already passed from death into life." John 5:24, Jesus' words

For God was in Christ, reconciling the world to himself, no longer counting people's sins against them. And he gave us this wonderful message of reconciliation. 2 Corinthians 5:19

Then he says, "I will never again remember their sins and lawless deeds." Hebrews 10:17

Christians come in all shapes, sizes, and colors

You cannot tell if a person is a Christian by his or her appearance. Some are short, some are tall, some have long hair, and some shave their heads. Many Christians dress conservatively, while others like to exhibit God's vibrant colors. We are all unique.

Christians are found in all denominations, but not all denominations are Christian. The test as to whether a person is a Christian is his or her assurance of salvation, not based on his or her own good deeds – but on his or her trusting in the life, death, and resurrection of Jesus Christ.

> *God saved you by his grace when you believed. And you can't take credit for this; it is a gift from God. Salvation is not a reward for the good things we have done, so none of us can boast about it.* Ephesians 2:8-9

Hallelujah!

PART FOUR
Salvation

Notes:

14

Original sin and the Old Covenant

*Original sin is that thing about man which makes him capable
of conceiving of his own perfection and incapable of achieving it.*

Karl Paul Reinhold Niebuhr (1892-1971)

Adam and Eve were the first two humans. From the very beginning, God differ-
entiated between what was right and wrong, but Adam and Eve disobeyed him.
This is known as *original sin*. The immediate effect of Adam and Eve's sin was that
they died spiritually. Because all of mankind are descendents of Adam and Eve, sin
entered the entire human race. This is referred to as imputed sin (impute means, to
attribute a fault or misconduct to another). Because of imputed sin, everyone is born
a sinner.

Approximately 2,500 years later, when the Israelites (Jews) came out of Egypt, God
gave them the Ten Commandments. These were just the beginning of God's given
laws. An additional 603 laws were given for the Jews to obey in order to gain favor
with God. Of those laws, 365 were the "shall-not" kind.

These laws are all described in the Old Testament Bible and are known as the Old
Covenant (covenant means agreement). In the Old Testament, believers in God offered continuous sacrifices to him in an attempt to have their sins forgiven. But these
sacrifices served only as a temporary cleansing of sins, and thus provided only temporary forgiveness.

Throughout the centuries, since the Israelites recognized their God, many Gentiles
have adopted the God of the Israelites as the one and only God, the Creator of all
things. He is known as the God of Abraham, Isaac, and Jacob.

God is infinitely holy and righteous, and he wants his human creation to be just as holy and righteous. However, we all know this is humanly impossible if the laws given to the Jews are used as the evaluation. If a conscientious person attempts to compile a list of his or her sins based on Old Testament laws, he would be overcome with guilt and failure.

> But those who depend on the law to make them right with God are under his curse, for the Scriptures say, "Cursed is everyone who does not observe and obey all the commands that are written in God's Book of the Law."
> Galatians 3:10

How can anyone ever be made right with God and not feel guilty? Worse than guilt, the punishment for breaking God's laws is death and separation from God in a place known as Eternal Hell. To keep from going to Hell, we sinners needed a way to become righteous.

The blood of lambs was commonly used for these temporary sacrifices, but God presented a new plan that would end this practice forever. His name was Jesus, and he was the ultimate and final Sacrificial Lamb. This new plan is referred to as the *New Covenant.*

> The old way, with laws etched in stone, led to death, though it began with such glory that the people of Israel could not bear to look at Moses' face. For his face shone with the glory of God, even though the brightness was already fading away. Shouldn't we expect far greater glory under the new way, now that the Holy Spirit is giving life? If the old way, which brings condemnation, was glorious, how much more glorious is the new way, which makes us right with God! In fact, that first glory was not glorious at all compared with the overwhelming glory of the new way. So if the old way, which has been replaced, was glorious, how much more glorious is the new, which remains forever!

> Since this new way gives us such confidence, we can be very bold. We are not like Moses, who put a veil over his face so the people of Israel would not see the glory, even though it was destined to fade away. But the people's minds were hardened, and to this day whenever the old covenant is being read, the same veil covers their minds so they cannot understand the truth. And this veil can be removed only by believing in Christ. Yes, even today when they read Moses' writings, their hearts are covered with that veil, and they do not understand.

But whenever someone turns to the Lord, the veil is taken away. For the Lord is the Spirit, and wherever the Spirit of the Lord is, there is freedom. So all of us who have had that veil removed can see and reflect the glory of the Lord. And the Lord — who is the Spirit — makes us more and more like him as we are changed into his glorious image. 2 Corinthians 3:7-18

The New Covenant is the Good News

The New Covenant is God's agreement that replaces the Old Covenant. It is not only for the Jews, but also for all of mankind. Those who accept the New Covenant with God are referred to as *Christians*. The New Covenant is explained in detail in the next chapter.

Notes:

15

The New Covenant – Salvation

The Gospel that represents Jesus Christ, not as a system of truth to be received, into the mind, as I should receive a system of philosophy,or astronomy, but it represents Him as a real, living, mighty Savior, able to save me now.

Catherine Booth (1829-1890) was the wife of the
founder of the Salvation Army.

The following passage explains the Old Testament (Old Covenant) and New Testament (New Covenant):

When Adam sinned, sin entered the world. Adam's sin brought death, so death spread to everyone, for everyone sinned. Yes, people sinned even before the law was given. But it was not counted as sin because there was not yet any law to break. Still, everyone died—from the time of Adam to the time of Moses—even those who did not disobey an explicit commandment of God, as Adam did. Now Adam is a symbol, a representation of Christ, who was yet to come. But there is a great difference between Adam's sin and God's gracious gift. For the sin of this one man, Adam, brought death to many. But even greater is God's wonderful grace and his gift of forgiveness to many through this other man, Jesus Christ. And the result of God's gracious gift is very different from the result of that one man's sin. For Adam's sin led to condemnation, but God's free gift leads to our being made right with God, even though we are guilty of many sins. For the sin of this one man, Adam, caused death to rule over many. But even greater is God's wonderful grace and his gift of righteousness, for all who receive it will live in triumph over sin and death through this one man, Jesus Christ.

Yes, Adam's one sin brings condemnation for everyone, but Christ's one act of righteousness brings a right relationship with God and new life for everyone.

Because one person disobeyed God, many became sinners. But because one other person obeyed God, many will be made righteous.

God's law was given so that all people could see how sinful they were. But as people sinned more and more, God's wonderful grace became more abundant. So just as sin ruled over all people and brought them to death, now God's wonderful grace rules instead, giving us right standing with God and resulting in eternal life through Jesus Christ our Lord. Romans 5:12-21

What is Christian salvation?

Salvation is the term used to describe the experience of being saved from eternal punishment in Hell by trusting in Jesus Christ's finished work as payment for all sins – past, present, and future.

You were dead because of your sins and because your sinful nature was not yet cut away. Then, God made you alive with Christ, for he forgave all our sins. He canceled the record of the charges against us and took it away by nailing it to the cross. Colossians 2:13-14

The *finished work* not only includes Jesus' death, which resulted in forgiveness for all sin, but also his resurrection, which gives us eternal Spiritual life. Many people believe that salvation is just the forgiveness of one's sins, but it is more than that. Salvation is being made alive in Christ as the result of one's Spiritual birth.

The following verse is a great place to begin our study:

"And she will have a son, and you are to name him Jesus, for he will save his people from their sins." Matthew 1:21

Jesus means "the Lord saves," as translated from the Hebrew word *Yeshua*.

For God made Christ, who never sinned, to be the offering for our sin, so that we could be made right with God through Christ. 2 Corinthians 5:21

Here is how it works

The plan is very simple.

"For God loved the world so much that he gave his one and only Son, so that everyone who believes in him will not perish but have eternal life. God sent

his Son into the world not to judge the world, but to save the world through him."

"There is no judgment against anyone who believes in him. But anyone who does not believe in him has already been judged for not believing in God's one and only Son." John 3:16-18, Jesus' words

The above passage explains Christianity in a nutshell, and is what differentiates Christianity from other belief systems. The unique quality of Christianity is that while other belief systems think their followers must perform in order to reach up to their god, Christianity embraces the fact that God loved us so much that he came down to us in the form of a man, named Jesus, and that he made all of the sacrifices necessary for those who believe to spend eternity with him in Heaven.

"I tell you the truth, those who listen to my message and believe in God who sent me have eternal life. They will never be condemned for their sins, but they have already passed from death into life." John 5:24, Jesus' words

We are made right with God by placing our faith in Jesus Christ. And this is true for everyone who believes, no matter who we are. Romans 3:22

All major world faiths except Christianity involve good behavior to receive God's favor for eternal life. Unlike the others, Christianity is not a school to reform behavior and to make immoral men moral. Christianity is a way that immoral people can spend eternity in Heaven with the Creator God, clothed in the righteousness of Jesus Christ. Christianity demands nothing more than faith. Good behavior is desirable, but not mandatory for salvation.

Jesus was God incarnate

Jesus Christ is the same yesterday, today, and forever. Hebrews 13:8

No theologian, scholar, historian, or other knowledgeable person questions the fact that Jesus existed. Atheists, agnostics, Jews, Muslims, and most other religions recognize Jesus as a true historical figure. The disagreement arises when one begins to consider Jesus' divinity.

A couple billion people believe he was God in the flesh. Contemporary scholars, who endorse the Bible as authoritative, accept the belief that through the power of the Holy Spirit, God became incarnate from the Virgin Mary, and he died on the Cross for the forgiveness of sin. They also believe he was resurrected so that believers may have eternal life with him in Heaven.

A few Bible verses that substantiate Jesus' divinity are as follows:

> In the beginning the Word already existed. The Word was with God, and the Word was God. He existed in the beginning with God. God created everything through him, and nothing was created except through him. John 1:1-3

> Though he was God,
>   he did not think of equality with God
>   as something to cling to.
> Instead, he gave up his divine privileges;
>   he took the humble position of a slave
>   and was born as a human being.
> When he appeared in human form,
>   he humbled himself in obedience to God
>   and died a criminal's death on a cross. Philippians 2:6-8

> For he has rescued us from the kingdom of darkness and transferred us into the Kingdom of his dear Son, who purchased our freedom and forgave our sins. Christ is the visible image of the invisible God.

> He existed before anything was created and is supreme over all creation, for through him God created everything in the heavenly realms and on earth. He made the things we can see and the things we can't see – such as thrones, kingdoms, rulers, and authorities in the unseen world. Everything was created through him and for him. Colossians 1:13-16

> And now in these final days, he has spoken to us through his Son. God promised everything to the Son as an inheritance, and through the Son he created the universe. Hebrews 1:2

> Because God's children are human beings – made of flesh and blood – the Son also became flesh and blood. For only as a human being could he die, and only by dying could he break the power of the Devil, who had the power of death. Hebrews 2:14

The above verses are either very true or absolute nonsense. I suggest you pray that God will reveal the truth to you, as he will.

Jesus became sin and was crucified

The Bible teaches that Jesus not only bore the punishment for our sins, he actually became sin. Jesus took all of our sins to the Cross in his body. Christ became sin for us so that we would have absolute righteousness. This is called *justification*, and it is a gift. It is by grace alone that we are justified, and the Bible says it has nothing to do with our behavior.

> *For God made Christ, who never sinned, to be the offering for our sin, so that we could be made right with God through Christ.* 2 Corinthians 5:21

Jesus took our place on the cross. Jesus was the perfect Lamb of God, who experienced death for all of the sins of mankind.

> *The next day John saw Jesus coming toward him and said, "Look! The Lamb of God who takes away the sin of the world!"* John 1:29

> *Christ suffered for our sins once for all time. He never sinned, but he died for sinners to bring you safely home to God. He suffered physical death, but he was raised to life in the Spirit.* 1 Peter 3:18

Jesus was a sinless man, and as a result, he was able to take the sin of the world onto himself immediately before he died.

Animal blood

God's prerequisite in the Old Testament for the forgiveness of sins was by the shedding of blood.

> *In fact, according to the law of Moses, nearly everything was purified with blood. For without the shedding of blood, there is no forgiveness.* Hebrews 9:22

The term *blood* has a special meaning in the Bible. Blood is the evidence of life, thus considered sacred, just as life is considered sacred. Because blood and life are considered sacred, Israel's priests used the blood of animals to prepare the sacrifices they offered to God for the benefit of the people.

> *Then slaughter the young bull in the Lord's presence, and Aaron's sons, the priests, will present the animal's blood by splattering it against all sides of the alter that stands at the entrance to the Tabernacle.* Leviticus 1:5

When the people of Israel were preparing to escape from Egypt, they were told to sprinkle blood on the doorframes of their houses to protect them as the Lord passed over Egypt and took the life of the oldest son in each family.

At Mount Sinai, blood was poured out to make firm the covenant between God and the Israelite people.

> *Then Moses took the blood from the basins and splattered it over the people, declaring, "Look, this blood confirms the covenant the Lord has made with you in giving you these instructions."* Exodus 24:8

Jesus' Blood

Because of the Old Testament blood sacrifices, the shed Blood of Jesus (who was God incarnate) did what the blood of animals could not do:

> *For everyone has sinned; we all fall short of God's glorious standard. Yet God, with undeserved kindness, declares that we are righteous. He did this through Christ Jesus when he freed us from the penalty for our sins. For God presented Jesus as the sacrifice for sin. People are made right with God when they believe that Jesus sacrificed his life, shedding his blood. This sacrifice shows that God was being fair when he held back and did not punish those who sinned in times past, for he was looking ahead and including them in what he would do in this present time. God did this to demonstrate his righteousness, for he himself is fair and just, and he declares sinners to be right in his sight when they believe in Jesus.* Romans 3:23-26

Everyone in the entire human race has sinned, and the only way a person can be redeemed is through a blood sacrifice. Because the Old Testament blood sacrifice was not sufficient to completely and permanently cleanse a person of their sinful nature, God came to Earth in the form of a baby named Jesus, foreknowing that non-believers would crucify him.

Jesus' Blood cleansed the world of all past, present, and future sins, enabling all who accept the Savior Jesus to receive eternal life.

Christ's sacrifice once and for all is the first half

Going through religious motions to get one's sins forgiven blasphemes Jesus' Blood sacrifice. According to God's standard of perfection, a person cannot do anything to make oneself blameless. Only the cleansing Blood that Jesus shed on the Cross, which was once and for all, perfects us.

The old system under the law of Moses was only a shadow, a dim preview of the good things to come, not the good things themselves. The sacrifices under that system were repeated again and again, year after year, but they were never able to provide perfect cleansing for those who came to worship. If they could have provided perfect cleansing, the sacrifices would have stopped, for the worshippers would have been purified once for all time, and their feelings of guilt would have disappeared.

But instead, those sacrifices actually reminded them of their sins year after year. For it is not possible for the blood of bulls and goats to take away sins.
Hebrews 10:1-4

Under the old covenant, the priest stands and ministers before the alter day after day, offering the same sacrifices again and again, which can never take away sins. But our High Priest offered himself to God as a single sacrifice for sins, good for all time. Then he sat down in the place of honor at God's right hand. There he waits until his enemies are humbled and made a footstool under his feet. For by that one offering he forever made perfect those who are being made holy. Hebrews 10:11-14

A few religions, including some that label themselves as Christian, still have priests that continue to stand before the altar day after day performing religious sacrifices in the hope of getting sins forgiven. This monotonous act is not only futile, but also blasphemous. Those who participate in this are claiming that the Blood of Jesus was insufficient in cleansing sins once and for all.

If you believe Jesus was God in the flesh and that he came to Earth to die on a cross to forgive you for your sins, then you're halfway to salvation.

Jesus' resurrection is the second half

Jesus' Blood paid for the sins of the world, but that is not all there is to salvation. In order to be saved, a person must also believe in Jesus' power to overcome death. On the third day after his crucifixion, Jesus arose from death. The resurrection of Jesus constitutes the most important proof of his deity.

Early on Sunday morning, as the new day was dawning, Mary Magdalene and the other Mary went out to visit the tomb.

Suddenly there was a great earthquake! For an angel of the Lord came down from heaven, rolled aside the stone, and sat on it. His face shone like lightening, and his clothing was as white as snow. The guards shook with fear when they saw him, and they fell into a dead faint.

Then the angel spoke to the women. "Don't be afraid!" he said. "I know you are looking for Jesus, who was crucified. He isn't here! He is risen from the dead, just as he said would happen. Come, see where his body was lying. And now, go quickly and tell his disciples he has risen from the dead, and he is going ahead of you to Galilee. You will see him there. Remember what I have told you." Matthew 28:1-7

The resurrection gives Christians eternal life

It is the resurrection that gives us spiritual and eternal life. Our sins were forgiven at the Cross, but we were not given eternal spiritual life until the resurrection of Jesus.

Many who refer to themselves as Christians insist that we must do something to gain salvation, and that once gained, salvation can be lost. This would mean that to regain our salvation Jesus would need to be slain, then rise from the dead again. That is not sound Christian doctrine, as God's one time sacrifice of his Son was enough.

If that had been necessary, Christ would have had to die again and again, ever since the world began. But now, once for all time, he has appeared at the end of the age, to remove sin by his own death as a sacrifice. Hebrews 9:26

The resurrection of Jesus Christ displayed the immeasurable power of God – who became a man, was crucified on a cross, and yet, had the power to resurrect himself. This proves that God can resurrect life after death. Jesus' resurrection substantiated the fact that he is God, and it is the basis of the Christian faith.

And if Christ has not been raised, then your faith is useless, and you are still guilty of your sins. 1 Corinthians 15:17

So you see, just as death came into the world through a man, now the resurrection from the dead has begun through another man. Just as everyone dies because we all belong to Adam, everyone who belongs to Christ will be given new life. 1 Corinthians 15:21-22

For sin is the sting that results in death, and the law gives sin its power. But thank God! He gives us victory over sin and death through our Lord Jesus Christ. 1 Corinthians 15:56-57

But God is so rich in mercy, and he loved us so much, that even though we were dead because of our sins, he gave us life when he raised Christ from the dead. (It is only by God's grace that you have been saved!) For he raised us from the dead along with Christ and seated us with him in the heavenly realms because we are united with Christ Jesus. Ephesians 2:4-6

God saved you by his grace when you believed. And you can't take credit for this; it is a gift from God. Salvation is not a reward for the good things we have done, so none of us can boast about it. Ephesians 2:8-9

It's a gift, but you must accept it

It is God's gift to those who accept it.

> *For the wages of sin is death, but the free gift of God is eternal life through Christ Jesus our Lord.* Romans 6:23

Once accepted, the recipient is referred to as a Christian for all eternity.

You receive it immediately

At the moment of belief one is saved. Below are two New Testament examples of how people were saved instantly:

Example 1: One day Jesus was in a house in Capernaum. A huge crowd of people had squeezed into the house to listen to him. Four men arrived, carrying a sick friend on a mat. They wanted Jesus to heal him, but could not get into the house. Looking around for another way, they climbed onto the roof and made a hole. Then they carefully lowered the paralyzed man into the room where Jesus was speaking.

> *Seeing their faith, Jesus said to the man, "Young man, your sins are forgiven."* Luke 5:20

In the example above, the first thing Jesus did was to forgive the man for his sins based strictly on faith. Then Jesus turned to the man and healed him. There was no condemnation and no payment of money. Just like coffee – it was instant.

Example 2: When Jesus was dying on the Cross, there were two thieves hanging on either side of him. One had faith that Jesus was God, and the other did not. To the one thief who had faith, Jesus said:

> *"I assure you, today you will be with me in paradise."* Luke 23:43

Jesus did not tell the thief on the Cross that he would have to wait for a church deacon to pray over him, or for a priest to give him blessings, or for a band of angels to vote. Jesus made the decision immediately, and that was that. No soul sleep, no purgatory, no holding cell, no cleaning up the thief – now!

The two examples above were before Jesus' death.

It is important to emphasize that no matter how many sins you have committed, how often, or the magnitude of the sins – you were forgiven immediately for all sins upon your trusting only in Jesus as your Savior – immediately. You will also experience immediate forgiveness for all sins committed after you have been saved. Many unlearned Christians deny that Jesus forgives so rapidly, but it is true. Making you suffer for a while is not Jesus' style.

Salvation cannot be lost

Permanent salvation is such a controversial subject that a separate chapter follows so that it may be discussed in detail. In the meantime, please try to comprehend the fact that once a person is saved, he or she is saved eternally. If you are already a saved person, but you are under the impression you can lose your salvation, then I ask you: Which of your sins did Jesus not die for?

Jesus' words regarding salvation

Based upon what God said and what Jesus did, there is only one method for acquiring eternal life in Heaven. It has nothing to do with being a good person or obeying rules. It is strictly by trusting in the sacrificial death of Jesus Christ, nothing more and nothing less.

Because Jesus is the one who made the ultimate sacrifice, his words must prevail. Let us see what he has to say.

> *"But everyone who denies me here on earth, I will also deny before my Father in heaven."* Matthew 10:33, Jesus' words

> *When Jesus heard this, he told them, "Healthy people don't need a doctor – sick people do. I have come to call not those who think they are righteous, but those who know they are sinners."* Mark 2:17

> *"For even the Son of Man, came not to be served but to serve others, and to give his life as a ransom for many."* Mark 10:45, Jesus' words

"Anyone who believes and is baptized will be saved. But anyone who refuses to believe will be condemned." Mark 16:16, Jesus' words

And Jesus said to the woman, "Your faith has saved you; go in peace."
Luke 7:50

"For the Son of Man, came to seek and save those who are lost." Luke 19:10, Jesus' words

Jesus replied, "I tell you the truth, unless you are born again, you cannot see the Kingdom of God." John 3:3

"But those who drink the water I give will never be thirsty again. It becomes a fresh, bubbling spring within them, giving them eternal life." John 4:14, Jesus' words

Then Jesus told her, "I Am the Messiah!" John 4:26

"I tell you the truth, those who listen to my message and believe in God who sent me have eternal life. They will never be condemned for their sins, but they have already passed from death into life." John 5:24, Jesus' words

"You search the Scriptures because you think they give you eternal life. But the Scriptures point to me!" John 5:39, Jesus' words

Jesus replied, "I am the bread of life. Whoever comes to me will never be hungry again. Whoever believes in me will never be thirsty. But you haven't believed in me even though you have seen me. However, those the Father has given me will come to me, and I will never reject them. For I have come down from heaven to do the will of God who sent me, not to do my own will. And this is the will of God, that I should not lose even one of all those he has given me, but that I should raise them up at the last day. For it is my Father's will that all who see his Son and believe in him should have eternal life. I will raise them up at the last day." John 6:35-40

"I tell you the truth, anyone who believes has eternal life. Yes, I am the bread of life! Your ancestors ate manna in the wilderness, but they all died. Anyone who eats the bread from heaven, however, will never die. I am the living bread that came down from heaven. Anyone who eats this bread will live forever; and this bread, which I will offer so the world may live, is my flesh."
John 6:47-51, Jesus' words

"Yes, I am the gate. Those who come in through me will be saved. They will come and go freely and will find good pastures. The thief's purpose is to steal and kill and destroy. My purpose is to give them a rich and satisfying life."
John 10:9-10, Jesus' words

Jesus replied, "I have already told you, and you don't believe me. The proof is the work I do in my Father's name. But you don't believe me because you are not my sheep. My sheep listen to my voice; I know them, and they follow me. I give them eternal life, and they will never perish. No one can snatch them away from me, for my Father has given them to me, and he is more powerful than anyone else. No one can snatch them from the Father's hand. The Father and I are one." John 10:25-30

Jesus told her, "I am the resurrection and the life. Anyone who believes in me will live, even after dying. Everyone who lives in me and believes in me will never ever die. Do you believe this, Martha?" John 11:25-26

"The time for judging this world has come, when Satan, the ruler of this world, will be cast out. And when I am lifted up from the earth, I will draw everyone to myself." John 12:31-32, Jesus' words

"The world's sin is that it refuses to believe in me." John 16:9, Jesus' words

Jesus is the only way

Jesus told him, "I am the way, the truth, and the life. No one can come to the Father except through me. If you had really known me, you would know who my Father is. From now on, you do know him and have seen him!" John 14:6-7

Many people become intolerant of Christians who proclaim that Christ is the only way to Heaven. That attitude makes Christians sound narrow-minded, bigoted, extreme, radical, prejudiced, and fanatical. I would rather be called narrow-minded than gamble with my eternal security. Why would anyone want to look elsewhere when Jesus is so readily available?

"But," you say, "what about all of those well-behaved, moral people around the world who do not know about Jesus or who do not believe he was God incarnate? I can't believe a loving God would let them burn in Hell!"

My answer is that although God is a loving God, he also destroyed the world with water once, destroyed two cities, and will come back to destroy the world again. He also allowed his Son to be humiliated, brutalized, and then nailed to the Cross to die so those who believe in his finished work may have eternal life. God has reasons for everything he does, and I decided years ago not to question his methods.

God knows all things, including who would and who will accept Jesus Christ as Savior. We must have faith that his decision will be fair and just to all who have not been exposed to Jesus.

What the Great Apostle Paul taught regarding salvation

The Apostle Paul is considered by many to be the greatest Christian who has ever lived. Here are some of Paul's teachings on salvation:

> *For I am not ashamed of this Good News about Christ. It is the power of God at work, saving everyone who believes – the Jew first and also the Gentile. This Good News tells us how God makes us right in his sight. This is accomplished from start to finish by faith. As the Scriptures say, "It is through faith that a righteous person has life."* Romans 1:16-17

> *But now God has shown us a way to be made right with him without keeping the requirements of the law, as was promised in the writings of Moses and the prophets long ago. We are made right with God by placing our faith in Jesus Christ. And this is true for everyone who believes, no matter who we are.* Romans 3:21-22

> *Can we boast, then, that we have done anything to be accepted by God? No, because our acquittal is not based on obeying the law. It is based on faith. So we are made right with God through faith and not by obeying the law.* Romans 3:27-28

> *When people work, their wages are not a gift, but something they have earned. But people are counted as righteous, not because of their work, but because of their faith in God who forgives sinners.* Romans 4:4-5

> *If God's promise is only for those who obey the law, then faith is not necessary and the promise is pointless. For the law always brings punishment on those who try to obey it. (The only way to avoid breaking the law is to have no law to break!)* Romans 4:14-15

> *Therefore, since we have been made right in God's sight by faith, we have peace with God because of what Jesus Christ our Lord has done for us.* Romans 5:1

So now there is no condemnation for those who belong to Christ Jesus. And because you belong to him, the power of the life-giving Spirit has freed you from the power of sin that leads to death. The Law of Moses was unable to save us because of the weakness of our sinful nature. So God did what the law could not do. He sent his own Son in a body like the bodies we sinners have. And in that body God declared an end to sin's control over us by giving his Son as a sacrifice for our sins. He did this so that the just requirement of the law would be fully satisfied for us, who no longer follow our sinful nature but instead follow the Spirit. Romans 8:1-4

What does all this mean? Even though the Gentiles were not trying to follow God's standards, they were made right with God. And it was by faith that this took place. But the people of Israel, who tried so hard to get right with God by keeping the law, never succeeded. Why not? Because they were trying to get right with God by keeping the law instead of by trusting in him. They stumbled over the great rock in their path. God warned them of this in the Scriptures when he said, "I am placing a stone in Jerusalem that makes people stumble, a rock that makes them fall. But anyone who trusts in him will never be disgraced." Romans 9:30-33

For Christ has already accomplished the purpose for which the law was given. As a result, all who believe in him are made right with God. Romans 10:4

For Christ didn't send me to baptize, but to preach the Good News – and not with clever speech, for fear that the cross of Christ would lose its power. The message of the cross is foolish to those who are headed for destruction! But we who are being saved know it is the very power of God. 1 Corinthians 1:17-18

Don't you realize that those who do wrong will not inherit the Kingdom of God? Don't fool yourselves. Those who indulge in sexual sin, or who worship idols, or commit adultery, or are male prostitutes, or practice homosexuality, or are thieves, or greedy people, or drunkards, or are abusive, or cheat people—none of these will inherit the Kingdom of God. Some of you were once like that. But you were cleansed; you were made holy; you were made right with God by calling on the name of the Lord Jesus Christ and by the Spirit of our God. 1 Corinthians 6:9-11

This means that anyone who belongs to Christ has become a new person. The old life is gone; a new life has begun!

And all of this is a gift from God, who brought us back to himself through Christ. And God has given us this task of reconciling people to him. For God was in Christ, reconciling the world to himself, no longer counting people's sins against them. And he gave us this wonderful message of reconciliation. So we are Christ's ambassadors; God is making his appeal through us. We speak for Christ when we plead, "Come back to God!" For God made Christ, who never sinned, to be the offering for our sin, so that we could be made right with God through Christ.   2 Corinthians 5:17-21

"You and I are Jews by birth, not 'sinners' like the Gentiles. Yet we know that a person is made right with God by faith in Jesus Christ, not by obeying the law. And we have believed in Christ Jesus, so that we might be made right with God because of our faith in Christ, not because we have obeyed the law. For no one will ever be made right with God by obeying the law."
Galatians 2:15-16

But those who depend on the law to make them right with God are under his curse, for the Scriptures say, "Cursed is everyone who does not observe and obey all the commands that are written in God's Book of the Law." So it is clear that no one can be made right with God by trying to keep the law. For the Scriptures say, "It is through faith that a righteous person has life." This way of faith is very different from the way of law, which says, "It is through obeying the law that a person has life."

But Christ has rescued us from the curse pronounced by the law. When he was hung on the cross, he took upon himself the curse for our wrongdoing. For it is written in the Scriptures, "Cursed is everyone who is hung on a tree." Through Christ Jesus, God has blessed the Gentiles with the same blessing he promised to Abraham, so that we who are believers might receive the promised Holy Spirit through faith.
Galatians 3:10-14

But when the right time came, God sent his Son, born of a woman, subject to the law. God sent him to buy freedom for us who were slaves to the law, so that he could adopt us as his very own children.   Galatians 4:4-5

And now you Gentiles have also heard the truth, the Good News that God saves you. And when you believed in Christ, he identified you as his own by giving you the Holy Spirit, whom he promised long ago. The Spirit is God's guarantee that he will give us the inheritance he promised and that he has purchased us to be his own people. He did this so we would praise and glorify him.   Ephesians 1:13-14

But God is so rich in mercy, and he loved us so much, that even though we were dead because of our sins, he gave us life when he raised Christ from the dead. (It is only by God's grace that you have been saved!) For he raised us from the dead along with Christ and seated us with him in the heavenly realms because we are united with Christ Jesus. So God can point to us in all future ages as examples of the incredible wealth of his grace and kindness toward us, as shown in all he has done for us who are united with Christ Jesus.

God saved you by his grace when you believed. And you can't take credit for this; it is a gift from God. Salvation is not a reward for the good things we have done, so none of us can boast about it. Ephesians 2:4-9

He cancelled the record of the charges against us and took it away by nailing it to Christ's cross. Colossians 2:14

For God chose to save us through our Lord Jesus Christ, not to pour out his anger on us. Christ died for us so that, whether we are dead or alive when he returns, we can live with him forever. 1 Thessalonians 5:9-10

I thank Christ Jesus our Lord, who has given me strength to do his work. He considered me trustworthy and appointed me to serve him, even though I used to blaspheme the name of Christ. In my insolence, I persecuted his people. But God had mercy on me because I did it in ignorance and unbelief. Oh, how generous and gracious our Lord was! He filled me with the faith and love that come from Christ Jesus.

This is a trustworthy saying, and everyone should accept it: "Christ Jesus came into the world to save sinners"—and I am the worst of them all.
1 Timothy 1:12-15

For there is only one God and one Mediator who can reconcile God and humanity – the man Christ Jesus. He gave his life to purchase freedom for everyone. This is the message God gave to the world at just the right time.
1 Timothy 2:5-6

For God saved us and called us to live a holy life. He did this, not because we deserved it, but because that was his plan from before the beginning of time—to show us his grace through Christ Jesus. And now he has made all of this plain to us by the appearing of Christ Jesus, our Savior. He broke the

*power of death and illuminated the way to life and immortality through the
Good News.* 2 Timothy 1:9-10

*But—"When God our Savior revealed his kindness and love, he saved us, not
because of the righteous things we had done, but because of his mercy. He
washed away our sins, giving us a new birth and new life through the Holy
Spirit. He generously poured out the Spirit upon us through Jesus Christ our
Savior. Because of his grace he declared us righteous and gave us confidence
that we will inherit eternal life."* Titus 3:4-7

More passages regarding salvation

*"Brothers, listen! We are here to proclaim that through this man Jesus there is
forgiveness for your sins. Everyone who believes in him is declared right with
God—something the law of Moses could never do.* Acts 13:38-39

*For God's will was for us to be made holy by the sacrifice of the body of Jesus
Christ, once for all time.* Hebrews 10:10

The reward for trusting him will be the salvation of your souls. 1 Peter 1:9

*In his kindness God called you to share in his eternal glory by means of
Christ Jesus. So after you have suffered a little while, he will restore, support,
and strengthen you, and he will place you on a firm foundation. All power to
him forever! Amen.* 1 Peter 5:10-11

You must die to the law

You should underline and highlight the following passages in your Bible. These two
passages make it clear how Christianity should be taught. Unfortunately, many
Christians have devised a deceitful, legalistic system within Christianity again.

*But now we have been released from the law, for we died to it and are
no longer captive to its power. Now we can serve God, not in the old way
of obeying the letter of the law, but in the new way of living in the Spirit.*
Romans 7:6

*For when I tried to keep the law, it condemned me. So I died to the law – I
stopped trying to meet all its requirements – so that I might live for God. My
old self has been crucified with Christ. It is no longer I who live, but Christ*

lives in me. So I live in this earthly body by trusting in the Son of God, who loved me and gave himself for me. Galatians 2:19-20

Galatianism

The term *Galatianism* was mentioned earlier in this book, but it is such an under-used and unrecognized term that it requires explanation and elaboration. Do not forget this term and its relevancy in Christendom.

A quick definition of *grace* is, "receiving something that is undeserved." Understanding its Biblical application in the doctrine of salvation requires further explanation. Grace is the formula for one's eternal destiny, resulting from the undeserved favor from God who justifies those who trust in the finished work of Jesus Christ as their only means for salvation. Justification is an instantaneous occurrence that results in eternal life.

> *"For God loved the world so much that he gave his one and only Son, so that everyone who believes in him will not perish but have eternal life. God sent his Son into the world not to judge the world, but to save the world through him."* John 3:16-17, Jesus' words

> *For God presented Jesus as the sacrifice for sin. People are made right with God when they believe that Jesus sacrificed his life, shedding his blood. This sacrifice shows that God was being fair when he held back and did not punish those who sinned in times past, for he was looking ahead and including them in what he would do in this present time. God did this to demonstrate his righteousness, for he himself is fair and just, and he declares sinners to be right in his sight when they believe in Jesus.* Romans 3:25-26

> *God saved you by his grace when you believed. And you can't take credit for this; it is a gift from God. Salvation is not a reward for the good things we have done, so none of us can boast about it.* Ephesians 2:8-9

Unfortunately, many people want to mix good deeds with the gift of grace, which makes God's simple plan confusing and complicated. This mixing of grace and works is called *Galatianism*. In existence since the beginning of Christian ministry, galatianism is demonstrated best in the book of *Galatians*.

Although many residents of Galatia had received and accepted the simplicity of the New Covenant, so-called "spiritual men" came on the scene teaching that new Christians needed to add some of the Old Covenant laws to the New Covenant freedom.

The great Apostle Paul boldly warned those of Galatia about the error of insisting that good deeds must be added to what Jesus had already done in order to obtain eternal life.

> *I am shocked that you are turning away so soon from God, who called you to himself through the loving mercy of Christ. You are following a different way that pretends to be the Good News but is not the Good News at all. You are being fooled by those who deliberately twist the truth concerning Christ.*
> Galatians 1:6-7

> *How foolish can you be? After starting your Christian lives in the Spirit, why are you now trying to become perfect by your own human effort?* Galatians 3:3

> *This way of faith is very different from the way of law, which says, "It is through obeying the law that a person has life."*

> *But Christ has rescued us from the curse pronounced by the law. When he was hung on the cross, he took upon himself the curse for our wrongdoing. For it is written in the Scriptures, "Cursed is everyone who is hung on a tree." Through Christ Jesus, God has blessed the Gentiles with the same blessing he promised to Abraham, so that we who are believers might receive the promised Holy Spirit through faith.* Galatians 3:12-14

These passages make it crystal clear that Christians are not saved by following religious rules; being a good person will not get you into Heaven.

Galatianism is one of the major reasons people are terrified of Jesus. Pathetically, they have heard that getting into Heaven requires insurmountable work, and they feel that they could never live up to the strict requirements – so they reject hearing about Jesus.

The world would be brimming with Christians (people who know Jesus personally) if church leaders would teach the truth of the New Testament rather than instill guilt by teaching laws that were demanded in the Old Testament. It is because of faulty teaching that most people reject this astonishing carpenter named Jesus, who died on a cross to forgive all of mankind for their sins.

A little about the Old Testament laws

Beginning with Adam and Eve, mankind has been of a sinful nature. Before the death of Jesus Christ, God gave mankind certain laws regarding our moral behavior.

God gave these laws so that people would have a guide to live by and a standard by which they might recognize God's purity and their sinfulness. There are 613 such laws, or commandments (including the Ten Commandments), stated in the Old Testament, but these laws were fulfilled by Jesus' death on the Cross.

> *For Christ has already accomplished the purpose for which the law was given. As a result, all who believe in him are made right with God.* Romans 10:4

> *Before the way of faith in Christ was available to us, we were placed under guard by the law. We were kept in protective custody, so to speak, until the way of faith was revealed.*

> *Let me put it another way. The law was our guardian until Christ came; it protected us until we could be made right with God through faith. And now that the way of faith has come, we no longer need the law as our guardian.* Galatians 3:23-25

> *He did this by ending the system of law with its commandments and regulations. He made peace between Jews and Gentiles by creating in himself one new people from the two groups.* Ephesians 2:15

Please notice the above verse states that the "Jewish law excluded the Gentiles." This means the Ten Commandments were not and are not laws for Gentiles. They are not now, nor have they ever been. Teaching that they were or are for Gentiles is counterfeit teaching.

The Jewish laws known as the Old Covenant that God gave to the Jews, were good, but because of mankind's sinful nature it was impossible for anyone to obey them. Notice I said *anyone*.

Warning

Always remember that because of human weakness, God made a New Covenant, which is simply your accepting the life, death, and resurrection of Jesus Christ as the only means for salvation. Please be warned that your church leaders may be guilty of adding laws, practices, customs, and traditions to their teachings that are not from the New Testament. It is your responsibility to ascertain if you are receiving the truth.

> *So Christ has truly set us free. Now make sure that you stay free, and don't get tied up again in slavery to the law.* Galatians 5:1

You must study your Bible to ascertain truth. Do not put all of your faith in another mortal, but depend on the Word of God and the Holy Spirit.

A story worth reading

> There was a man named Nicodemus, a Jewish religious leader who was a Pharisee. After dark one evening, he came to speak with Jesus. "Rabbi," he said, "we all know that God has sent you to teach us. Your miraculous signs are evidence that God is with you."
>
> Jesus replied, "I tell you the truth, unless you are born again, you cannot see the Kingdom of God."
>
> "What do you mean?" exclaimed Nicodemus. "How can an old man go back into his mother's womb and be born again?"
>
> Jesus replied, "I assure you, no one can enter the Kingdom of God without being born of water and the Spirit. Humans can reproduce only human life, but the Holy Spirit gives birth to spiritual life. So don't be surprised when I say, 'You must be born again.' The wind blows wherever it wants. Just as you can hear the wind but can't tell where it comes from or where it is going, so you can't explain how people are born of the Spirit." John 3:1-8

NOTE: In the passage above, where it says *water*, many Bible scholars agree it is not referring to "baptism with water," which would be in conflict with other New Testament passages that do not state that water baptism is needed for salvation. The term *water* here is referring to the water-like fluid released when the amniotic sac breaks prior to a pregnant woman birthing a child.

Hundreds of millions of individuals like you and me have embraced this passage and will attest to knowing, beyond the shadow of a doubt, that they have received the Holy Spirit, and have been assured by him they are going to Heaven.

The proof is in the receiving

10 days after witnessing Jesus ascending into Heaven, the apostles began to celebrate the Jewish feast of Pentecost, along with Jews from many nations who had come to Jerusalem for this festive occasion.

On Sunday morning Jesus' followers met together, when suddenly the sound of a mighty wind filled the house. In amazement, they watched what appeared to be tongues of fire blowing from Heaven and permeating the house. These flames of fire settled on each of them, filling them with the Holy Spirit.

> *Then Peter said to them, "Repent, and let every one of you be baptized in the name of Jesus Christ for the remission of sins; and you shall receive the gift of the Holy Spirit."* Acts 2:38 (KJV)

About 3,000 people became believers that day.

> *Those who believed what Peter said were baptized and added to the church that day—about 3,000 in all.* Acts 2:41

This was the beginning of the Christian Church. You can be a part of the Church that will enjoy eternal life based on the death, burial, and resurrection of Jesus Christ.

> *But to all who believed him and accepted him, he gave the right to become children of God. They are reborn—not with a physical birth resulting from human passion or plan, but a birth that comes from God.* John 1:12-13

> *But you are not controlled by your sinful nature. You are controlled by the Spirit if you have the Spirit of God living in you. (And remember that those who do not have the Spirit of Christ living in them do not belong to him at all.)* Romans 8:9

> *There is no longer Jew or Gentile, slave or free, male and female. For you are all one in Christ Jesus.* Galatians 3:28

One powerful verse

Hopefully by now you are a believer who wants to spend eternity with God. The great Apostle Paul provided us with a verse that has been the formula for millions who, throughout the last 2,000 years, have made the declaration. That powerful Scripture can be found in the book of Romans:

> *For it is by believing in your heart that you are made right with God, and it is by confessing with your mouth that you are saved.* Romans 10:10

Although God made the offer, you make the decision

God so loved the world that he created a plan that would allow those who accept Jesus Christ as Savior to spend eternity in Heaven. God's plan is so simple that *you* make the final decision regarding your destiny. You can make that decision right now. It has nothing to do with how good you have been or how good you will be. It is contingent on your faith in Jesus Christ as your Savior. Immediately upon making your declaration, you will be as white as the wind-driven snow. God will remember your sins no longer. Pretty simple, huh? It is going to Hell that takes a lot of work. Make the right choice, and make it now.

The sinner's prayer

The following confession is similar to that which millions have prayed and they have received eternal life with God. No fancy oration is necessary, so do not make it too complicated. It should be simple and to the point because God knows what is in your heart. If you sincerely mean the words that you are about to pray, you will then be *born again* – it is that easy. It is hard to believe, but it is true!

> God,
>
> I know that I am a sinner and in need of salvation. I don't know much about religion, but I am going to trust that your Son Jesus Christ died to pay a debt that I cannot pay. From now and forever I am trusting in Jesus' death, burial and resurrection as payment in full for my sins and for my eternal life in Heaven. Thank you, Jesus, for loving and forgiving me!
>
> Amen.

So that you may KNOW

If you have said the above prayer with meaning or if you believe that Jesus is your only means of salvation, you have eternal life.

> *I have written this to you who believe in the name of the Son of God, so that you may know you have eternal life.* 1 John 5:13

Notes:

16

Occasional doubting is normal

There's something in every atheist, itching to believe, and something in every believer, itching to doubt.

Mignon McLaughlin (1913-1983)

There is a difference between doubting and disbelief. Everyone occasionally has doubts in both the existence of God and the divinity of the man named Jesus. Just as it would not be possible to have cold without hot, it would not be possible to have faith without doubt.

Even those who walked, talked, ate, laughed, and cried with Jesus occasionally had doubts. Then, he would perform another miracle and they would be believers again, for a while. Jesus understood doubt then, and he understands now, so do not feel guilty.

One reason Jesus was crucified was that he claimed to be the king of the Jews. He was continuously called upon to prove his power, and he obliged time and time again by performing feats that would be impossible by an ordinary man. Yet human doubt cost him his life.

Doubting Thomas, an apostle and friend of Jesus, was also skeptical:

> *One of the twelve disciples, Thomas (nicknamed the Twin), was not with the others when Jesus came. They told him, "We have seen the Lord!"*
>
> *But he replied, "I won't believe it unless I see the nail wounds in his hands, put my fingers into them, and place my hand into the wound in his side."*

Eight days later the disciples were together again, and this time Thomas was with them. The doors were locked; but suddenly, as before, Jesus was standing among them. "Peace be with you," he said. Then he said to Thomas, "Put your finger here, and look at my hands. Put your hand into the wound in my side. Don't be faithless any longer. Believe!"

"My Lord and my God!" Thomas exclaimed.

Then Jesus told him, "You believe because you have seen me. Blessed are those who believe without seeing me." John 20:24-29

Notice the very last verse, *"Blessed are those who believe without seeing me."* Although written more than 2,000 years ago, this story is typical and applicable.

Doubt is acceptable, but rejection isn't

Jesus is very forgiving, but he draws the line at rejection. The following passage is often incorrectly interpreted to mean that a person's good behavior is the narrow gate, and that those who live a moral life will obtain eternal life in Heaven.

"You can enter God's Kingdom only through the narrow gate. The highway to hell is broad, and its gate is wide for the many who choose that way. But the gateway to life is very narrow and the road is difficult, and only a few ever find it." Matthew 7:13-14, Jesus' words

The correct meaning is that the narrow way is faith in Jesus as one's Savior. Believing there are many paths to Heaven is the highway to Hell. To seek another path is to belittle Jesus' sacrifice. A person who rejects God's beloved Son is condemned. The following passages speak for themselves.

"But everyone who denies me here on earth, I will also deny before my Father in heaven." Matthew 10:33, Jesus' words

"There is no judgment against anyone who believes in him. But anyone who does not believe in him has already been judged for not believing in God's one and only Son." John 3:18, Jesus' words

Jesus told him, "I am the way, the truth, and the life. No one can come to the Father except through me." John 14:6

"The world's sin is that it refuses to believe in me." John 16:9, Jesus' words

"There is salvation in no one else! God has given no other name under heaven by which we must be saved." Acts 4:12

If a person could get to Heaven by being good, then there would have been absolutely no reason for Jesus. If eternal life was possible without belief in Jesus, then he had little purpose. God does allow moral people to go to Hell, but they make the choice. Make the right one. Of course, none of us has the right to judge another's destiny, but as Christians, we do have the responsibility to share our belief with those who do not know Jesus.

Ask yourself this question: If I were to die this very moment, would I go to Heaven? If the answer is no, or you are unsure, then it is time for you to trust Jesus' finished work.

Knowing about Jesus isn't enough

If you know about Jesus, go to church, sing songs of praise, try to live by the Ten Commandments, wear a gold cross on a chain around your neck, decorate nicely at Christmas time – this may not be enough. Although commendable, these nice things are not the necessary ingredients for being a Christian. They look good, and they may impress everyone around you, but the only thing that makes a person a Christian is the Holy Spirit living in that person.

Notes:

17

A saved person never becomes *unsaved*

Christ allows His money to be taken from Him, but never His sheep.
Pasquier Quesnel (1634-1719)

Many Christians live guilt-filled lives because they fail to understand the truth about salvation. They constantly wonder if they are doing enough to pay for their own sins. If you are a saved person and you are under the impression you can lose your salvation, then I ask you: Which of your sins did Jesus not die for?

If you believe that salvation can be lost, you do not understand the purpose and power of Jesus' Blood. It is a Biblical fact that someone cannot lose his or her salvation. If after reading this chapter, you don't agree that once you are saved, you are always saved, you are probably just being stubborn.

Ask yourself

I want you to ask yourself if you honestly think it would make sense for God to provide us with a revolving-door salvation plan. Consider this:

> You wake up in the morning saved, but catch a glimpse of an attractive member of the opposite gender on TV while you are dressing for work. Because lust is a sin, of course, you instantly lose your salvation. In desperation, you fall on your face begging God's forgiveness, hoping that he understands.

> When that confession session is over, you get into your car and head for work. A reckless driver goes through a red light and almost hits you, and you responsively yell an obscene word. Back again to the confession and begging for God's forgiveness, as you worry about losing your salvation.

Throughout the rest of the day you experience many thoughts that are not in agreement with being a good Christian, plus you have done things that you know disappointed God. When you lay your head on the pillow that night, you are not sure if you would go to Heaven if you die in your sleep.

God did not send his Son to the Cross so you would have to lay there and wonder how many times you moved in and out of salvation that day.

No matter how hard we try, our lives are filled with sessions of sin, including our sinful thoughts. Most people know they are sinners, but unless they thoroughly understand God's total forgiveness, they can become overwhelmed by guilt, accompanied by doubting their salvation.

Uncertainty of one's standing with God is a pity for both the Christian and for the Carpenter who willingly gave his life on the Cross. If a Christian doubts his or her salvation, they are simultaneously insulting our Savior! Jesus did not die on the Cross so that his people could live their lives instilled with guilt and uncertainty. Either salvation is a gift, or it is not. If a person must work to keep his or her salvation, then it is works-based, and not a gift. Yet, the Bible tells us it is a *free* gift.

> *For the wages of sin is death, but the free gift of God is eternal life through Christ Jesus our Lord.* Romans 6:23

> *Can we boast, then, that we have done anything to be accepted by God? No, because our acquittal is not based on obeying the law. It is based on faith.* Romans 3:27

Sin cannot send a person to Hell

Sin cannot send someone to Hell because all of mankind's sins were paid for on the Cross. God said he would remember them no more because they were nailed to the Cross with Jesus!

> *When people work, their wages are not a gift, but something they have earned. But people are counted as righteous, not because of their work, but because of their faith in God who forgives sinners. David also spoke of this when he described the happiness of those who are declared righteous without working for it:*

"Oh, what joy for those
whose disobedience is forgiven,
whose sins are put out of sight.
Yes, what joy for those
whose record the Lord has cleared of sin." Romans 4:4-8

So, if it is not sin that sends a person to Hell, what is it? There is only one thing that can cause an individual eternal suffering, and Jesus makes it crystal clear.

"But everyone who denies me here on earth, I will also deny before my Father
in heaven." Matthew 10:33, Jesus' words

The only thing that can send someone to Hell is the denial that Jesus is the only way to righteousness with God. Once a person is saved, his salvation is irrevocable because salvation is a new birth. Miraculously, unlike that of a person's natural birth, which results in eventual physical death, salvation is a Spiritual birth that results in eternal life.

For you have been born again, but not to a life that will quickly end. Your
new life will last forever because it comes from the eternal, living word of
God. 1 Peter 1:23

False teaching

Many Clergy mislead their flock by teaching a false doctrine that salvation can be lost because of sin. This erroneous teaching began when the Apostles were teaching the New Covenant of salvation by faith, because people could not believe salvation could be so uncomplicated. People do not want to accept the truth if it conflicts with how they think it should be. In Paul's letter to the Galatians, he was explicit that God's New Covenant not be altered.

Dear brothers and sisters, I want you to understand that the gospel message
I preach is not based on mere human reasoning. I received my message from
no human source, and no one taught me. Instead, I received it by direct
revelation from Jesus Christ. Galatians 1:11-12

By faith alone

The fact that Christians are saved only by faith is the most difficult concept for Christians to comprehend because it is so simple and it seems too good to be true.

We mortals are so accustomed to being rewarded for our good deeds and punished for our transgressions that it seems incomprehensible we could spend eternity in Heaven just by our faith. However, Jesus tells it differently.

> *"For God loved the world so much that he gave his one and only Son, so that everyone who believes in him will not perish but have eternal life. God sent his Son into the world not to judge the world, but to save the world through him."* John 3:16-17, Jesus' words

Jesus goes on to say.

> *"However, those the Father has given me will come to me, and I will never reject them."* John 6:37, Jesus' words

> *I have written this to you who believe in the name of the Son of God, so that you may know you have eternal life.* 1 John 5:13

Jesus said, "No one will snatch them away from me." We can backslide from our attempting to be good Christians (referred to as *discipleship*), but we cannot backslide from salvation because when you become a part of him, you stay a part of him.

> *The human body has many parts, but the many parts make up one whole body. So it is with the body of Christ. Some of us are Jews, some are Gentiles, some are slaves, and some are free. But we have all been baptized into one body by one Spirit, and we all share the same Spirit.* 1 Corinthians 12:12-13

Sealed with the Holy Spirit

Immediately when a person accepts Jesus as their Savior, that person is sealed with the Holy Spirit. And the Holy Spirit does not depart the believer; he does not come and go.

> *"As I began to speak,"* Peter continued, *"the Holy Spirit fell on them, just as he fell on us at the beginning. Then I thought of the Lord's words when he said, 'John baptized with water, but you will be baptized with the Holy Spirit.' And since God gave these Gentiles the same gift he gave us when we believed in the Lord Jesus Christ, who was I to stand in God's way?"* Acts 11:15-17

> *And Christ lives within you, so even though your body will die because of sin, the Spirit gives you life because you have been made right with God. The Spirit of God, who raised Jesus from the dead, lives in you. And just as God*

raised Christ Jesus from the dead, he will give life to your mortal bodies by this same Spirit living within you. Romans 8:10-11

It is God who enables us, along with you, to stand firm for Christ. He has commissioned us, and he has identified us as his own by placing the Holy Spirit in our hearts as the first installment that guarantees everything he has promised us. 2 Corinthians 1:21-22

And now you Gentiles have also heard the truth, the Good News that God saves you. And when you believed in Christ, he identified you as his own by giving you the Holy Spirit, whom he promised long ago. The Spirit is God's guarantee that he will give us the inheritance he promised and that he has purchased us to be his own people. He did this so we would praise and glorify him. Ephesians 1:13-14

And do not bring sorrow to God's Holy Spirit by the way you live. Remember, he has identified you as his own, guaranteeing that you will be saved on the day of redemption. Ephesians 4:30

And God has given us his Spirit as proof that we live in him and he in us.
1 John 4:13

All sins are equal

Christ's body is not a revolving door that we must exit because we commit a major sin, as all sins are equal in God's eyes.

For the person who keeps all of the laws except one is as guilty as a person who has broken all of God's laws. James 2:10

Though we are all as guilty as murderers, the power of Jesus' Blood cleanses *all* sins.

"Brothers, listen! We are here to proclaim that through this man Jesus there is forgiveness for your sins. Everyone who believes in him is declared right with God—something the law of Moses could never do." Acts 13:38-39

For God's will was for us to be made holy by the sacrifice of the body of Jesus Christ, once for all time. Hebrews 10:10

All praise to God, the Father of our Lord Jesus Christ. It is by his great mercy that we have been born again, because God raised Jesus Christ from the dead. Now we live with great expectation, and we have a priceless

> *inheritance—an inheritance that is kept in heaven for you, pure and undefiled, beyond the reach of change and decay.* 1 Peter 1:3-4

> *In his kindness God called you to share in his eternal glory by means of Christ Jesus. So after you have suffered a little while, he will restore, support, and strengthen you, and he will place you on a firm foundation. All power to him forever! Amen.* 1 Peter 5:10-11

Hopefully, by now you understand.

A license to sin?

There are Christians who take advantage of grace and use it as a license to sin. In essence, such a Christian is saying, "Christians can sin more, but enjoy it less." Christians enjoy sin less than those who have not been saved because of the indwelling and conviction of the Holy Spirit.

> *But now we have been released from the law, for we died to it and are no longer captive to its power. Now we can serve God, not in the old way of obeying the letter of the law, but in the new way of living in the Spirit.*
> Romans 7:6

The Apostle Paul struggled

The Apostle Paul was saved, yet he was very forthright about his struggles. Do not ever forget what you are about to read, as it should comfort you to know that weaknesses are present in all of us, including those whom God has personally chosen.

The following passage makes it quite clear that Paul continued to sin, even at the height of his ministry. Yet, Paul remained saved. You are no different.

> *I have discovered this principle of life—that when I want to do what is right, I inevitably do what is wrong. I love God's law with all my heart. But there is another power within me that is at war with my mind. This power makes me a slave to the sin that is still within me. Oh, what a miserable person I am! Who will free me from this life that is dominated by sin and death? Thank God! The answer is in Jesus Christ our Lord. So you see how it is: In my mind I really want to obey God's law, but because of my sinful nature I am a slave to sin.* Romans 7:21-25

There is no condemnation for those who believe

So now there is no condemnation for those who belong to Christ Jesus.
Romans 8:1

Two judgments (know these)

Another piece of evidence reinforces the fact that salvation cannot be lost. There are two final judgments, rather than the customary one judgment that most people assume. The myth that, as the criteria for eternal life in Heaven, someday each of us will stand before God and our good behavior will be compared to our bad behavior is false.

The *Biblical fact* is there are two judgments:

1. The Judgment Seat of Christ (AKA Christ's Judgment and/or Bema Seat) is for those who have been saved by grace through faith, and it is to determine the rewards for those who have trusted Jesus as Savior.

For we must all stand before Christ to be judged. We will each receive whatever we deserve for the good or evil we have done in this earthly body.
2 Corinthians 5:10

There will be no judgment here for sin because the Christian's sin is remembered no more. This judgment is to determine the rewards for the good deeds, or discipleship, of the Christian prior to his or her death.

2. The Great White Throne Judgment is for those who have rejected Christ as Savior, and who are going to Hell regardless of their life's works, or lack thereof. These may be very fine, moral people who have tried to work their way to Heaven rather than trusting in Jesus. At the time of an individual's death, if that person has not trusted Jesus Christ as Savior, he or she will receive eternal punishment, as explained in the next passage.

And I saw a great white throne and the one sitting on it. The earth and sky fled from his presence, but they found no place to hide. I saw the dead, both great and small, standing before God's throne. And the books were opened, including the Book of Life. And the dead were judged according to what they had done, as recorded in the books. The sea gave up its dead, and death and the grave gave up their dead. And all were judged according to their deeds. Then death and the grave were thrown into the lake of fire. This lake of fire

> *is the second death. And anyone whose name was not found recorded in the*
> *Book of Life was thrown into the lake of fire.* Revelation 20:11-15

Christians go directly to Heaven

For those who have accepted Jesus as their Savior, the following applies:

> *So we are always confident, even though we know that as long as we live in*
> *these bodies we are not at home with the Lord. For we live by believing and*
> *not by seeing. Yes, we are fully confident, and we would rather be away from*
> *these earthly bodies, for then we will be at home with the Lord.*
> 2 Corinthians 5:6-8

As seen in the above text, the moment we are absent from our bodies, we are present with the Lord. A minority of Christian teachers believe we will go into soul sleep until the final resurrection, but most believe that Jesus' words to the thief on the Cross makes it clear that we immediately ascend to Heaven upon our death.

> *And Jesus replied, "I assure you, today you will be with me in paradise."*
> Luke 23:43

As a Christian, you will be judged and rewarded according to your deeds, but your deeds will not be the criteria God uses to welcome you into his home. Eternal life is purely based on your faith in Jesus Christ as your Savior.

Have you rejected Jesus?

Have you rejected Jesus as your only means for salvation by depending on your good deeds to receive eternal life in Heaven? Even if you are one of those who believe you are saved, but are under the impression you can lose your salvation, then you may not truly be saved. A person is only saved by total trust in Jesus as his or her Savior.

Sabbath rest

Sabbath rest is the term used to describe *current and eternal* rest in Christ experienced by the Christian. Sabbath rest quiets a guilty conscience, stills troubling thoughts, and gives hope in desperation. In Christ we find complete rest today and forever. This term should not be confused with resting on Sunday. Sabbath rest is what those who understand salvation, and who have accepted Jesus as their Savior, experience when they cease from their own efforts for salvation and depend on the work of Christ. It is also when a Christian allows the Holy Spirit to work through them in matters of morals and discipleship.

> *Then Jesus said, "Come to me, all of you who are weary and carry heavy burdens, and I will give you rest. Take my yoke upon you. Let me teach you, because I am humble and gentle at heart, and you will find rest for your souls. For my yoke is easy to bear, and the burden I give you is light."*
> Matthew 11:28-30

The Apostle Paul shares his weakness with the world as he experienced Sabbath rest.

> *Each time he said, "My grace is all you need. My power works best in weakness." So now I am glad to boast about my weaknesses, so that the power of Christ can work through me. That's why I take pleasure in my weaknesses, and in the insults, hardships, persecutions, and troubles that I suffer for Christ. For when I am weak, then I am strong.* 2 Corinthians 12:9-10

Notes:

18

What is sin?

You can never tell the sinner from the Christian. They drink the same drinks and smoke the same cigars.

Aimee Semple McPherson (1890-1944)

One of my colleagues criticized me because a portion of what is written in this chapter I also wrote in another chapter that condemned some churches, denominations, and Christians for their piety. As a Christian evangelist for 30 years, I have learned that some things require repeating.

Churches frequently do not explain sin comprehensively

Many Christians are notorious for harping on the subject of sin probably because they really do not know its Biblical definition.

Self-righteous Christians describe smoking, drinking, swearing, and gambling as sins, but these habits are not always considered sinful to God. Mankind is not always "man-kind." Sometimes Christians impose their interpretations of morality on one another in an unkindly way. Too often, the net effect is scaring people into thinking they are not worthy of God's love. This is of epidemic proportion and the more we push people away from God, the closer we push them to evil. It is evil that results in terrorism, drug addiction, prostitution, school children killing one another, corporations being drained by executives, and many more evils.

Many churches have invented sins that are not Biblical

We depend on our church leaders to be Biblically accurate. Sadly, throughout the centuries, self-seeking church leaders have invented non-Biblical sins based on what they consider personally offensive and what they think should also be offensive to God, regardless of their Biblical accuracy. They have compiled a continuous list of human behaviors and labeled them *sin* for everyone. Thisv is a disastrous blunder on the part of church leaders because it causes many people to reject Jesus based on false information. Creating undeserved guilt and unworthiness in people should not be the function of a church.

Contrary to what many churches teach, what is sin for one person may not be sin for another. For example, having a couple beers (the Bible says not to get drunk) may not be sin for the person who has control of his alcohol consumption and who has not been convicted by the Holy Spirit not to drink. However, another individual may have a drinking problem, or may be convicted by the Spirit not to drink. It is not a sin to drink for the first man, but it is for the second. There are many more examples.

To compound this problem, many churches neglect discussing the role of the Holy Spirit in the Christian's life. The Bible states that we are to learn from one another, but makes it clear that a Christian's ultimate counselor is the Holy Spirit. Church leaders make leadership errors, but the Holy Spirit's guidance is flawless. The Holy Spirit works differently in each person's life, convicting each individual to the path he is to follow. Therefore, what is sin for one person may be different from what is sin for another, as defined by the Holy Spirit.

What is sin?

Theologians have been tossing the subject of sin around for years. I once hear it said, "If you laid all of the tens of thousands of theologians, both contemporary and historical, end to end they still would not reach a conclusion."

The subject of sin is somewhat difficult to write about because it has so many implications. The term *sin* is derived from the Greek word *hamartia*, which means, "to miss the mark." The *mark*, in this case, is the standard of perfection established by God and evidenced by Jesus. Viewed in that light, it is clear that we are all sinners.

> *For everyone has sinned; we all fall short of God's glorious standard.*
> Romans 3:23

Sin is an offense against God. When a sin is deliberate in action – such as murder, stealing, lying, or adultery – it is referred to as a *sin of commission*. If it is something we should have done, but did not, such as feeding a poor person, it is referred to as a *sin of omission*. Both are punishable by death and eternity in Hell.

Based on the account of Adam and Eve, the Bible indicates that sin is disobeying God. The moment Adam and Eve ate from the tree that God commanded them not to, sin was born. The sin was the act of disobeying. From that point until the very last chapter of the New Testament, examples of sin are found continuously and condemned. Adam and Eve's act, the *original sin*, was handed down to all mankind throughout the ages. It is referred to as *imputed sin*.

Although the word *sin* is used hundreds of times throughout both the Old and New Testaments, nowhere in the Scriptures do we find a precise dictionary definition. To ascertain the actual meaning of sin, one must understand both the history and the future of mankind.

In a nutshell, sin means to do something contrary to the will of God. However, what is contrary to the will of God for one person may not be the same for another. It is impossible not to sin, primarily because we are imperfect creations. No matter how hard we try, we are going to sin.

Imputed sin

Imputed sin is the reason none are worthy of the glory of God, until we are saved by the Blood of Jesus, which is referred to as *imputed righteousness*. Although it may not seem fair in our eyes, Adam's sin became our sin (imputed sin). Furthermore, although it may not seem possible in our eyes, Jesus' righteousness became our righteousness (imputed righteous).

It is Christ's imputed righteousness that finds the Christian not guilty, and the punishment of death and eternity in Hell is exchanged for eternal life in Heaven. King David spoke of this, when he said:

> "Oh, what joy for those
>   whose disobedience is forgiven,
>   whose sins are put out of sight.
> Yes, what joy for those
>   whose record the Lord has cleared of sin." Romans 4:7-8

Sin is sin

We live in a culture where the concept of sin has become entangled in legalistic arguments over right and wrong. Many of us consider violations of the Ten Commandments as sin, and we have the tendency to think of murder and adultery as major sins compared with lying, cursing, or idolatry, which are considered minor. Specifically, the Bible is unclear as to exactly what behavior, or lack of behavior, constitutes sin.

In our mortal minds, most of us believe there are little and big sins. But in God's mind, all sins are equal. Whether it is telling a little fib, lusting, robbing a bank, or murder – sin is sin.

> *For the person who keeps all of the laws except one is as guilty as a person who has broken all of God's laws.* James 2:10

That is right – God does not differentiate between one sin and another. We mortals think cheating on our income tax is the American thing to do, but consider adultery as the act of an immoral person. In God's eyes, both are equal, just as stealing a pencil from work is as sinful as murder. You may consider yourself a good person, but God does not.

What is sin for one Christian, may not be sin for another

Christians have a personal relationship with Jesus Christ via the Holy Spirit, who resides in the Christian and who is her or his personal counselor. Our personal convictions are conveyed upon us through that relationship. This means that what the Holy Spirit communicates to me may not be the same as what the Holy Spirit communicates to you.

The Holy Spirit may convict me to volunteer in helping to feed the poor, but may not convict you to help in that same mission. The Holy Spirit treats and convicts each person individually. For me not to feed the poor would be a sin, but may not be a sin for you.

A more serious example would be that a person may be convicted by the Holy Spirit to go to war and fight for his or her country, while another Christian is convicted to serve by working in a hospital. Killing on the battlefield would not be a sin for one Christian, but it would be a sin for the other Christian.

I am sure many Christians will not like what I have to say here, but it is the truth. Many social issues are labeled sinful in Christendom that I believe may not be sinful, depending on the person involved. These things include the playing of musical instruments, dancing, uttering an occasional swear-word, drinking a few beers, or even placing an affordable wager on the outcome of a football game. Personally, I am guilty of all of the above. But I do them in moderation, and I do not consider them sinful behavior for me personally. The Lord has allowed me certain liberties, and I feel very confident that if these were activities in which he wanted me to stop, he would stop me in one way or another. He has not convicted me to change my behavior in these areas. One or all of these activities or behaviors may be sinful for someone else who has different convictions.

I understand conviction because this book is the result of my conviction to spend 10 years pecking away at my computer compiling a book about Jesus. Anyone who knows me well would agree that writing a book about Jesus is not my style. I would swear on a stack of Bibles that this book is the result of a conviction from God, and not of my choosing. For me to *not* write this book would be a sin.

I have been convicted to participate in other Christian endeavors and activities in which I had no choice. I fought the convictions, but the Lord won. My ignoring God's convictions would have been a sin.

I believe in free will, but I know there have been times in my life when God's will overrode my desires. There are other times when I am permitted to be me. Although most of our choices may be personal preferences, the Holy Spirit may aggressively influence our choices. These choices then become Holy Spirit convictions. Willfully ignoring those convictions separate us from God – and that is what defines sin.

> *But the Holy Spirit produces this kind of fruit in our lives: love, joy, peace, patience, kindness, goodness, faithfulness, gentleness, and self-control.*
> *There is no law against these things!* Galatians 5:22-23

Live your life with Holy Spirit conviction and you will experience all of these qualities.

Christianity is freedom from religious demands

Many people are scared from Jesus because just the simple mention of his name reminds them of their sins. This is very sad. The name of Jesus should be a reminder of God's overwhelming love for us and his forgiveness for our sins, not a reminder of how bad we are or how guilty we should feel. The New Testament refers to the forgiveness of sin more than it does sin itself, and that is the reason to not be afraid.

Christian freedom does not mean we no longer sin or have the desire to sin. But it does mean that a process toward excellence has begun in each Christian, and that as we grow in our faith, our sin nature becomes less and less as we gradually develop the nature of Christ.

Love

> *Most important of all, continue to show deep love for each other, for love covers a multitude of sins.* 1 Peter 4:8

The only unforgivable sin

> *"So I tell you, every sin and blasphemy can be forgiven—except blasphemy against the Holy Spirit, which will never be forgiven. Anyone who speaks against the Son of Man can be forgiven, but anyone who speaks against the Holy Spirit will never be forgiven, either in this world or in the world to come."* Matthew 12:31-32, Jesus' words

This passage was Jesus' response to the Jewish religious leaders, who were stating that Jesus' ability to cast out demons was from power he was receiving through Satan, rather than power from the Holy Spirit. It is also the passage that is used throughout Christianity to express that all of mankind's sins except blaspheming the Holy Spirit were forgiven on the Cross.

However, the esteemed theologian Dr. Charles C. Ryrie states in his *Study Bible*:

> Technically, according to the scribes, blasphemy involved direct and explicit abuse of the divine name. Jesus here teaches that it may be the reviling of God by attributing the Spirit's work to Satan. The special circumstances involved in this blasphemy cannot be duplicated today; therefore, this sin cannot now be committed. Jesus exhorted the Pharisees to turn and be justified (vv. 33, 37). *Page 1534*

The American Bible Society *NIV Learning Bible* states:

> The sin of blasphemy, or speaking against the Holy Spirit, is a complete turning away from God. Those who reject God also reject God's forgiveness. **Page 1874**

The *Illustrated Davis Dictionary of the Bible* defines Blasphemy against the Holy Ghost as:

> …attributing the miracles of Christ, which were wrought by the Spirit of God, to Satanic power. **Page 103**

I don't think so

I do not think a Christian can commit the unforgivable sin. The remark that Jesus made was not to people who had been saved – it was made to unbelievers. And it was made before Jesus went to the Cross, where he paid for all of the sins of mankind.

Throughout the Scriptures Jesus makes it very clear that a saved individual cannot become unsaved. We are saved by the permanent indwelling of the Holy Spirit, and there is no Biblical support, or instance, of the Holy Spirit leaving a person once that baptism has taken place. The Bible makes it clear that the only way a person can suffer eternally is by rejecting the Holy Spirit.

Notes:

19

You will continue to sin after you are saved

Either sin is with you, lying on your shoulders,
or it is lying on Christ, the Lamb of God.

Martin Luther (1483-1546)

According to the Scriptures, it is impossible to live without sinning.

As the Scriptures say,
 "No one is righteous—
 not even one." Romans 3:10

If we claim we have no sin, we are only fooling ourselves and not living in the truth. 1 John 1:8

If it were possible to live a sinless life, then Jesus Christ died for nothing!

Understand what "repent" means!

Before I became a Christian, for years I constantly heard that to be a Christian one must "repent of sin." Christians explained this phrase to me as meaning that a Christian must not sin. I wanted to be right with God, but I knew that my carnal nature was not capable of becoming sinless. It was not until I was 34 years old that I learned the phrase "repent of sin" is not Biblical. That was my turning point.

The misconception I had about the Biblical term *repent* kept me from learning about Jesus. I am certain this same misconception has scared, and will continue to scare, many from enjoying the freedom provided by our Savior. There are many who will never know Jesus because they have been frightened by a phrase that is used inappropriately.

The following is a typical example of a verse that is misinterpreted. Many, at first glance, believe it means to repent of sin.

> *Then Peter said to them, "Repent, and let every one of you be baptized in the name of Jesus Christ for the remission of sins; and you will receive the gift of the Holy Spirit."* Acts 2:38 (NKJV)

This verse does not say "repent of sin." Yes the term *repent* is used, but not in the context erroneously taught by those who insist that Christians must live sinless lives.

One must understand the meaning of the word *repent*. It is a mistake to go to a modern dictionary to find the meaning of a word that was used 2,000 years ago. Repent comes from the Greek word *metanoia*, which means "a change of mind." It was used frequently by the Apostle Paul to convince the Jews that they must change their minds, from depending on the laws (i.e. the Ten Commandments) to obtain favor with God, to accepting Jesus as the Messiah. It is one's belief in Jesus that redeems; Jesus was the fulfillment of the law. That means, Jesus did what man could not do.

NOTE: Speaking of the Ten Commandments – most people do not realize they were not given to non-Jews. The commandments were given only to the Jews. Gentiles were never under these laws, and following Jesus' death on the Cross, Jews were also freed from legal bondage. If you are under the impression that by your feebly attempting to live, by obeying the commandments, you will go to Heaven, you are dead wrong. That is not the way to receive life eternal.

Yes, the Bible says we are to strive to be moral, but as I have said thousands of times since 1980, "If we could stop sinning, then Christ died for nothing." Think about that.

> *I do not treat the grace of God as meaningless. For if keeping the law could make us right with God, then there was no need for Christ to die.*
> Galatians 2:21

The Apostle Paul was a sinner

Many of us feel very unworthy of God's love and forgiveness, but even the Apostle Paul, who many believe was the greatest Christian who has ever lived, was in bondage to sin. The following words were written by Paul 25 years after the beginning of his ministry. This proves that even after years of being a Christian, we are all vulnerable.

So the trouble is not with the law, for it is spiritual and good. The trouble is with me, for I am all too human, a slave to sin. I don't really understand myself, for I want to do what is right, but I don't do it. Instead, I do what I hate. But if I know that what I am doing is wrong, this shows that I agree that the law is good. So I am not the one doing wrong; it is sin living in me that does it.

And I know that nothing good lives in me, that is, in my sinful nature. I want to do what is right, but I can't. I want to do what is good, but I don't. I don't want to do what is wrong, but I do it anyway. But if I do what I don't want to do, I am not really the one doing wrong; it is sin living in me that does it.

I have discovered this principle of life—that when I want to do what is right, I inevitably do what is wrong. I love God's law with all my heart. But there is another power within me that is at war with my mind. This power makes me a slave to the sin that is still within me. Oh, what a miserable person I am! Who will free me from this life that is dominated by sin and death? Romans 7:14-24

Jesus Christ was the answer for Paul's sins

Thank God! The answer is in Jesus Christ our Lord. So you see how it is: In my mind I really want to obey God's law, but because of my sinful nature I am a slave to sin. Romans 7:25

The only antidote for Paul's struggles was Jesus Christ. Jesus Christ is the cure for everyone's struggles.

So now there is no condemnation for those who belong to Christ Jesus. And because you belong to him, the power of the life-giving Spirit has freed you from the power of sin that leads to death. The law of Moses was unable to save us because of the weakness of our sinful nature. So God did what the law could not do. He sent his own Son in a body like the bodies we sinners have. And in that body God declared an end to sin's control over us by giving his Son as a sacrifice for our sins. He did this so that the just requirement of the law would be fully satisfied for us, who no longer follow our sinful nature but instead follow the Spirit. Romans 8:1-4

It is a gift!

Jesus became sin

The Bible teaches that Jesus took *all* of our sins to the Cross in his body. Christ became sin for us so that we would have absolute righteousness. This is called justification, and it is what saves. When we are justified, it means that we are made righteous through grace because of the Blood of Christ. The Christian's righteousness is imputed by God because of his love for us. It is free and is not earned. It is by grace alone that we are justified, and the Bible says it has nothing to do with our behavior.

> *God made him who had no sin to be sin for us, so that in him we might become the righteousness of God.* 2 Corinthians 5:21 (NIV)

> *He canceled the record of the charges against us and took it away by nailing it to the cross.* Colossians 2:14

Many Christians live guilt-filled lives because they don't understand the truth. The truth is that God does not remember our sins because they were nailed to the Cross with Jesus!

> *"Oh, what joy for those*
> *whose disobedience is forgiven,*
> *whose sins are put out of sight.*
> *Yes, what joy for those*
> *whose record the Lord has cleared of sin."*
> Romans 4:7-8

Grace is truly amazing

Grace is receiving something that is undeserved. From a Christian perspective, grace is what God shows to humans by offering salvation through the death, burial, and resurrection of Jesus Christ.

The following are just a few of many Bible passages that make it clear we are saved by grace:

> *But now God has shown us a way to be made right with him without keeping the requirements of the law, as was promised in the writings of Moses and the prophets long ago. We are made right with God by placing our faith in Jesus Christ. And this is true for everyone who believes, no matter who we are.*
> Romans 3:21-22

> *And since it is through God's kindness, then it is not by their good works. For in that case, God's grace would not be what it really is—free and undeserved.*
> Romans 11:6

God saved you by his grace when you believed. And you can't take credit for this; it is a gift from God. Salvation is not a reward for the good things we have done, so none of us can boast about it.
Ephesians 2:8-9

The Old Testament prepared the world for the forthcoming Savior Jesus Christ. The entire New Testament is dedicated to teaching the grace of that Savior.

Too much grace?

Christians frequently chastise me for emphasizing grace, saying I encourage people to sin. An irate church lady once criticized the late, renowned evangelist Dwight L. Moody for the way he preached. His answer to her was, "I like the way I'm doing it better than the way you're not doing it."

Cool! At least I am evangelizing and winning souls to Jesus. Stating that I emphasize grace too much is ridiculous. If I taught differently, I would by lying. Unlike many Christians, I am not scaring people from the Savior who died on the Cross to pay for our sins.

Many preachers love to instill fear by avoiding the powerful saving subjects of grace and the Holy Spirit, even though fear is opposite to what the Scriptures teach. Instilling fear in people by lying doesn't work. It chases would-be Christians from knowing Jesus, which usually results in more sin, including the unpardonable sin of rejecting Jesus. The immoral behavior of a person will not cause their eternal punishment, but rejecting Jesus will.

Rather than scaring people from Jesus by lecturing about Old Testament and man-made laws, the Apostle Paul attracted his listeners to the Savior by sharing the reality of abundant grace.

God's law was given so that all people could see how sinful they were. But as people sinned more and more, God's wonderful grace became more abundant. So just as sin ruled over all people and brought them to death, now God's wonderful grace rules instead, giving us right standing with God and resulting in eternal life through Jesus Christ our Lord.
Romans 5:20-21

If Paul can teach it, so can I.

Improving behavior

When people become Christians, to show their appreciation for what God provided through Jesus Christ, most attempt to make moral improvements. This is not always easy.

The best way for a person to change is to replace the bad behavior with something superior. There is nothing more superior than to allow Jesus' Spirit to be one's personal Counselor. People need to allow Jesus to live through them via the Holy Spirit, rather than to make feeble attempts at changing their own behavior. The flesh is weak, but the Spirit is strong. Once a person begins to allow the Holy Spirit to work through them, the more moral they become, and the less they enjoy immorality.

Listen to the Spirit, not the flesh

It is nonsense to suppose that all Christians must think and act exactly alike. Christians have the Holy Scriptures to guide them and they are given the Holy Spirit as their personal counselor.

> *"And I will ask the Father, and he will give you another Advocate, who will never leave you. He is the Holy Spirit, who leads into all truth. The world cannot receive him, because it isn't looking for him and doesn't recognize him. But you know him, because he lives with you now and later will be in you." John 14:16-17, Jesus' words*

> *"But when the Father sends the Advocate as my representative—that is, the Holy Spirit—he will teach you everything and will remind you of everything I have told you.*

> *"I am leaving you with a gift—peace of mind and heart. And the peace I give is a gift the world cannot give. So don't be troubled or afraid." John 14:26-27, Jesus' words*

> *But people who aren't spiritual can't receive these truths from God's Spirit. It all sounds foolish to them and they can't understand it, for only those who are spiritual can understand what the Spirit means.* 1 Corinthians 2:14

> *But you have received the Holy Spirit, and he lives within you, so you don't need anyone to teach you what is true. For the Spirit teaches you everything you need to know, and what he teaches is true—it is not a lie. So just as he has taught you, remain in fellowship with Christ.* 1 John 2:27

Sublimate

One of the meanings of *sublimate* is to transfer a harmful thought or act into one of value. It is the transfer of one energy into another. This process can be utilized to grow Spiritually.

The Apostle Peter demonstrated the difference between carnal and Spiritual thinking when he walked a short distance on the water, then sank. Peter was doing fine until he turned his thoughts from his faith in Jesus to his own carnality. This same transfer of thought from Jesus to ourselves is what causes us to sink.

When we find ourselves in moral dilemmas, if we listen intently to the Spirit and respond obediently, we will make the right decision. But when we listen to the flesh, down we go.

> *So I say, let the Holy Spirit guide your lives. Then you won't be doing what your sinful nature craves.* Galatians 5:16

Peter failed and so will you. But the more you try, the more you will grow.

> *But the Holy Spirit produces this kind of fruit in our lives: love, joy, peace, patience, kindness, goodness, faithfulness, gentleness, and self-control. There is no law against these things!* Galatians 5:22-23

Learning to live in the way God wants us to live is a growth process. The more we learn to listen to the Holy Spirit, the more we begin to live beneficial lives – leaving behind our carnality. There may be periods of slow yet steady growth, and periods of spectacular growth. Whatever the case, accept and submit to it.

When volunteering in a hospital, if you are of the male gender, rather than lusting about the presence of pretty nurses, use that same energy to pray with a patient. It does not always work, but it is worth a try. God understands our weaknesses. If you are of the female gender, use the same technique when drooling over a handsome doctor. Such acts are *sublimation.*

No more guilt

> *"Brothers, listen! In this man Jesus there is forgiveness for your sins. Everyone who believes in him is <u>freed from all guilt</u> and declared right with God – something the Jewish law could never do."* Acts 13:38-39 (NLT 1996)

In the above passage, I underlined *freed from all guilt* to emphasize that fact. Many Christians experience psychological problems because they have a faulty understanding of the Christian faith. Some have erroneously interpreted certain Bible passages, and others have been taught incorrectly. A Christian should be guilt-free. Jesus did not die on the Cross so his sheep would have to pop pills or live in mental institutions. His death was to free people from condemnation, oppression, and guilt. Jesus said it, and I believe it.

> *"So if the Son sets you free, you are truly free."* John 8:36, Jesus' words

Although your goal should be to follow the Spirit and modify your behavior, there will be times when you succumb to the flesh. Remember, if it were possible to live sinless lives, then Christ died for nothing. You will have remorse for your shortcomings and conviction from the Holy Spirit to improve, but if you correctly understand the forgiveness that accompanies Christianity, you will have no guilt.

There is a distinct difference between guilt, remorse, and conviction. Guilt is crippling, remorse is constructive, and conviction is action. Guilt is a powerful weapon used by Satan to accuse, torment, and berate his victims. Satan is an accuser, a tempter, and a liar.

Jesus' death on the Cross was the substitutionary atonement for our sins. In the Christian community, this means that we are made righteous through grace because of the Blood of Christ. The Christian's righteousness is imputed by God. That is awesome! Every sin you have ever committed, or are presently committing, or ever will commit is forgiven and forgotten. The following are God's words, as quoted by Paul in Hebrews 8:12:

> *"And I will forgive their wickedness,*
> *   and I will never again remember their sins."*

If God forgets your sins, by feeling guilty you are telling Jesus that what he did was not sufficient. Because God has forgiven you, you must forgive yourself.

In conclusion

> *Do not love this world nor the things it offers you, for when you love the*
> *world, you do not have the love of the Father in you. For the world offers only*
> *a craving for physical pleasure, a craving for everything we see, and pride*
> *in our achievements and possessions. These are not from the Father, but are*
> *from this world.* 1 John 2:15-16

20

You never have to ask forgiveness again[4]

Sinners need a Savior. Christ is that Savior and the only valid one. Through faith I receive Him and His forgiveness. Then the sin problem is solved, and I can be fully assured of going to heaven.

Charles C. Ryrie (born 1925)

We are taught from childhood to ask for forgiveness every time we do wrong. Therefore, it seems natural for us to ask God continually for his forgiveness. Asking forgiveness is common courtesy, but it does not make sense to ask constantly for forgiveness once you have been forgiven.

The New Testament makes it clear that Christ's death on the Cross paid for all of our sins once and for all. Yet many folks continually ask God to forgive them. Over and over again, they keep asking God to forgive them. This insult to Christ's Blood can probably be blamed on the misinterpretation of one isolated Bible verse that has influenced millions of people to believe they must constantly re-crucify Christ by asking for God's forgiveness:

> *But if we confess our sins to him, he is faithful and just to forgive us our sins and to cleanse us from all wickedness.* 1 John 1:9

If a person reads this lone verse, it can be misinterpreted to sound like constant confession is necessary for forgiveness. Even many church leaders have never studied the meaning of this verse, so they also interpret it incorrectly. Never base belief

---

4   Because so many people are so seriously confused regarding the subject of confession, a separate chapter is provided. One's belief that he or she must constantly confess may be an indication that person may not be saved.

systems on what a person or people tell you. Base it on truth. No one person has all the answers, but there is one that will show you the truth – and Jesus is the truth.

One of the difficulties when reading the Bible is that we often use one passage to establish doctrine without studying other verses and passages that pertain to a particular topic. Doctrine should not be established using one lone verse if dozens of other passages are inconsistent with its interpretation. In this case, the Bible is very explicit that Jesus' shed Blood finalized the forgiveness of all sin. The Bible must be *studied*, not read.

To understand what 1 John 1:9 means, we must understand for whom it was written. The letters in the New Testament were written to Christian leaders who would read them to many people with varying beliefs: Christian believers, Jews, idol worshipers, atheists, agnostics, and those of other beliefs. Because John knew that non-believers would be present and that they were probably immoral, he articulated that we are all sinners in need of forgiveness. The Christians and Jews knew they were sinners, so John clearly was not addressing them.

It is obvious from the beginning of the book of 1 John that its author was trying to convince listeners that Jesus was God incarnate, that Jesus was of flesh, and that Jesus' Blood cleansed us from every sin.

John said if they thought they had no sin, they were wrong. His stating that they must confess their sins meant that they must be aware they were sinners, and must recognize their need of forgiveness from God, the Creator of the world and everything in it. Of course, that still applies today for those who think they have no sin.

When researching the book of 1 John, you will learn that one of the groups that John was addressing was a sect called Gnostics, who are still present today. Gnosticism is a society that describes the physical world as evil and the spiritual world as good. They believe that Jesus only "appeared" as a fleshly being, but in fact, he was not a man of flesh, he was totally Spiritual. Because of their emphasis on the spiritual world, they teach that moral rules are only for those who cannot see beyond the physical level of life.

1 John 1:9 is the only place that confession and forgiveness are mentioned simultaneously in the New Testament. Therefore, the verse is not applicable to those who have already been saved. Once a person has been saved, there is no further need to ask forgiveness.

Furthermore, John did not say one must continually confess their sins, nor did John say one must continually ask forgiveness. Additionally, John did not say one must confess one's sins to another human. However, Christians are given the authority and responsibility to tell people that they have been forgiven as the result of Jesus' Blood. From cover to cover, the New Testament emphasizes that our sins were forgiven once and for all on the Cross.

If you are one of those who believe you must constantly confess your sins to be forgiven, you don't fully comprehend the magnitude, significance, and finality of the Cross. This could indicate that you really are not saved, if you are depending on your confessions and works, rather than your faith. Perhaps it is time to re-examine your faith to reinforce that you are totally depending on what Jesus did, and not your own works, for your salvation. The Apostle Paul called attention to this in his letter to the Galatians.

> *I am shocked that you are turning away so soon from God, who called you to himself through the loving mercy of Christ. You are following a different way that pretends to be the Good News but is not the Good News at all. You are being fooled by those who deliberately twist the truth concerning Christ.*
>
> *Let God's curse fall on anyone, including us or even an angel from heaven, who preaches a different kind of Good News than the one we preached to you.* Galatians 1:6-8

God has forgotten your sins

> *For God was in Christ, reconciling the world to himself, no longer counting people's sins against them. And he gave us this wonderful message of reconciliation.* 2 Corinthians 5:19

The verse above says, "no longer counting people's sins against them." If God is no longer counting our sins, then do not insult him by continually asking forgiveness. You have been forgiven once and forever.

> *We are made right with God by placing our faith in Jesus Christ. And this is true for everyone who believes, no matter who we are.* Romans 3:22

> *So we praise God for the glorious grace he has poured out on us who belong to his dear Son. He is so rich in kindness and grace that he purchased our freedom with the blood of his Son and forgave our sins.* Ephesians 1:6-7

You were dead because of your sins and because your sinful nature was not yet cut away. Then God made you alive with Christ, for he forgave all our sins. He canceled the record of the charges against us and took it away by nailing it to the cross. Colossians 2:13-14

He himself is the sacrifice that atones for our sins—and not only our sins but the sins of all the world. 1 John 2:2

Do not be hardheaded. There is no need to ask Jesus to die on the cross again, and again, and again. The issue of asking forgiveness was completed at the Cross.

It's not semantics

If you think there is no difference between asking for forgiveness and thanking Jesus for forgiveness, you are wrong. Once you get into the habit of constantly thanking Jesus rather than continually asking forgiveness, you will soon begin to feel the complete peace and freedom that accompanies Christianity.

You will never fully understand the power of the Blood until you fully feel the enormity and finality of God's forgiveness.

Jesus knew that his mission was now finished, and to fulfill Scripture he said, "I am thirsty." A jar of sour wine was sitting there, so they soaked a sponge in it, put it on a hyssop branch, and held it up to his lips. When Jesus had tasted it, he said, "It is finished!" Then he bowed his head and released his spirit. John 19:28-30

It is finished! Jesus said it, and I believe it.

You should have no guilt

"Brothers, listen! We are here to proclaim that through this man Jesus there is forgiveness for your sins. Everyone who believes in him is declared right with God—something the law of Moses could never do. Acts 13:38-39

Always remember that God's grace is greater than your sins. God has acquitted you. Of course, you will have regrets about the immorality in your life, but knowing that you have been completely exonerated will set you free from all guilt. Guilt is a tool of Satan utilized to take your eyes off Jesus. Scripture says there is no condemnation to those who are in Christ Jesus. If God does not condemn you, then you certainly should not condemn yourself.

Bask in God's forgiveness

If you are a saved person, and you are under the impression you can lose your salvation, then I ask you again: Which of your sins did Jesus not pay for?

It is difficult to imagine you have been forgiven for everything you have done, everything you are doing, and everything you will ever do. When you grasp this phenomenal concept, you will be so amazed that you will bask in having been forgiven. Once that happens, you will do three things: You will become a disciple of Christ, you will be able to forgive yourself, and you will be able to forgive others. Our God is awesome.

Now, shout it from the rooftops

> *Jesus came and told his disciples, "I have been given all authority in heaven and on earth. Therefore, go and make disciples of all the nations, baptizing them in the name of the Father and the Son and the Holy Spirit."*
> Matthew 28:18-19

Now that you know the truth, the whole truth, and nothing but the truth, it is time to share this *Good News*.

In addition to the Apostles, Jesus sent out 72 disciples to deliver the Good News. He may have sent more that are not recorded in the Bible. It does not take a rocket scientist to ascertain that Jesus wants the Good News to be shared by as many as have the courage. Are you one of them?

> *The Lord now chose seventy-two other disciples and sent them ahead in pairs to all the towns and places he planned to visit. These were his instructions to them: "The harvest is great, but the workers are few. So pray to the Lord who is in charge of the harvest; ask him to send more workers into his fields. Now go, and remember that I am sending you out as lambs among wolves."*
> Luke 10:1-3

We are ambassadors

> *For God was in Christ, reconciling the world to himself, no longer counting people's sins against them. And he gave us this wonderful message of reconciliation. So we are Christ's ambassadors; God is making his appeal through us. We speak for Christ when we plead, "Come back to God!" For God made Christ, who never sinned, to be the offering for our sin, so that we could be made right with God through Christ.* 2 Corinthians 5:19-21

Notes:

21

Fall out of fellowship with Jesus?

Jesus knew that his mission was now finished, and to
fulfill Scripture he said, "I am thirsty." A jar of sour wine was
sitting there, so they soaked a sponge in it, put it on a
hyssop branch, and held it to his lips. When Jesus
had tasted it, he said, "It is finished!"
Then he bowed his head and released his spirit.

John 19:28-30

Please take the time to read the passage above and contemplate the pain and suffering that Jesus endured for you. He did this, knowing everything that you would ever do throughout your lifetime, to express his *agape* love for you. The Greek word *agape*, when used to describe God's love for mankind, is unlike our English word *love*, which is used to refer to romantic feelings, friendship, or brotherly love. Agape love is unique because it describes the fact that God does not merely love – God *is* love.

God's love is displayed most clearly at the Cross, where Christ died for unworthy people. We are incapable of comprehending God's love for us, but it is not a love that has conditions attached or degrees based upon our earthly performance. God does not love us a lot one moment, then just a little the next. God's love is unconditional.

For years after I was saved, I heard Christians warn one another that they had better walk the straight and narrow or they would fall out of fellowship with Christ. That sounded logical, so I never doubted or questioned it.

Because I have always been such an imperfect human, I began to study the topic of fellowship with Jesus in the Word of God. As a new Christian, I wondered daily, sometimes hourly, if I was still in fellowship with Jesus because I lusted, cussed when I hit my thumb with a hammer, coveted, was prideful at times, and so forth. Plus, I had broken most of the Jewish Ten Commandments numerous times. But, I found hope:

> *When we were utterly helpless, Christ came at just the right time and died for us sinners. Now, most people would not be willing to die for an upright person, though someone might perhaps be willing to die for a person who is especially good. But God showed his great love for us by sending Christ to die for us while we were still sinners. And since we have been made right in God's sight by the blood of Christ, he will certainly save us from God's condemnation. For since our friendship with God was restored by the death of his Son while we were still his enemies, we will certainly be saved through the life of his Son. So now we can rejoice in our wonderful new relationship with God because our Lord Jesus Christ has made us friends of God.*
> Romans 5:6-11

Believe me when I tell you that I would not be entitled to be in fellowship with Jesus at most times. I did not even deserve to be saved. But now I am his child and his friend, and as the above passage says, "For since we were restored to friendship with God by the death of his Son." Our fellowship is based completely on the work of Jesus. Once we completely understand this, we can truly enjoy our relationship with him without the constant worry of being flesh and blood.

Jesus loves us in spite of ourselves, so there is no such thing as falling out of fellowship with him. Jesus is not an instiller of guilt, but a purveyor of forgiveness. He is stable in his attitude and his mood is not affected by our transgressions.

If anyone tells you that you can fall from fellowship with the Lord, tell him or her that his or her opinion is anti-Biblical. God may not agree with your behavior, but unlike our fellow humans, he is always your friend and confidant. Reciprocate!

22

Church attendance, baptism, communion, and tithing are not necessary for salvation

*Thousands have gone to heaven who
never read one page of the Bible.*

Francis A. Baker (1820-1865)

I warned you in the beginning of this book that there would be some repetition. Remember my example using the first four books of the New Testament (Matthew, Mark, Luke, and John) as being somewhat repetitive?

This chapter recaps much of what you have read. Excuse me for insisting that you get it right; if there are redundancies in this chapter it was done with good intention. I would much rather be thorough than have to apologize in a revised edition of this book for having left something out.

Jesus did it all

In the Bible-believing Christian Church there are no sacraments, ordinances, duties, rites, or rituals required for a person to receive the free gift of eternal life in Heaven. A Christian is saved by grace – an unmerited gift. The following passage given to us from the Apostle Paul should clarify that nothing saves us except "grace":

> *I do not treat the grace of God as meaningless. For if keeping the law could make us right with God, then there was no need for Christ to die.* Galatians 2:21

Throughout the centuries, since Jesus paid for the sins of all mankind by giving his life on the Cross, and since he was resurrected so that all who believe will have eternal life in Heaven, many churches and denominations have added rituals to

Christianity to make it seem more sacred. Rituals make some people feel warm and fuzzy, so most congregations do not question the soundness by searching the Scriptures for validation. Adding rituals to what Jesus Christ did is deceptive.

> *For I am not ashamed of this Good News about Christ. It is the power of God at work, saving everyone who believes—the Jew first and also the Gentile. This Good News tells us how God makes us right in his sight. This is accomplished from start to finish by faith. As the Scriptures say, "It is through faith that a righteous person has life."* Romans 1:16-17

Four popular Christian practices that many believe to be necessary for God's favor are church attendance, baptism, Holy Communion, and tithing. People love to formulate man-made laws and rituals, especially when it pertains to religion. Because Christianity is not a religion, there are no rituals, ceremonies, or sacraments required. Notice the word *required*.

> *But now God has shown us a way to be made right with him without keeping the requirements of the law, as was promised in the writings of Moses and the prophets long ago. We are made right with God by placing our faith in Jesus Christ. And this is true for everyone who believes, no matter who we are.* Romans 3:21-22

Hallelujah – "No matter what we have done." Although there is nothing that must be done to receive eternal salvation, there are observances the Christian should consider as part of his or her worship program. However, it is important to remember that although Jesus respects rites and rituals, he continuously criticized one's placing too much emphasis on overt acts rather than on matters of the heart. Jesus is more concerned with the spiritual condition of a person than he is their repetitious observances.

Church attendance

The words *Church* and *church* are used frequently throughout this book. When capitalized, it means the entire body of Christ's believers. When lowercase, it refers to a building with attendees who profess to be Christians. The term *church* means, "a group of people who are called together." *Church attendance* means, "a collective body of believers who meet regularly in a building that is designated for public study, prayer, and worship."

It is important to understand that, after the death of Jesus, many people began to meet and to partake in Christian fellowship. It is also important to understand that eternal life is attained by faith in Jesus Christ alone. No amount of church attendance will earn eternity in Heaven, nor will the lack of church attendance result in the loss of salvation.

For believers, attending church is an expression of our faith in Jesus as our Savior. It is a place where we can gather with fellow believers to worship God, pray to God, learn more about God, and serve one another. These passages suggest church attendance:

> *"I also tell you this: If two of you agree here on earth concerning anything you ask, my Father in heaven will do it for you. For where two or three gather together as my followers, I am there among them."* Matthew 18:19-20, Jesus' words

> *For you have been called to live in freedom, my brothers and sisters. But don't use your freedom to satisfy your sinful nature. Instead, use your freedom to serve one another in love.* Galatians 5:13

> *So faith comes from hearing, that is, hearing the Good News about Christ.* Romans 10:17

> *I am fully convinced, my dear brothers and sisters, that you are full of goodness. You know these things so well you can teach each other all about them.* Romans 15:14

> *And let us not neglect our meeting together, as some people do, but encourage one another, especially now that the day of his return is drawing near.* Hebrews 10:25

The Bible suggests Christians meet, but there is no designated building, time, or number of people who must attend.

> *In the same way, some think one day is more holy than another day, while others think every day is alike. You should each be fully convinced that whichever day you choose is acceptable.* Romans 14:5

Baptism

The term *baptism* is commonly misunderstood. People frequently associate the term baptism with water baptism. *Baptize* generally means "to immerse," but the immersion can be with many substances. There are several baptisms taught in the Bible, but the two that determine one's eternal destination are the *Holy Spirit baptism*, and the *baptism of fire* – not water baptism.

In approximately 313 AD the new Roman Emperor, Constantine, had a very realistic vision of a fiery red cross. On that cross was written, "By this thou shalt conquer." Constantine interpreted the dream that he should give up paganism and become a Christian. He called a council and the first hierarchy was formed. Consequently, Christ was dethroned to make Constantine the head of the church. This hierarchy is identified as the indefinite beginnings of what is now the Catholic, or "universal church."

Because of the adoption of baptismal regeneration, Constantine (not being a Christian yet) was in a quandary. "If I am saved from my sins by water baptism, what is to become of my sins which I may commit after I am baptized?" He finally decided to unite with the Christians and put off baptism until just before his death. Does it make sense that we should wait until we think we are ready to die to be water baptized? No. It is not water baptism that saves us.

Those who are baptized in the Holy Spirit go to Heaven, but those who are baptized with fire go to Hell. John the Baptist prepared the way for Jesus by telling people:

> "I baptize with water those who repent of their sins and turn to God. But someone is coming soon who is greater than I am—so much greater that I'm not worthy even to be his slave and carry his sandals. He will baptize you with the Holy Spirit and with fire. He is ready to separate the chaff from the wheat with his winnowing fork. Then he will clean up the threshing area, gathering the wheat into his barn but burning the chaff with never-ending fire." Matthew 3:11-12

Holy Spirit baptism takes place the very instant a person proclaims Jesus Christ as their Savior. Fire baptism is a reference to the future judgment for those who do not have the indwelling of Jesus' Holy Spirit.

> And God will provide rest for you who are being persecuted and also for us when the Lord Jesus appears from heaven. He will come with his mighty angels, in flaming fire, bringing judgment on those who don't know God and on those who refuse to obey the Good News of our Lord Jesus. They will be punished with eternal destruction, forever separated from the Lord and from his glorious power. When he comes on that day, he will receive glory from his holy people—praise from all who believe. And this includes you, for you believed what we told you about him. 2 Thessalonians 1:7-10

Holy Spirit baptism

> *Then Peter said to them, "Repent and let every one of you be baptized in the name of Jesus Christ for the remission of sins; and you shall receive the gift of the Holy Spirit."* Acts 2:38 (NKJV)

The term *repent* in the verse above means "to change one's mind from believing they can merit Heaven by following laws to accepting Jesus as their only means of salvation." Notice it also states that the Holy Spirit is a gift.

> *Some of us are Jews, some are Gentiles, some are slaves, and some are free. But we have all been baptized into one body by one Spirit, and we all share the same Spirit.* 1 Corinthians 12:13

It is being a part of Jesus Christ's body as the result of Spiritual baptism that makes a person a Christian – not being immersed in water. Water baptism is commonly referred to as an outward expression of an inward confession. It usually takes place within a few weeks after one's Holy Spirit baptism, but it is not necessary for salvation. In Acts 10:47 Peter asked:

> *"Can anyone object to their being baptized, now that they have received the Holy Spirit just as we did?"*

In this passage, the people were clearly saved and received the Holy Spirit before ever being water baptized.

It is also very important to understand that the greatest apostle who ever lived was Paul, and he made this statement:

> *For Christ didn't send me to baptize, but to preach the Good News—and not with clever speech, for fear that the cross of Christ would lose its power.*
> 1 Corinthians 1:17

Though Paul did baptize some, it is clear from his statement that he did not consider water baptism necessary for salvation.

Eternal life is attained by faith in Jesus Christ alone, so no amount of dunking in or sprinkling of water will contribute to salvation.

Infant baptism is a ceremony that was never practiced in the New Testament (early church) and is very contrary to accepted fundamental doctrine. Salvation is by one method only: *mature* belief in the life, death, and resurrection of the Lord Jesus Christ. Infants do not have the capacity for that *mature* faith. Infant baptism is a fuzzy and sweet ceremony, but it does not save a soul.

Holy Communion

Jesus' final meal with his followers in Jerusalem the evening before his crucifixion on the orders of Pilate around AD 30 is called the Last Supper. During the meal, Jesus said he is to be remembered by breaking bread and sharing a cup of wine – inspiring the central ritual of Christianity variously called the *Eucharist, Mass, Lord's Supper,* or *Holy Communion.*

Knowing that he was soon to die, Jesus chose to celebrate a final Passover with his beloved disciples. Then, at the proper time, Jesus and the 12 apostles sat down together at the table, probably located at the upper room on Mount Zion.

> *Then he took a cup of wine and gave thanks to God for it. Then he said, "Take this and share it among yourselves. For I will not drink wine again until the Kingdom of God has come."*
>
> *He took some bread and gave thanks to God for it. Then he broke it in pieces and gave it to the disciples, saying, "This is my body, which is given for you. Do this to remember me."*
>
> *After supper he took another cup of wine and said, "This cup is the new covenant between God and his people—an agreement confirmed with my blood, which is poured out as a sacrifice for you."* Luke 22:17-20

It is from this act that we partake in the Lord's Supper, an expression of faith that is celebrated in most Christian denominations. However, like most aspects of our faith, there are many differences of opinion regarding who, why, when, what, and where.

Who

Christians agree that we should all partake, but some churches are pretty picky regarding who they will serve (which doesn't seem very Christian to me, since it's God's Church and not theirs). Some only serve to members of their particular church or denomination, and others believe only those who are "worthy" should be permitted. The Apostle Paul indicated that some people in the Church of Corinth got sick, and some died as a result of their disrespect for the Lord's Supper.

However, this does not mean that only those without sin can come to the table, because if that were the case, none could come. It is only those who know they are not worthy, but who understand and accept Jesus' Blood sacrifice as their absolute payment for sin, who should participate.

Why

The purpose is fourfold:

1. Commemorates the sacrificial death of Jesus Christ
2. Provides Spiritual strength to the person taking the bread
3. Reaffirms a commitment to Christ
4. Accentuates the Spiritual union of believers

The death of Christ, his broken body, and spilt Blood are the foundation of the Christian faith. Without it, we are not saved and have no redemption. We must always be aware of the true meaning of our living in Christ. As partakers of his flesh and Blood, we should examine ourselves regarding our sincerity.

When

This varies from denomination to denomination, from church to church, from pastor to pastor, and from person to person. There is nothing Biblical that suggests its frequency, just that it is expected. It is important that the Lord's Supper has nothing to do with salvation, and there is no mention of its benefits *per se* in the Scriptures, other than being an important ceremony. Nor does Jesus threaten damnation for lack of participation. Its frequency should be between you and the Holy Spirit.

What

Although throughout history the Church traditionally used wine, non-alcoholic grape juice became increasingly popular in Protestant churches in England during the temperance movement and in the United States in the late 19th and early 20th centuries. Because of so many problems with alcoholism, many churches have switched to grape juice.

Where

This symbol of one's faith can be done at any time, at any place, and most agree does not necessitate administration by a member of clergy.

Misconceptions

The Lord's Supper does nothing toward forgiving, because all sins were forgiven at the Cross.

The use of leavened or unleavened bread should not be a doctrinal issue.

As with most issues, Christians debate the nature of the bread and wine (the elements). Does the wine actually turn into Jesus' Blood? Does the bread actually turn into Jesus' body? Are these foods just symbols?

These are issues that divide the body of Christ, and although they should not to be shrugged off, they should be open to personal interpretation. I doubt Jesus will penalize you if your opinion is incorrect.

Tithing commanded? Not so.

Many are under the false impression that God commanded from the beginning that we "tithe" 10 percent of our income, and that "rule" remains in effect today. God never commanded in the New Testament (New Covenant) that anyone tithes. However, many preachers present the act of tithing as a Scriptural imperative.

The Old Testament stories regarding tithing do not coincide with what many preachers present to their congregations today. Tithing is too often presented to parishioners as a law from God, rather than the privilege of giving. Under the *New Covenant*, tithing is not a law, although it is sometimes presented as such to keep church coffers full.

The giving of gifts to the church and to the needy is the expression of one's love of God and the love of one's fellow man, and it should be done with a joyful heart.

> *You must each decide in your heart how much to give. And don't give reluctantly or in response to pressure. "For God loves a person who gives cheerfully."* 2 Corinthians 9:7

Exploring the Old Testament regarding tithing

The word *tithe* comes from an old English word that actually means "tenth." So when we are referring to tithing we are talking about giving one-tenth. I prefer to use the word *give* because tithe has the connotation of not only demanding a certain amount, but also limiting the amount to 10 percent.

As we explore the Scriptures, we will find that it gets much more complicated than that. There are several stories that describe Abraham and Jacob offering a portion of their blessings. Let us examine the Scriptures. The following is the first story mentioned in the Bible regarding tithing:

> After Abram returned from his victory over Kedorlaomer and all his allies, the king of Sodom went out to meet him in the valley of Shaveh (that is, the King's Valley).
>
> And Melchizedek, the king of Salem and a priest of God Most High, brought Abram some bread and wine. Melchizedek blessed Abram with this blessing:
>
> > "Blessed be Abram by God Most High,
> >   Creator of heaven and earth.
> > And blessed be God Most High,
> >   who has defeated your enemies for you."
>
> Then Abram gave Melchizedek a tenth of all the goods he had recovered.
>
> The king of Sodom said to Abram, "Give back my people who were captured. But you may keep for yourself all the goods you have recovered."
>
> Abram replied to the king of Sodom, "I solemnly swear to the Lord, God Most High, Creator of heaven and earth, that I will not take so much as a single thread or sandal thong from what belongs to you. Otherwise you might say, 'I am the one who made Abram rich.' I will accept only what my young warriors have already eaten, and I request that you give a fair share of the goods to my allies—Aner, Eshcol, and Mamre." Genesis 14:17-24

Abram (later changed to Abraham) gave 10 percent of everything he had won in one battle to Melchizedek, who was the king of Salem and a priest of God. Nothing here states that Abram ever tithed on a regular basis. The next story also comes from the Book of Genesis, Chapter 28, verses 20-22:

> Then Jacob made this vow: "If God will indeed be with me and protect me on this journey, and if he will provide me with food and clothing, and if I return safely to my father's home, then the Lord will certainly be my God. And this memorial pillar I have set up will become a place for worshiping God, and I will present to God a tenth of everything he gives me."

God did not tell Jacob that if he tithed he would bless Jacob; rather, Jacob told God that if God blessed him first, then Jacob would give God a tithe.

Notice that the last paragraph in the passage below states that this was a command given to the Israelites, not to the Gentile or to the Christian.

> *"One tenth of the produce of the land, whether grain from the fields or fruit from the trees, belongs to the Lord and must be set apart to him as holy. If you want to buy back the Lord's tenth of the grain or fruit, you must pay its value, plus 20 percent. Count off every tenth animal from your herds and flocks and set them apart for the Lord as holy. You may not pick and choose between good and bad animals, and you may not substitute one for another. But if you do exchange one animal for another, then both the original animal and its substitute will be considered holy and cannot be bought back."*

> *These are the commands that the Lord gave through Moses on Mount Sinai for the Israelites.* Leviticus 27:30-34

I like the following passage, especially the part about the beer.

> *"You must set aside a tithe of your crops—one-tenth of all the crops you harvest each year. Bring this tithe to the place the Lord your God chooses for his name to be honored, and eat it there in his presence. This applies to your tithes of grain, new wine, olive oil, and the firstborn males of your flocks and herds. The purpose of tithing is to teach you always to fear the Lord your God.*

> *"Now the place the Lord your God chooses for his name to be honored might be a long way from your home. If so, you may sell the tithe portion of your crops and herds and take the money to the place the Lord your God chooses. When you arrive, use the money to buy anything you want—an ox, a sheep, some wine, or beer. Then feast there in the presence of the Lord your God and celebrate with your household. And do not forget the Levites in your community, for they have no inheritance as you do.*

> *"At the end of every third year bring the tithe of all your crops and store it in the nearest town. Give it to the Levites, who have no inheritance among you, as well as to the foreigners living among you, the orphans, and the widows in your towns, so they can eat and be satisfied. Then the Lord your God will bless you in all your work."* Deuteronomy 14:22-29 (NLT 1996)

> *The people of Israel responded immediately and generously by bringing the first of their crops and grain, new wine, olive oil, honey, and all the produce of their fields. They brought a large quantity—a tithe of all they produced.* 2 Chronicles 31:5

"Should people cheat God? Yet you have cheated me!

"But you ask, 'What do you mean? When did we ever cheat you?'

"You have cheated me of the tithes and offerings due to me. You are under a curse, for your whole nation has been cheating me. Bring all the tithes into the storehouse so there will be enough food in my Temple. If you do," says the Lord of Heaven's Armies, "I will open the windows of heaven for you. I will pour out a blessing so great you won't have enough room to take it in! Try it! Put me to the test! Your crops will be abundant, for I will guard them from insects and disease. Your grapes will not fall from the vine before they are ripe," says the Lord of Heaven's Armies. Then all nations will call you blessed, for your land will be such a delight," says the Lord of Heaven's Armies.
Malachi 3:8-12

The law of tithing is historic, confusing, and not applicable for Christians. Remember, God gave us a new covenant through Jesus, and it is not based on rule-keeping. Jesus himself was extremely critical of the Pharisees for the importance they placed on the details of the law, while overlooking the big picture. Here are the words of Jesus:

"What sorrow awaits you teachers of religious law and you Pharisees. Hypocrites! For you are careful to tithe even the tiniest income from your herb gardens, but you ignore the more important aspects of the law—justice, mercy, and faith. You should tithe, yes, but do not neglect the more important things. Blind guides! You strain your water so you won't accidentally swallow a gnat, but you swallow a camel!

"What sorrow awaits you teachers of religious law and you Pharisees. Hypocrites! For you are so careful to clean the outside of the cup and the dish, but inside you are filthy—full of greed and self-indulgence! You blind Pharisee! First wash the inside of the cup and the dish, and then the outside will become clean, too.

"What sorrow awaits you teachers of religious law and you Pharisees. Hypocrites! For you are like whitewashed tombs—beautiful on the outside but filled on the inside with dead people's bones and all sorts of impurity. Outwardly you look like righteous people, but inwardly your hearts are filled with hypocrisy and lawlessness." Matthew 23:23-28, Jesus' words

Yes, Jesus loves to see the poor fed, the sick cared for, the homeless given shelter, and the Church growing, but he wants these things done cheerfully from the heart and not because he commanded it.

Jesus presents a new way and a bigger picture

The 10 percent figure that most fund-raisers use is really an Old Testament number that is inappropriately used today. There is no certain percentage that Christians must give, as Paul tells us in his letter to the Corinthians:

> Remember this—a farmer who plants only a few seeds will get a small crop. But the one who plants generously will get a generous crop. You must each decide in your heart how much to give. And don't give reluctantly or in response to pressure. "For God loves a person who gives cheerfully." And God will generously provide all you need. Then you will always have everything you need and plenty left over to share with others. As the Scriptures say,
>
> "They share freely and give generously to the poor.
> Their good deeds will be remembered forever."
>
> For God is the one who provides seed for the farmer and then bread to eat. In the same way, he will provide and increase your resources and then produce a great harvest of generosity in you.
>
> Yes, you will be enriched in every way so that you can always be generous. And when we take your gifts to those who need them, they will thank God. So two good things will result from this ministry of giving—the needs of the believers in Jerusalem will be met, and they will joyfully express their thanks to God.
>
> As a result of your ministry, they will give glory to God. For your generosity to them and to all believers will prove that you are obedient to the Good News of Christ. And they will pray for you with deep affection because of the overflowing grace God has given to you. Thank God for this gift too wonderful for words! 2 Corinthians 9:6-15

If you are not comfortable digging deep, keep it in your pocket, or just give a smaller amount until you are comfortable. Also, it says you should make up your own mind as to how much you give. The 10 percent number that is so often used as a commandment is an Old Testament figure. You may give more or less – but give cheerfully.

So, what is the big picture?

The big picture has to do with loving the Lord and loving one another.

> *"Watch out! Don't do your good deeds publicly, to be admired by others, for you will lose the reward from your Father in heaven. When you give to someone in need, don't do as the hypocrites do—blowing trumpets in the synagogues and streets to call attention to their acts of charity! I tell you the truth, they have received all the reward they will ever get. But when you give to someone in need, don't let your left hand know what your right hand is doing. Give your gifts in private, and your Father, who sees everything, will reward you."* Matthew 6:1-4, Jesus' words

> *Then Jesus said to his disciples, "If any of you wants to be my follower, you must turn from your selfish ways, take up your cross, and follow me. If you try to hang on to your life, you will lose it. But if you give up your life for my sake, you will save it. And what do you benefit if you gain the whole world but lose your own soul. Is anything worth more than your soul? For the Son of Man will come with his angels in the glory of his Father and will judge all people according to their deeds. And I tell you the truth, some standing here right now will not die before they see the Son of Man coming in his Kingdom."* Matthew 16:24-28

> *"Sell your possessions and give to those in need. This will store up treasure for you in heaven! And the purses of heaven never get old or develop holes. Your treasure will be safe; no thief can steal it and no moth can destroy it. Wherever your treasure is, there the desires of your heart will also be."* Luke 12:33-34, Jesus' words

> *Then he turned to his host. "When you put on a luncheon or a banquet,"* he said, *"don't invite your friends, brothers, relatives, and rich neighbors. For they will invite you back, and that will be your only reward. Instead, invite the poor, the crippled, the lame, and the blind. Then at the resurrection of the righteous, God will reward you for inviting those who could not repay you."* Luke 14:12-14

> *"So now I am giving you a new commandment: Love each other. Just as I have loved you, you should love each other. Your love for one another will prove to the world that you are my disciples."* John 13:34-35, Jesus' words

In these expressions from Jesus Christ, he makes no mention of a certain percentage. Conversely, he is adamant regarding heartfelt love and charity for one another.

Jesus wants to live in your heart, allowing his Spirit to tell you what missions he has specifically for you.

Paul said

> *Now regarding your question about the money being collected for God's people in Jerusalem. You should follow the same procedure I gave to the churches in Galatia. On the first day of each week, you should each put aside a portion of the money you have earned. Don't wait until I get there and then try to collect it all at once.* 1 Corinthians 16:1-2

> *Whatever you give is acceptable if you give it eagerly. And give according to what you have, not what you don't have. Of course, I don't mean your giving should make life easy for others and hard for yourselves. I only mean that there should be some equality.* 2 Corinthians 8:12-13

Give till it hurts

Jesus Christ gave to you until it hurt, and you should reciprocate generously.

> *You know the generous grace of our Lord Jesus Christ. Though he was rich, yet for your sakes he became poor, so that by his poverty he could make you rich.* 2 Corinthians 8:9

> *We know what real love is because Jesus gave up his life for us. So we also ought to give up our lives for our brothers and sisters. If someone has enough money to live well and sees a brother or sister in need but shows no compassion—how can God's love be in that person?* 1 John 3:16-17

Crooks in the pulpit

One of the major complaints from non-Christians is that Christians are always soliciting money. Many believe because a ministry is huge, it is because they are swindlers. While there are a few swindlers, God knows whom they are and he will deal with them.

> *You see, we are not like the many hucksters who preach for personal profit. We preach the word of God with sincerity and with Christ's authority, knowing that God is watching us.* 2 Corinthians 2:17

Crooks have always existed in every walk of life, including the ministry. Be diligent not to confuse the message with the messenger. Although you may not trust a famed preacher, it does not mean his message is wrong. Whether it is the little church on Elm or the satellite giant, all ministries need support, so do not hesitate to send a check if they have helped you, or if you believe they are helping others.

I once heard an evangelist on television begging for contributions to pay the monthly bills. He told folks that if they planted a seed of $1,000, the Lord would give them tenfold. I immediately picked up the phone and called his 800 number. I told the operator I wanted to help them pay their bills, but instead of my sending them $1,000 and getting back $10,000, I was willing to have them send me $1,000, so they would get the $10,000. She hung up on me.

It's not yours to begin with

You are not giving the Lord two percent, 10 percent, or 40 percent of what is yours – it is all his. He is merely allowing you to use it, so be generous.

> *For what gives you the right to make such a judgment? What do you have that God hasn't given you? And if everything you have is from God, why boast as though it were not a gift?* 1 Corinthians 4:7

Everything else belongs to God.

 **Notes:**

23

Invite Jesus into your heart?

One such term or expression is 'Ask Jesus into your heart.' The same expression is sometimes phrased, 'Ask Jesus into your life', or 'Invite Jesus into your heart.' Nowhere does one find anything like this in the Bible. The Bible says, 'Believe on the Lord Jesus Christ, and thou shalt be saved (Acts 16:31).' Why don't we use Bible terms? Why not drop the unclear ones?

Dr. Hank Lindstrom (1940-2008)

Nowhere in the Bible does it say that a person is saved by inviting Jesus into their heart. In the world of Christianity you will often hear the phrase "invite Jesus Christ into your heart" as the method by which an individual receives salvation. This phrase is used frequently by evangelists indicating the act is necessary for salvation. This is technically not true because it is not something we do for God that saves us, but our belief in what Jesus did for us. Although inviting Jesus into our hearts sounds good, it is not how we are saved. However, because God knows all, if you extend the invitation to Jesus, I feel very confident that he will understand that you are accepting him as your Savior. So do not worry about the preciseness of the process you use. It is our belief – a function of our brain – that saves us, and not something we do.

Then why do people say this?

They say it probably because that thought has been handed down from person to person, although it lacks accuracy. It sounds so sweet that nobody has taken the time to research its truthfulness.

Furthermore, it probably started because the term *heart* is used frequently through-out the Bible. In *Strong's Exhaustive Concordance of the Bible*, which is a listing of primary words contained in the King James Version of the Bible, the *brain* is not mentioned once, whereas *heart* is cited more than 800 times.

Why *heart* was used instead of *brain*

If the heart is purely an organ used to pump blood throughout the body, then why wasn't the term *brain* used? Isn't it our brain that makes rational, intelligent deci-sions? Here is the answer:

> According to scientist's recent discoveries, our hearts play just as much an important part in our evaluations and appropriate actions as our brains. In fact, maybe more.

To get a more clear understanding of the term *heart*, when used to describe some-thing other than a pumping organ, I will present a fascinating story about a heart transplant patient, followed by an interesting theory by Dr. Don Colbert, M.D.

When author and scientist Paul Pearsall was speaking to an international group of psychologists, psychiatrists, and social workers in Houston, Texas, he talked about his belief in the central role of the heart in both physical and spiritual life. A physi-cian came up to the microphone to share her story, sobbing as she spoke:

> I have a patient, an eight-year-old little girl who received the heart of a murdered ten-year-old girl. Her mother brought her to me when she started screaming at night about her dreams of the man who had murdered her donor. She said her daughter knows who it was. After several sessions, I just could not deny the reality of what this child was telling me. Her mother and I finally decided to call the police and, using the descriptions from the little girl, they found the murderer. He was easily convicted with the evidence my patient provided. The time, the weapon, the place, the clothes he wore, what the little girl he killed had said to him…everything the little heart transplant recipient reported was completely accurate.

The following paragraphs are from a very interesting book titled *Deadly Emotions*, by Dr. Don Colbert.

> Even before the brain of a fetus forms, a tiny heart begins to beat. Scientists don't know what makes it begin its long journey of beating for seventy, eighty, or more

years. Medical practitioners use the word "autorhythmic" to describe how a heart begins beating all by itself.

While the source of the heart's beating is found within the heart itself, researchers believe the brain controls the timing of each beat. Even so, a heart does not need to be "hardwired" to the brain to continue a steady, rhythmical beating. When a surgeon is harvesting a heart for transplantation, he severs the nerves running to the deceased person's brain. He then places the heart into another person's chest and restores the beat. Surgeons do not know how to reconnect the nerves of the newly installed heart to the brain, so a connection between the two organs is lost, at least temporarily. Nevertheless, the new heart that is jump-started continues to beat, beat, beat.

How can this be? In recent years neuroscientists have discovered that the heart has it's own independent nervous system. At least forty thousand nerve cells (neurons) exist in a human heart. That's the same amount found in various subcortical (beneath the cerebral cortex) centers of the brain. In other words, the heart is more than a mere biological pump. These abundant nerve cells give it a thinking, feeling capability.

The heart's "brain" and the nervous system relay messages back and forth to the brain in the skull, creating a two-way communication between these two organs. In the 1970's physiologists John and Beatrice Lacey of the Fels Research Institute found a flaw in current popular thinking about the brain. The popular approach was to assume that the brain made all of the body's decisions. The Lacey's research indicated otherwise.

Specifically, these researchers found that while the brain may send instructions to the heart through the nervous system, the heart doesn't automatically obey.

Instead, the heart seems to respond at times as if it is "considering" the information that it has received. Sometimes when the brain sends an arousal signal to the body in response to external stimuli, the heart speeds up, as might be expected. On other occasions, however, the heart slows down while all other organs are aroused as expected.

The selectivity of the heart's response suggested to the Laceys that the heart does not mechanically respond to the brain's signals. Rather, the heart seems to have an opinion of its own, which it communicates back to the brain.

What was even more interesting in the Laceys' research was the fact that the messages that the heart sent to the brain seemed to be ones that the brain not only understood but obeyed. In effect, heart and brain hold an intelligent dialogue. At times the heart submits to the brain, and on occasions the brain seems to submit to the heart. The messages from the heart appear to be capable of affecting an individual's behavior.

The ultimate "real you" is a composite of what your heart tells your brain, your brain tells your heart, and your will decides to believe, say, and do. **Pages 141 and 142**

The Bible never fails us

Heart, when used in the Bible, refers to the Christian's personal characteristics. It means mind, soul, spirit, or one's entire emotional nature in understanding – both good and bad. The heart is the organ that is said to have the ability to reason, question, meditate, motivate, and think. All of these mental processes in today's world are normally associated with one's brain, and not the heart.

How is your heart? Jesus can soften it. Having a soft heart does not mean that one has a weak mind! When a Christian's heart is softened, his character is simultaneously strengthened.

24

Misunderstood passages regarding salvation

Which sins didn't Jesus die for?

Common Sense

Knowing what the Bible says and knowing what it means are two different things. It requires the Spirit of God living in the reader to understand its meaning.

Some religions claim the name *Christian* but deny the sufficiency of Jesus' finished work on the Cross as payment in full for one's sins. They recognize his brutal death as only part of the recipe, and teach that we humans must add good works to what Jesus did. This is not logical, nor does it agree with the Holy Scriptures.

Always remember, when interpreting the Scriptures you cannot use a few confusing verses to contradict the aggregate message of Jesus' death, burial, and resurrection. The entire New Testament message focuses on Jesus Christ's finished work. So anyone who attempts to diminish the completeness of his mission is flirting with blasphemy. When a person becomes a Christian, that individual becomes a part of Christ's body (the Church), and although that person will continue to sin carnally, God holds him blameless Spiritually.

> *Christ is also the head of the church,*
> *which is his body.*
> *He is the beginning,*
> *supreme over all who rise from the dead*
> *So he is first in everything.*
> *For God in all his fullness*
> *was pleased to live in Christ,*

and through him God reconciled
  everything to himself.
 He made peace with everything in heaven and on earth
  by means of Christ's blood on the cross.

This includes you who were once far away from God. You were his enemies,
separated from him by your evil thoughts and actions. Yet now he has
reconciled you to himself through the death of Christ in his physical body.
As a result, he has brought you into his own presence, and you are holy and
blameless as you stand before him without a single fault. Colossians 1:18-22

Notice the last verse that states, "...you are holy and blameless as you stand before him without a single fault." This means that Jesus faced death, as God, so we who trust only in Jesus for redemption can be assured that his sacrifice was complete and that he truly removed our sin. Once a person is saved, that person is holy and blameless forever.

When I am explaining salvation strictly by faith, others use the following passages to discredit Jesus' Blood by insisting these stipulate works in addition to his Blood.

Matthew 5:48

"But you are to be perfect, even as your Father in heaven is perfect." Jesus'
words

Matthew Chapters 5-7 contain verses from Jesus' hyperbolic (meaning embellished to create a strong impression) *Sermon on the Mount.* This discourse by Jesus requires intense theological interpretation because its content is not typical of the style of our Savior. Many theologians agree that Jesus painted a picture of unobtainable perfection to emphasize that God desires obedience of the heart, not the appearance of obedience as displayed by the religious leaders of the day. Please remember, Jesus' entire ministry was in anticipation of his death, which was the ultimate manifestation of grace. Jesus makes this clear in Matthew 5:17:

"Don't misunderstand why I have come. I did not come to abolish the law
of Moses or the writings of the prophets. No, I came to accomplish their
purpose."

You must understand that mankind cannot become perfect, as stated in Matthew 5:48, so Jesus' statement must have a deeper message. That message is that only

Christ has met this standard, and it is only by becoming part of his body that our spirit is considered perfect. The following verse should clarify this immediately.

> *For God made Christ, who never sinned, to be the offering for our sin, so that we could be made right with God through Christ.* 2 Corinthians 5:21

Matthew 7:13-14

> *"Enter through the narrow gate. For wide is the gate and broad is the road that leads to destruction, and many enter through it. But small is the gate and narrow the road that leads to life, and only a few find it."* Jesus' words (NIV)

These verses, also a part of the *Sermon on the Mount*, are a consummation of Christ's entire existance. Many people interpret the "narrow gate" as meaning those with the fewest sins. Not true. Jesus is stating that belief in him as the Messiah is the only (narrow) way to have a relationship with God.

We live in a world where many people believe there are multiple paths that lead to God. According to Jesus, who is God, there is only one path. That path is him and only him.

Matthew 7:21

Also from the Sermon on the Mount:

> *"Not everyone who calls out to me, 'Lord! Lord!' will enter the Kingdom of Heaven. Only those who actually do the will of my Father in heaven will enter."* Jesus' words

Jesus is not suggesting that works merit salvation, but that true faith will not fail to produce good works. Keep in mind that when we are saved, our new Counselor is the Holy Spirit, who influences our decisions, although we are continually influenced by our carnal nature. Therefore, because of the influence of the Spirit, we will produce good works.

Matthew 7:24-27

Also from the *Sermon on the Mount*:

> *"Anyone who listens to my teaching and follows it is wise, like a person who builds a house on solid rock. Though the rain comes in torrents and the*

floodwaters rise and the winds beat against that house, it won't collapse because it is built on bedrock. But anyone who hears my teaching and doesn't obey it is foolish, like a person who builds a house on sand. When the rains and floods come and the winds beat against that house, it will collapse with a mighty crash." Jesus' words

The "house built on solid rock" represents living an obedient life. The obedience necessitates trusting in Jesus for salvation, at which time the Holy Spirit immediately indwells the believer, and it is by obeying the Holy Spirit that God is pleased. Those who ignore the Spirit do not lose their salvation, but they do not receive the peace that accompanies living a Spiritual life.

Matthew 25:1-12

The explanation to this parable is in Matthew 25:13, which is warning us to be prepared for the return of Jesus Christ. Only those who have been saved will enter his Kingdom. It does not mean a person can lose his or her salvation.

Matthew 25:31-46

"When the Son of man shall come in his glory, and all the holy angels with him, then shall he sit upon the throne of his glory:

And before him shall be gathered all nations: and he shall separate them one from another, as a shepherd divideth his sheep from the goats:

And he shall set the sheep on his right hand, but the goats on the left.

Then shall the King say unto them on his right hand, Come, ye blessed of my Father, inherit the kingdom prepared for you from the foundation of the world:

For I was an hungred, and ye gave me meat: I was thirsty, and ye gave me drink: I was a stranger, and ye took me in:

Naked, and ye clothed me: I was sick, and ye visited me: I was in prison, and ye came unto me.

Then shall the righteous answer him, saying, Lord, when saw we thee an hungred, and fed thee? or thirsty, and gave thee drink?

When saw we thee a stranger, and took thee in? Or naked, and clothed thee?

Or when saw we thee sick, or in prison, and came unto thee?

And the King shall answer and say unto them, Verily I say unto you, Inasmuch as ye have done it unto one of the least of these my brethren, ye have done it unto me.

Then shall he say also unto them on the left hand, Depart from me, ye cursed, into everlasting fire, prepared for the devil and his angels:

For I was an hungred, and ye gave me no meat: I was thirsty, and ye gave me no drink:

I was a stranger, and ye took me not in: naked, and ye clothed me not: sick, and in prison, and ye visited me not.

Then shall they also answer him, saying, Lord, when saw we thee an hungred, or athirst, or a stranger, or naked, or sick, or in prison, and did not minister unto thee?

Then shall he answer them, saying, Verily I say unto you, Inasmuch as ye did it not to one of the least of these, ye did it not to me.

And these shall go away into everlasting punishment: but the righteous into life eternal." Jesus' words (KJV)

Many people interpret these passages incorrectly, thinking that Jesus is separating all people, throughout history based on their good deeds. The incorrect interpretation is that God will allow those with good deeds into Heaven, but cast those without good deeds into Hell. This is wrong. He is only judging a small group of people, from a specific time period, and he is separating them as believers and non-believers, not by their works. Good works do not save us, but good works are a manifestation of the believer's faith.

These passages are referring to the judgment of nations (some Bible scholars state that the word *nations* refers to people and some to Gentiles), which is an event that will occur seven years after the Rapture, immediately following Armageddon and the Second Coming of Jesus Christ to the earth. As Jesus Christ sets up his earthly 1,000-year kingdom, his first order of business will be to judge everyone alive at this time and eliminate the unsaved from entering the millennium. This judgment will be immediate, and there will be no time for the unsaved to receive Christ; it will be too late. God gathers the nations, but it is the individual people within the various nations that are judged, not the nations.

The sheep are the righteous who were made right via their faith, not by their works. The goats are the unrighteous because of their disbelief, not because of a lack of works.

> *So we are made right with God through faith and not by obeying the law.*
> Romans 3:28

The sheep (the righteous) will be allowed to enter the millennium, but the goats (the unrighteous) will be sent away to face destruction by eternal fire.

The sheep are those who have cared for the "least of these my brothers and sisters" who are the Jews. There will be 144,000 virgin Jewish men (Revelation 7:4 and 14:4) who preach the gospel of Jesus Christ during the seven-year tribulation. And those who respond to the message of salvation will so appreciate receiving the message that they will protect the Jews just as they were protected during the time of Hitler's dictatorship. The goats, who will reject the message of the gospel, are those who will show hatred toward the Jews.

It will be the Antichrist's determination to destroy the Jews, just as many were destroyed by Hitler during World War II. Anti-Semitism will be worldwide. Many Christians will refuse to take the mark of the beast and will help the Jews, just as in Nazi Germany. They will visit those who are in prisons, hide those in need of security, and comfort the hurting.

Luke 10:25-27

> *One day an expert in religious law stood up to test Jesus by asking him this question: "Teacher, what should I do to inherit eternal life?"*
>
> *Jesus replied, "What does the law of Moses say? How do you read it?"*
>
> *The man answered, "'You must love the Lord your God with all your heart, all your soul, all your strength, and all your mind.' And, 'Love your neighbor as yourself.'"*

Jesus was speaking to an expert in religious law, so Jesus answered him according to the law. You must also keep in mind that this was prior to Jesus' death and resurrection, so Jesus spoke in legal terms familiar to the person with whom he was speaking. Notice Jesus did not talk about the multiple laws of those days, but just spoke of the one law that still exists as you read this. Of course, that is the law of love. A true Christian has the law of love written in his heart, which was not available prior to Jesus' resurrection.

Christ was very clear about loving one another throughout his teachings, and in John 13:34-35 he commands us to love one another, to prove to the world we are his disciples. Paul's words sum it up very well:

> *Owe nothing to anyone—except for your obligation to love one another. If you love your neighbor, you will fulfill the requirements of God's law.* Romans 13:8

John 8:11

> *"No, Lord," she said.*
>
> *And Jesus said, "Neither do I. Go and sin no more."*

The last words of Jesus in this story were, "Go and sin no more." The novice Christian often quotes this statement in an attempt to claim that once a person is saved, that person should never sin again – which is absurd.

Jesus is speaking to a woman caught committing adultery, who was brought to Jesus by the Pharisees, the religious teachers (religious policemen), expecting her to be given the traditional punishment for an adulterer – death by being stoned.

The Pharisees were constantly testing Jesus, and this was an opportunity to put him to the test again. Following Jesus' suggestion that he who is sinless should cast the first stone, the accusers left. Then Jesus told her to *"Go and sin no more."* Jesus knew that it was not possible for her to stop sinning, so most scholars agree that Jesus' words were not meant literally, and that Jesus meant for her to cease her adulterous acts.

In 1 John 1:8, John the apostle says, "If we say we have no sin, we are only fooling ourselves and refusing to accept the truth." No matter what anyone tells you, it is impossible to stop sinning, so Jesus could not have meant that literally. Yes, as Christians, we should constantly be trying to improve ourselves, but if you think you can live a sinless life, you are only fooling yourself and refusing to accept the truth.

NOTE: Always remember, there is no difference in God's eyes between a small sin and a large sin.

For the person who keeps all of the laws except one is as guilty as a person who has broken all of God's laws. James 2:10

Acts 2:38

Then Peter said to them, "Repent, and let every one of you be baptized in the name of Jesus Christ for the remission of sins; and you shall receive the gift of the Holy Spirit." (NKJV)

We must understand the meaning of the word *repent*. It is a mistake to go to a modern dictionary to find the meaning of a word that was used 2,000 years ago. The term *repent* comes from the Greek word *metanoia*, which means: "a change of mind." The original Greek word was translated into "repentance," but does not mean one must turn from, or be sorrowful for sin! It means "...a change of mind from the adherence to religious laws for eternal life, to that of only trusting in what God has done through the life, death, and resurrection of Jesus the Jewish Messiah." In the Bible, "repentance" is not referring to morals, bad habits, good behavior, sitting in church, or anything else. It is about trusting only in the free gift of eternal life from the bloody, beaten, belittled, scorned young man named Jesus, who said, "It is finished," before he struggled for his last breath.

Repentance is not to be confused with *penitence*, which is "sorrow for sin."

This verse does not say "repent of your sins." Yes, the term "repent" is used, but it is not used in the context erroneously taught by those who love to add works to salvation. The phrase "repent of sin" is not in the Bible. Uneducated Christians like to say a person must repent of their sins to be saved, and you may even hear renowned preachers say the same thing. But that does not make it Biblical. It is one of those phrases that has been used for so long by so many people that it has become accepted as true, although it is not.

Stop and think about it: If Jesus' death paid for all of mankind's sin, then sin is not a factor in salvation. Therefore, a change in behavior (i.e., turning from sinning) is not a precursor to salvation. A person can turn from sinning and not be a Christian, and a person can be saved without a change in behavior.

Being sorry for one's sins is one thing, but believing that one must repent or do something for salvation is ludicrous. We are saved only by the death and resurrection of Jesus. It is not our sins that send us to Hell, as they were absolved on the Cross. It is our disbelief in Jesus' finished work that keeps us from enjoying eternity in Heaven.

He himself is the sacrifice that atones for our sins—and not only our sins but the sins of all the world. 1 John 2:2

What this passage means is exactly what it says, "He takes away not only our sins but the sins of all the world." Therefore, it should be clear that a person does not go to Hell because of their sins – their sins were paid for.

When we place our faith in Jesus only as having taken our place on the Cross and bearing the penalty for our sins, then we are repenting from the false notion there is something we can do to save ourselves. It never ceases to amaze me how important people want to make themselves, when it is all about what Jesus did.

Philippians 2:12

The mistake the novice makes in understanding the following verse is the mistake of thinking that "work out your salvation" means "work for your salvation":

> *Wherefore, my beloved, as ye have always obeyed, not as in my presence only, but now much more in my absence, work out your own salvation with fear and trembling.* (KJV)

Notice that I used this verse as it appears in the KJV. The words "work" and "out" are used in several other translations, but not all.

The following is from the *NLT*:

> *Dear friends, you always followed my instructions when I was with you. And now that I am away, it is even more important. Work hard to show the results of your salvation, obeying God with deep reverence and fear.*

The publishers of the *New Living Translation* substituted "work out" with "put into action."

Paul is telling the Philippians that because they (we) live in a world of "crooked and perverse" people, we as Christians, who have been saved, should live lives that represent Christ.

The *Message Bible* says it this way:

> *Now that I am separated from you, keep it up. Better yet, redouble your efforts. Be energetic in your life of salvation, reverent and sensitive before God.*

The next verse, which states that God is working in you, will help to clarify the meaning of "work out." It is God working in us that gives us the desires and abilities to do what he wants us to do.

Hebrews 6:4-6

> *For it is impossible to bring back to repentance those who were once enlightened—those who have experienced the good things of heaven and shared in the Holy Spirit, who have tasted the goodness of the word of God and the power of the age to come – and who then turn away from God. It is impossible to bring such people back to repentance; by rejecting the Son of God, they themselves are nailing him to the cross once again and holding him up to public shame.*

This is a difficult passage to interpret, but it does not teach that we can lose our salvation. The following are two possible interpretations.

> 1. This passage refers to unbelievers who are influenced by the truth of the gospel, but who have not trusted in Jesus Christ as Savior. They are intellectually persuaded but spiritually uncommitted, which is the case with many living today.

> Churches are filled with those who know about Jesus, but they do not know Jesus. They go through the motions and celebrate the holidays, yet they reject the idea of being born again. A person must come all the way to Christ in complete trust, or for them there is no hope for forgiveness because they reject him with full knowledge and conscious experience.

> 2. The other interpretation suggests that this passage is written about Christians. According to this interpretation, the author of Hebrews is setting up a hypothetical statement that if a Christian falls away, it would be impossible to renew his salvation. That's because Christ died once for sin and if his "one-time" sacrifice is insufficient, then there is no hope at all. Believing that Jesus must be crucified over and over again is not logical and borders on heresy and blasphemy.

James 2:26

> *Just as the body is dead without breath, so also faith is dead without good works.*

"Faith without works is dead" is probably the most commonly misunderstood expression in the New Testament. It is imperative to realize that James was writing to Jewish Christians, those who were already saved. He addresses them as *brethren*. James is not telling them how to receive eternal life, as they are already saved, but he is telling them how to live a life of discipleship. In today's vernacular, we say that *talk is cheap* – and that is exactly what James was saying. There is definitely a difference between salvation and discipleship, and James was emphasizing God's desire for his people to follow his Son's teachings as disciples.

It is extremely important to note that in James 2:10 he also wrote that a person who breaks one law is as guilty as one who breaks them all. This makes it clear that people who want to keep the Old Testament law must keep all of the law, not merely part of it. Two verses later James states that Christians will be judged by the "law of love."

James' points are excellent, but confusing, so they should not be used as a weapon to distort grace.

1 John 1:9

What I have written here is indeed a repetition of what I wrote earlier, but I do not consider it a redundancy. Millions of Christians are under the false assumption that they must continually confess their sins to be forgiven. I am very impatient with those who underestimate the forgiveness at the Cross, so I will say it again and again. The following verse is misunderstood. Rather than confess over and over again, say, "Thank you Lord Jesus, thank you Lord Jesus, thank you Lord Jesus."

> *But if we confess our sins to him, he is faithful and just to forgive us our sins and to cleanse us from all wickedness.* 1 John 1:9

Before a Bible reader makes a doctrinal decision, the reader must know the audience of the letter to which the passage is written and understand the writer's intent. One of the difficulties of reading the Bible is that we often use one passage to establish doctrine without studying other verses and passages. Doctrine should not be the result of using one lone verse.

This verse does not mean that a Christian must continually confess his or her sins to be forgiven. We know that our sins were paid for when Jesus died on the Cross. There are many verses that make this fact crystal clear, so all of these verses combined make it very obvious that 1 John 1:9 must have another meaning.

To understand what 1 John 1:9 means, we must understand for whom it was written. The letters in the New Testament were written to Christian leaders who would read them to many people with varying beliefs: Christian believers, Jews, idol worshipers, atheists, agnostics, and those of other beliefs.

It is obvious from the introduction that the Book of 1 John was trying to convince listeners that Jesus was God incarnate, that Jesus was of flesh, and that Jesus' Blood cleansed us from every sin. Because John knew non-believers would be present and that they were probably immoral, he articulated that we are all sinners in need of forgiveness.

John said if they thought they had no sin, they were wrong. This clearly indicates he was speaking to individuals who were probably not Christians or Jews. His stating that we must confess our sins means that we must be aware we are sinners, and we must recognize we are in need of forgiveness from God, the Creator of the world and everything in it.

If you research the Book of 1 John, you will learn that one of the groups that John was addressing was a sect called Gnostics, who are still present today. Gnosticism is a society that describes the physical world as evil and the spiritual world as good. They believe that Jesus only appeared as a fleshly being – but in fact he was not a man of flesh, he was totally spiritual. Because of their emphasis on the spiritual world, they teach that moral rules are only for those who cannot see beyond the physical level of life.

This verse, 1 John 1:9, is the only place that confession and forgiveness are mentioned simultaneously in the New Testament. Therefore, the verse is not applicable to those who have already been saved. Asking forgiveness is good unless you have already been forgiven.

I recently heard a prominent Christian pastor tell the story of his 100-year-old father who became burdened with guilt from ungodly things that he had done in his younger years. To help him through his guilt, he told his wife that he was going to begin asking God for forgiveness. His wife told him that he would do no such thing, but that if he wanted to begin praising God for the forgiveness he had already received at the Cross, she would respect his endeavor.

We are taught from childhood to ask for forgiveness every time we do wrong. This is common courtesy, but it does not make sense to constantly ask forgiveness once you have been forgiven!

Revelation 3:15-16

Jesus' words are as follows:

> *"I know all the things you do, that you are neither hot nor cold. I wish that you were one or the other! But since you are like lukewarm water, neither hot nor cold, I will spit you out of my mouth!"*

This verse is another case of the reader needing to know the story behind the story. In this scenario, Jesus was speaking to the Christian church of Laodicea, a very prosperous banking center for all of Asia Minor. As is so often the case with success, Laodicea became self-important and arrogant – both qualities that are in direct conflict with God's desires. We humans are usually guilty of seeking better things, but God is impressed only in those of us who are enthusiastic about serving him. This is the case with many churches today, which leave Jesus out of the equation. Jesus' saying that he would spit them out was a metaphor meaning their complacency made him sick to the point of vomiting.

In closing

We are made alive with Christ.

> *But God is so rich in mercy, and he loved us so much, that even though we were dead because of our sins, he gave us life when he raised Christ from the dead. (It is only by God's grace that you have been saved!) For he raised us from the dead along with Christ and seated us with him in the heavenly realms because we are united with Christ Jesus.* Ephesians 2:4-6

When a person is saved, he or she becomes one with Christ Jesus. So in order for a saved person to be denied eternal life in Heaven, Jesus must also deny himself – which is ludicrous. Once we are saved, we are always saved. Jesus promised us that he would never cast us out.

If you are a saved person, and you are under the impression you can lose your salvation, then I ask you: Which of your sins did Jesus not die for? The Blood of Jesus covers them all.

 **<u>Notes:</u>**

PART FIVE

Jesus

Notes:

25

Jesus

*Christians believe that Jesus Christ is the son
of God because He said so.*

C. S. Lewis (1898-1963)

Jesus would probably win the prize for being the most controversial figure who ever lived. He is loved and hated by many. He was so important that they restarted the calendar to begin with the year of his birth. Few question the fact that Jesus existed and most non-Christian religious leaders recognize Jesus as a true historical figure, but the disagreement is whether he was God incarnate. This chapter will establish he was.

This chapter is an inclusive history of Jesus' life, which had no beginning and has no end. Because Jesus is God, the Creator of all things, the account begins in the book of Genesis and ends in the book of Revelation. This is being written so that you may know more about him, but if you want to know him personally, you may do so by simply accepting him as your Savior, at which time his Spirit will come to live in you, giving you the contentment of knowing you have eternal life. God loves you so much that he made it extremely easy.

ONE SOLITARY LIFE

Here is a young man who was born in an obscure village, the child of a peasant woman. He grew up in another village. He worked in a carpenter shop. He was thirty, and then for three years he was an itinerant preacher. He never wrote a book. He never held an office. He never owned a home. He never had a family. He never went to college. He never put his foot inside a big city. He never traveled

200 miles from the place where he was born. He never did one of the things that usually accompany greatness. He had no credentials but himself. While he was still a young man the tide of public opinion turned against him. His friends ran away. He was turned over to his enemies. He went through the mockery of a trial. He was nailed to a cross between two thieves. While he was dying, his executioners gambled for the only piece of property he had on earth, and that was his coat… when he was dead he was laid in a borrowed grave through the pity of a friend. Nineteen centuries wide have come and gone, and today he is the central figure of the human race and the leader of the column of progress. I am far within the mark when I say that all the armies that ever marched, and all the navies that ever sailed, and all the parliaments that ever sat, and all the kings that ever reigned, put together, have not affected the life of man upon this earth as has that ONE SOLITARY LIFE.

The essay above, titled "One Solitary Life," can be found in various forms. I found this one years ago, but I cannot remember exactly where or when. When I began writing this book, I researched its author via Google and found that Dr. James Allan Francis originally wrote "One Solitary Life," but apparently in a different version. This little story was an influence in leading me to believe Jesus was who he said he was – God.

Jesus was and is God

Jesus was God, is God, and always will be God. He was not one of many prophets that God sent to earth to provide philosophy.

> *In the beginning the Word already existed.*
> *The Word was with God,*
> *and the Word was God.*
> *He existed in the beginning with God.*
> *God created everything through him,*
> *and nothing was created except through him.*
> *The Word gave life to everything that was created,*
> *and his life brought light to everyone.*
> *The light shines in the darkness,*
> *and the darkness can never extinguish it.*

> *God sent a man, John the Baptist, to tell about the light so that everyone might believe because of his testimony. John himself was not the light; he was simply a witness to tell about the light. The one who is the true light, who gives light to everyone, was coming into the world.*

*He came into the very world he created, but the world didn't recognize
him. He came to his own people, and even they rejected him. But to all who
believed him and accepted him, he gave the right to become children of God.
They are reborn—not with a physical birth resulting from human passion or
plan, but a birth that comes from God.* John 1:1-13

Though he was God,
 he did not think of equality with God
 as something to cling to.
Instead, he gave up his divine privileges;
 he took the humble position of a slave
 and was born as a human being.
When he appeared in human form,
 he humbled himself in obedience to God
 and died a criminal's death on a cross. Philippians 2:6-8

Christ is the visible image of the invisible God.
 He existed before anything was created and is supreme
over all creation,
for through him God created everything
 in the heavenly realms and on earth.
 He made the things we can see
 and the things we can't see—
such as thrones, kingdoms, rulers, and authorities in the unseen world.
 Everything was created through him and for him.
He existed before anything else,
 and he holds all creation together. Colossians 1:15-17

*And without controversy great is the mystery of godliness: God was manifest
in the flesh, justified in the Spirit, seen of angels, preached unto the Gentiles,
believed on in the world, received up into glory.* 1 Timothy 3:16 (KJV)

*And now in these final days, he has spoken to us through his Son. God
promised everything to the Son as an inheritance, and through the Son he
created the universe.* Hebrews 1:2

*Because God's children are human beings—made of flesh and blood—the
Son also became flesh and blood. For only as a human being could he die,
and only by dying could he break the power of the devil, who had the power of
death.* Hebrews 2:14

Jesus Christ is the same yesterday, today, and forever. Hebrews 13:8

Jesus Christ is truly God, the second person of the Trinity – who with the Father and the Holy Spirit, always was, is, and always will be.

> *Jesus replied, "Have I been with you all this time, Philip, and yet you still don't know who I am? Anyone who has seen me has seen the Father! So why are you asking me to show him to you? Don't you believe that I am in the Father and the Father is in me? The words I speak are not my own, but my Father who lives in me does his work through me. Just believe that I am in the Father and the Father is in me. Or at least believe because of the work you have seen me do."* John 14:9-11

He has two natures as both God and man simultaneously

You will have to admit, the people of Jesus' time had reasons for doubting his deity. This can be a stumbling block for many who, like the rest of us, have infinitesimal divine perception. However, once it is accepted based strictly on faith, and not reason, it will begin to be understood as taught by the Holy Spirit.

Hypostasis means "that which lies beneath as basis or foundation." In Christianity, hypostasis is used to describe the reality of the two distinct natures that co-existed in Jesus, as both God and man. Jesus was 100 percent man and 100 percent God simultaneously. Some misinformed individuals think of him as half God and half man. But once a Christian knows Jesus personally, they comprehend and appreciate his dual nature. For instance, when Jesus was dying on the Cross, it was the sacrificial man who died. When he arose from being dead, it was his divine nature that allowed him to overcome death. Now you know.

The Old Testament prophesied about Jesus

Jesus did not just pop into town unexpectedly. His life was predestined from the beginning of time, as prophesized in the Old Testament. According to Josh McDowell in *The New Evidence that Demands a Verdict*, there are more than 300 prophecies (Page 164). Some are as follows:

Would be born in Bethlehem

> *But you, O Bethlehem Ephrathah,*
> *   are only a small village among all the people of Judah.*
> *Yet a ruler of Israel will come from you,*
> *   one whose origins are from the distant past.*

The people of Israel will be abandoned to their enemies
*   until the woman in labor gives birth.*
Then at last his fellow countrymen
*   will return from exile to their own land.*
And he will stand to lead his flock with the Lord's strength,
*   in the majesty of the name of the Lord his God.*
Then his people will live there undisturbed,
*   for he will be highly honored around the world.* Micah 5:2-4

Would be born of a virgin

All right then, the Lord himself will give you the sign. Look! The virgin will conceive a child! She will give birth to a son and will call him Immanuel (which means 'God is with us'). Isaiah 7:14

Would be a descendant of King David

For a child is born to us,
*   a son is given to us.*
The government will rest on his shoulders.
*   And he will be called:*
Wonderful Counselor, Mighty God,
*   Everlasting Father, Prince of Peace.*
His government and its peace
*   will never end.*
He will rule with fairness and justice from the throne of his ancestor David
*   for all eternity.*
The passionate commitment of the Lord of Heaven's Armies
*   will make this happen!* Isaiah 9:6-7

Would ride into Jerusalem on a donkey

Rejoice, O people of Zion!
*   Shout in triumph, O people of Jerusalem!*
* Look, your king is coming to you.*
*   He is righteous and victorious,*
* yet he is humble, riding on a donkey—*
*   riding on a donkey's colt.*
I will remove the battle chariots from Israel
*   and the warhorses from Jerusalem.*
* I will destroy all the weapons used in battle,*
*   and your king will bring peace to the nations.*

His realm will stretch from sea to sea
*   and from the Euphrates River to the ends of the earth.* Zechariah 9:9-10

Would be beaten and have his side pierced

He was despised and rejected—
*   a man of sorrows, acquainted with deepest grief.*
We turned our backs on him and looked the other way.
*   He was despised, and we did not care.*
Yet it was our weaknesses he carried;
*   it was our sorrows that weighed him down.*
And we thought his troubles were a punishment from God,
*   a punishment for his own sins!*
But he was pierced for our rebellion,
*   crushed for our sins.*
He was beaten so we could be whole.
*   He was whipped so we could be healed.* Isaiah 53:3-5

"Then I will pour out a spirit of grace and prayer on the family of David and on the people of Jerusalem. They will look on me whom they have pierced and mourn for him as for an only son. They will grieve bitterly for him as for a firstborn son who has died." Zechariah 12:10

Will be the foundation for the new people of Jerusalem

Therefore, this is what the Sovereign Lord says:
*   "Look! I am placing a foundation stone in Jerusalem,*
*   a firm and tested stone.*
It is a precious cornerstone that is safe to build on.
*   Whoever believes need never be shaken.* Isaiah 28:16

Exhibits A, B, and C

There are distinguishable characteristics or circumstances that set Jesus apart from other historical religious figures, new-age religious figures, or from anyone, anywhere. See if you do not agree.

Exhibit A - Jesus' mother was a virgin

Many find this difficult to believe. It does sound strange, but once a person accepts Jesus as their Savior, the Holy Spirit begins to reveal astonishing truths, making the virgin part believable. God can do anything.

Exhibit B - Jesus performed miracles

Each time the skeptics requested further proof from Jesus, he would perform another miracle. He healed the sick, walked on water, made the blind see, raised the dead, fed 4,000 people with seven loaves of bread, calmed a storm, and even predicted his own death. God can do anything.

Exhibit C - Jesus rose from the dead

There were many people who witnessed this conquering event. Jesus was tested repeatedly and he passed every test. Yet the Jews still refused to believe him – so they crucified him. He passed that test, which established he had triumph over death. God can do anything.

Jesus' early days

Jesus was born in a manger in Bethlehem, although some scholars believe he was born in Nazareth. Jesus' mother was a teenage girl named Mary, who was a virgin impregnated by the Spirit of God. Mary wedded Joseph, a carpenter, who became Jesus' foster father.

The baby in the manger was named *Jesus* because an angel of the Lord told Joseph in a dream that this should be the name of the Son of Mary. *Jesus* is translated from the original Aramaic *Yehowshuwa*, meaning "YHWH" (Lord), which stands for salvation. Although his given name was Jesus, throughout the Bible Jesus was referred to by more than 300 different names.

He officially received the name *Jesus* at the age of eight days, when his circumcision was performed. What Jesus was (the Christ) became (sort-of) his last name, although not technically. Christ, or *Christos* in Greek, translates the Hebrew word *messiah* (which means anointed) and refers to the ancient manner of crowning kings.

Christ is not the last name of Jesus – it is his title. Much like King David, President Obama, or Reverend Billy Graham, all of whom have titles. There are different ways of addressing a person with a title. That is why Jesus is sometimes referred to as *Christ Jesus*, when one wants to emphasize his divinity. When one wants to emphasize his humanity, *Jesus Christ* is the preferred order. When one wants to emphasize his lordship, *Lord Jesus* is often used. This is an often-confused thing, wherein people believe Christ to be Jesus' last name, but that is not the case.

Jesus had brothers and sisters

The Bible tells us that Joseph and Mary had additional children; meaning Jesus had brothers and sisters. Jesus' brothers were James, Joseph, Simon, and Judas. His sisters' names are not mentioned.

> *Then they scoffed, "He's just the carpenter's son, and we know Mary, his mother, and his brothers—James, Joseph, Simon, and Judas. All his sisters live right here among us. Where did he learn all these things?"*
> Matthew 13:55-56

> *Then Jesus' mother and brothers came to see him, but they couldn't get to him because of the crowd. Someone told Jesus, "Your mother and your brothers are outside, and they want to see you."* Luke 8:19-21

> *After the wedding he went to Capernaum for a few days with his mother, his brothers, and his disciples.* John 2:12

> *They all met together and were constantly united in prayer, along with Mary the mother of Jesus, several other women, and the brothers of Jesus.* Acts 1:14

> *Don't we have the right to live in your homes and share your meals? Don't we have the right to bring a Christian wife with us as the other apostles and the Lord's brothers do, and as Peter does?* 1 Corinthians 9:4-5

> *The only other apostle I met at that time was James, the Lord's brother.*
> Galatians 1:19

Some theologians claim Jesus had no siblings and that those understood to be brothers and sisters were his cousins. Other theologians argue that Jesus did have brothers and sisters, but they were Joseph's children from a previous marriage. Neither of these speculations has much weight. Jesus was a relative, probably a cousin, to John the Baptist, who was chosen by God to prepare the way for the Jewish Messiah, Jesus Christ.

A regular kid in most ways

As a child, Jesus probably played games similar to hopscotch and jacks. Archaeologists have found whistles, rattles, hoops, spinning toys, and toy animals on wheels that were probably kept in his play box, if they had play boxes in those days.

As a young carpenter Jesus and his earthly father Joseph would probably have constructed farm tools (carts, plows, winnowing forks, and yokes), house parts (doors, frames, posts, and beams), furniture, and kitchen utensils. I find it interesting that tradesman were recognizable by the symbols they wore – such as tailors sticking needles in their tunics, dyers wearing colored rags, and carpenters wearing wood-chips behind their ears. Consequently, Jesus probably wore a woodchip behind his ear.

There are no stories regarding Jesus' childhood until he reached age 12, when he accompanied his Jewish parents on their yearly trip to the Temple in Jerusalem. Left in the city by mistake, he was discovered by his parents discussing the finer points of the Torah (Jewish law) with the scribes and rabbis. This was apparently the first sign of his mission. The New Testament then falls silent about Jesus.

Jesus' physical appearance

The Bible is not very specific regarding Jesus' appearance, so any attempt to recon-struct him is speculation. However, there are several references in the Old Testa-ment to the Messiah being beautiful. The Book of Psalms refers to him as "bright and morning star, fairer than 10,000." However, Isaiah 53:2 says, "There was nothing beautiful or majestic about his appearance, nothing to attract us to him." Appar-ently, he was not a handsome man.

Children seemed to be attracted to him, so we can assume he was not scary looking. Most historians believe that because he was Jewish he would be dark skinned and haired. His hair was probably medium in length.

Jesus' ministry

Jesus' story picks up when he was 30

John the Baptist was a prophet sent by God to carry out a Jewish form of baptism in the Jordan River. But his primary mission was to speak of the coming of the King-dom of God. Because the Jews were suffering under the pressure of the Romans, Jewish expectations of the Messiah and God's Kingdom were very high at the time. By stirring them up, John the Baptist was preparing the way for Jesus – the Jewish Messiah.

Cousin John baptized Jesus prior to Jesus beginning his ministry.

> Then Jesus went from Galilee to the Jordan River to be baptized by John. But John tried to talk him out of it. "I am the one who needs to be baptized by you," he said, "so why are you coming to me?"

But Jesus said, "It should be done, for we must carry out all that God requires." So John agreed to baptize him.

After his baptism, as Jesus came up out of the water, the heavens were opened and he saw the Spirit of God descending like a dove and settling on him. And a voice from heaven said, "This is my dearly loved Son, who brings me great joy." Matthew 3:13-17

Jesus was sinless, so his water baptism demonstrated that it is not water that cleanses our sins, but it is the Holy Spirit baptism that identifies members of the Body of Christ.

C'mon boys, let's make history!

A *disciple* is one who follows the teachings of Jesus. An *apostle* is one who is chosen and sent by Jesus. There were originally 12 apostles, but most theologians believe the Scriptures reveal there could have been as many as 18. The following verses are referring to Jesus' apostles.

"Look, I am sending you out as sheep among wolves. So be as shrewd as snakes and harmless as doves. But beware! For you will be handed over to the courts and will be flogged with whips in the synagogues. You will stand trial before governors and kings because you are my followers. But this will be your opportunity to tell the rulers and other unbelievers about me. When you are arrested, don't worry about how to respond or what to say. God will give you the right words at the right time. For it is not you who will be speaking—it will be the Spirit of your Father speaking through you." Matthew 10:16-20, Jesus' words

Jesus called out to them, "Come, follow me, and I will show you how to fish for people!" Mark 1:17

And he called his twelve disciples together and began sending them out two by two, giving them authority to cast out evil spirits. He told them to take nothing for their journey except a walking stick—no food, no traveler's bag, no money. He allowed them to wear sandals but not to take a change of clothes. Mark 6:7-9

Jesus originally chose 12 men. However, he knew that one of his followers, named Judas, would betray him. Following this betrayal Judas hung himself, but the remaining 11 chose a replacement, named Matthias. Many scholars surmise that Matthias was not God's choice. Therefore, the Apostle Paul replaced Matthias, while Matthias faded into the background.

The Savior's ministry took place primarily in the area of the Sea of Galilee, approximately 120 miles north of his birthplace. This entire area was in the region of Palestine, which is east of the Mediterranean Sea and west of the Jordan River.

Jesus was new age for his era

Jesus' message was so *new age* (not orthodox) that it sounded as if he was making a mockery of God. "How dare this carpenter try to reform a religion that took thousands of years to establish," was the thought of most.

The Jews were very set in their ways and were occasionally very faithful to God. However, suddenly this very controversial revolutionary man began telling everyone he was the Jewish Messiah. But if he was the Messiah, where was the grandeur? The people were looking for flamboyancy, not humility. The thought was that Jesus was making a fool of himself and of his fellow Jews.

They insisted Jesus demonstrate proof – he did

The purpose of his miracles was twofold: to help people, but also to prove his divinity. All the miracles of Jesus pointed to him as the Messiah. He did not just heal the sick and raise the dead for the purpose of taking suffering away, but to produce the credentials of his Kingdom.

> *"Don't believe me unless I carry out my Father's work. But if I do his work, believe in the evidence of the miraculous works I have done, even if you don't believe me. Then you will know and understand that the Father is in me, and I am in the Father."* John 10:37-38, Jesus' words

The four gospels record about 35 separate miracles Jesus performed. These were not the only ones he did, but the specific ones the writers picked out under the guidance of the Holy Spirit to represent his ministry. But there were more that were never recorded.

> *The disciples saw Jesus do many other miraculous signs in addition to the ones recorded in this book. But these are written so that you may continue to believe that Jesus is the Messiah, the Son of God, and that by believing in him you will have life by the power of his name.* John 20:30-31

The following is a partial list of his miracles, accompanied by the corresponding Scripture reference where the stories of these miracles begin.

1. Stilling the storm (Matthew 8:23, Mark 4:35, Luke 8:22)
2. Feeding the 5,000 (Matthew 14:13, Mark 6:30, Luke 9:10)
3. Defying gravity (Matthew 14:25, Mark 6:48)
4. Feeding the 4,000 (Matthew 15:32, Mark 8:1)
5. Temple tax in the fish's mouth (Matthew 17:24)
6. Withering the fig tree (Matthew 21:18, Mark 11:12)
7. Filling the nets (Luke 5:1)
8. Whooping it up (John 2:1)
9. More fish (Luke 21:1)
10. Healing a leper (Matthew 8:2, Mark 1:40, Luke 5:12)
11. Healing a centurion's servant (Matthew 8:5, Luke 7:1)
12. Healing Peter's mother-in-law (Matthew 8:14, Mark 1:30, Luke 4:38)
13. Shooing away demons (Matthew 8:16, Mark 1:32, Luke 4:40)
14. Healing a paralytic (Matthew 9:2, Mark 2:3, Luke 5:18)
15. More healing (Matthew 9:20, Mark 5:25, Luke 8:43)
16. Letting the blind see (Matthew 9:27)
17. Healing a hand (Matthew 12:9, Mark 3:1, Luke 6:6)
18. Healing the Gentile woman's daughter (Matthew 15:21, Mark 7:24)
19. Casting out more demons (Matthew 17:14, Mark 9:17, Luke 9:38)
20. More blind see (Matthew 20:30, Mark 10:46, Luke 18:35)
21. Works on the Sabbath (Luke 14:1)
22. Heals more lepers (Luke 17:11)
23. Attaching an ear (Luke 22:51)
24. More healing (John 5:1)
25. Raising a daughter from the dead (Matthew 9:18, Mark 5:22, Luke 8:40)
26. Raising a son from the dead (Luke 7:11)
27. Raising Lazarus from the dead (John 11:38)

Jesus healed every kind of disease and every kind of sickness among the people – some because of the person's belief, some by touching the person, and some by the person just touching the fringe of Jesus' cloak.

> *Everyone tried to touch him, because healing power went out from him, and he healed everyone.* Luke 6:19

In Matthew 8:5-13, Jesus healed a centurion servant without even being present. He healed by touch and from a distance, demonstrating that he is the Lord of space and time. Jesus even had control over nature by calming the seas.

> *Then Jesus got into the boat and started across the lake with his disciples. Suddenly, a fierce storm struck the lake, with waves breaking into the boat. But Jesus was sleeping. The disciples went and woke him up, shouting, "Lord, save us! We're going to drown!"*
>
> *Jesus responded, "Why are you afraid? You have so little faith!" Then he got up and rebuked the wind and waves, and suddenly there was a great calm.*
>
> *The disciples were amazed. "Who is this man?" they asked. "Even the winds and waves obey him!"* Matthew 8:23-27

Even death was subject to Jesus' authority. On three occasions, he raised someone from the dead: These three included, Jairus' daughter, who had just died, the widow's son in the village of Nain who was already in the coffin, and his friend, Lazarus, who Jesus left dead for four days as the ultimate proof that he could raise someone whose corpse had started to rot. All the miracles defied natural laws.

NOTE: It was Jewish belief that the soul departed the person three days after death. So a resurrection after three days would have truly been a miracle in the Jewish mind during the first century AD.

Jesus' character

Jesus, although God, was a common man who loved common people, and the common people loved him. He healed the sick, fed the hungry, raised the dead, walked on water, and heightened the self-esteem of sinners.

Our supposed Christian country, the United States of America, knows more about Elvis Presley than they do the Savior. I have asked thousands of folks who consider themselves Christians if they knew the first miracle that Jesus performed. Surprisingly, very few were able to give me the correct answer.

Jesus' first miracle proved he wasn't a prude

Jesus performed his first miracle at the wedding in Cana.

The next day there was a wedding celebration in the village of Cana in Galilee. Jesus' mother was there, and Jesus and his disciples were also invited to the celebration. The wine supply ran out during the festivities, so Jesus' mother told him, "They have no more wine."

"Dear woman, that's not our problem," Jesus replied. "My time has not yet come."

But his mother told the servants, "Do whatever he tells you."

Standing nearby were six stone water jars, used for Jewish ceremonial washing. Each could hold twenty to thirty gallons. Jesus told the servants, "Fill the jars with water." When the jars had been filled, he said, "Now dip some out, and take it to the master of ceremonies." So the servants followed his instructions.

When the master of ceremonies tasted the water that was now wine, not knowing where it had come from (though, of course, the servants knew), he called the bridegroom over. "A host always serves the best wine first," he said. "Then, when everyone has had a lot to drink, he brings out the less expensive wine. But you have kept the best until now!"

This miraculous sign at Cana in Galilee was the first time Jesus revealed his glory. And his disciples believed in him. John 2:1-11

This is one of the most revealing stories about the personality of Jesus. It demonstrates that he had the ability to do, that which was supernatural. It also shows he was not opposed to partying and enjoying alcoholic beverages. Jesus could have stood on a table and screamed for everyone's attention, and lectured about the offense of consuming wine, and ordered those enjoying the party to go home – but he did not.

Instead of turning the water to wine he could have simply removed impurities from the water, added some essential nutrients, and added a few drops of lemon to give it a little pizzazz – but he did not. He was so cool!

If anyone tries to tell you it was not wine, do not believe him or her. If anyone tells you the percentage of alcohol was extremely low, do not believe that either – it was wine. However, there is absolutely nothing in the Bible that suggests that Jesus abused wine. In fact, Jesus warns against getting drunk.

"Watch out! Don't let your hearts be dulled by carousing and drunkenness, and by the worries of this life. Don't let that day catch you unaware, like a

trap. For that day will come upon everyone living on the earth."
Luke 21:34-35, Jesus' words

They called Jesus a drunkard

Palestine was primarily agricultural land, with three main types of crops: grain, olives, and grapes used in winemaking. Wine was a common drink that was undoubtedly consumed by our Savior, which is why they called him a *drunkard*.

> *"The Son of Man, on the other hand, feasts and drinks, and you say, 'He's a glutton and a drunkard, and a friend of tax collectors and other sinners!' But wisdom is shown to be right by its results."* Matthew 11:19, Jesus' words

What Jesus is telling us is that true wisdom is more than yielding to popularity. His message also indicates that no matter how hard we try, we will be criticized – especially by the pious.

Jesus got angry

When Jesus cleared the temple of the money changers and animal-sellers, he displayed considerable anger caused by his disappointment that supposed Godly men were using his Father's house for merchandising.

> *Jesus entered the Temple and began to drive out all the people buying and selling animals for sacrifice. He knocked over the tables of the money changers and the chairs of those selling doves.* Matthew 21:12

Another time Jesus showed anger was in the synagogue of Capernaum, when the Pharisees demonstrated their hard hearts by refusing to answer Jesus' questions.

> *Jesus went into the synagogue again and noticed a man with a deformed hand. Since it was the Sabbath, Jesus' enemies watched him closely. If he healed the man's hand, they planned to accuse him of working on the Sabbath.*
>
> *Jesus said to the man with the deformed hand, "Come and stand in front of everyone." Then he turned to his critics and asked, "Does the law permit good deeds on the Sabbath, or is it a day for doing evil? Is this a day to save life or to destroy it?" But they wouldn't answer him.*

He looked around at them angrily and was deeply saddened by their hard hearts. Then he said to the man, "Hold out your hand." So the man held out his hand, and it was restored! At once the Pharisees went away and met with the supporters of Herod to plot how to kill Jesus. Mark 3:1-6

Jewish law prohibited practicing medicine on the Sabbath, but Jesus was more about compassion than he was of the countless Jewish laws. Jesus' critics were determined to stop him from deviating from their customs, but he has proven throughout the last 2,000 years that he cannot be stopped.

Jesus and prophecy

Among other prophecies, Jesus even spoke of his coming death and resurrection prophetically.

And he said, "Yes, it was written long ago that the Messiah would suffer and die and rise from the dead on the third day. Luke 24:46

He predicted the circumstances surrounding his death, and who would be involved.

From then on Jesus began to tell his disciples plainly that it was necessary for him to go to Jerusalem, and that he would suffer many terrible things at the hands of the elders, the leading priests, and the teachers of religious law. He would be killed, but on the third day he would be raised from the dead. Matthew 16:21

Jesus also predicted that the timing of his death would occur during the Passover celebration, and it would be by means of crucifixion.

When Jesus had finished saying all these things, he said to his disciples, "As you know, Passover begins in two days, and the Son of Man will be handed over to be crucified." Matthew 26:1-2

Despite Jesus' best efforts, he was still judged, and then crucified

Jesus knew that he had aroused bitter opposition, especially from the religious leaders. His claim to be God, accompanied by his liberalized New Covenant, had most people stunned. At their insistence, he constantly yielded to their demands of demonstrating supernatural feats, but obviously, this failed. Jesus was not what the masses wanted the Messiah to be, so he was placed on trial.

His appearance before Pilate was to defend three charges: first, that he had mis-led the people; second, that he had encouraged the people not to pay their taxes to Rome; and third, that he had falsely claimed to be the King of the Jews. They thought he was so radical, so different and so unique that they tortured him, and then nailed him on a cross.

> *Then Pilate went back into his headquarters and called for Jesus to be brought to him. "Are you the king of the Jews?" he asked him.*
>
> *Jesus replied, "Is this your own question, or did others tell you about me?"*
>
> *"Am I a Jew?" Pilate retorted. "Your own people and their leading priests brought you to me for trial. Why? What have you done?"*
>
> *Jesus answered, "My Kingdom is not an earthly kingdom. If it were, my followers would fight to keep me from being handed over to the Jewish leaders. But my Kingdom is not of this world."*
>
> *Pilate said, "So you are a king?"*
>
> *Jesus responded, "You say I am a king. Actually, I was born and came into the world to testify to the truth. All who love the truth recognize that what I say is true."* John 18:33-37
>
> *Then Pilate had Jesus flogged with a lead-tipped whip. The soldiers wove a crown of thorns and put it on his head, and they put a purple robe on him. "Hail! King of the Jews!" they mocked, as they slapped him across the face.* John 19:1-3

For this, Jesus was condemned to death, beaten, then taken to a hill named Golgotha and nailed to a cross.

A wealthy follower of Jesus, Joseph of Arimathea, asked Pontius Pilate for the body of Jesus, wrapped it in a linen shroud, and placed it in a tomb that he had prepared. Multiple guards were placed at the door to make sure that no followers of Jesus could steal the body.

Jesus became sin

The Bible teaches that Jesus took all of our sins to the Cross in his body. Christ became sin for us so that we would have absolute righteousness. This is called *justification*,

212 JESUS CHRIST IS THE EASY AND ONLY WAY TO HEAVEN

and it is a gift (gifts are free). It is by grace alone that we are justified, and the Bible says it has nothing to do with our behavior.

> *For God made Christ, who never sinned, to be the offering for our sin, so that we could be made right with God through Christ.* 2 Corinthians 5:21

> *He canceled the record of the charges against us and took it away by nailing it to the cross.* Colossians 2:14

Many Christians live guilt-filled lives because they do not understand the truth. The truth is that God does not remember our sins because they were nailed to the Cross with Jesus!

> *"Oh, what joy for those*
> > *whose disobedience is forgiven,*
> > *whose sins are put out of sight.*
> *Yes, what joy for those*
> > *whose record the Lord has cleared of sin."* Romans 4:7-8

Jesus' Blood

Jesus' shed Blood did what the blood of animals could not do.

> *For everyone has sinned; we all fall short of God's glorious standard. Yet God, with undeserved kindness, declares that we are righteous. He did this through Christ Jesus when he freed us from the penalty for our sins. For God presented Jesus as the sacrifice for sin. People are made right with God when they believe that Jesus sacrificed his life, shedding his blood. This sacrifice shows that God was being fair when he held back and did not punish those who sinned in times past, for he was looking ahead and including them in what he would do in this present time. God did this to demonstrate his righteousness, for he himself is fair and just, and he declares sinners to be right in his sight when they believe in Jesus.* Romans 3:23-26

Christ's sacrifice: once and for all

We are perfected only by the cleansing Blood that Jesus shed on the Cross, which was once and for all.

> *The old system under the law of Moses was only a shadow, a dim preview of the good things to come, not the good things themselves. The sacrifices under that system were repeated again and again, year after year, but they were*

never able to provide perfect cleansing for those who came to worship. If they could have provided perfect cleansing, the sacrifices would have stopped, for the worshipers would have been purified once for all time, and their feelings of guilt would have disappeared.

But instead, those sacrifices actually reminded them of their sins year after year. For it is not possible for the blood of bulls and goats to take away sins.
Hebrews 10:1-4

Under the old covenant, the priest stands and ministers before the altar day after day, offering the same sacrifices again and again, which can never take away sins. But our High Priest offered himself to God as a single sacrifice for sins, good for all time. Then he sat down in the place of honor at God's right hand. There he waits until his enemies are humbled and made a footstool under his feet. For by that one offering he forever made perfect those who are being made holy. Hebrews 10:11-14

There continues to be religions, including some that label themselves as Christian, whose priests continue to stand before the alter day after day performing religious rituals. This monotonous act is not only futile but is also blasphemous. Those who participate in this are claiming that the Blood of Jesus was insufficient in cleansing sins once and for all.

If you believe Jesus was God in the flesh and that he came to earth to die on a cross to forgive you for your sins, then you are halfway to salvation.

A dead man walked – The Resurrection

Jesus' resurrection is the second half of what one must believe to be saved

In Christendom, many believe that Christ's sacrificial death was all that was necessary for their eternal life. Christ's death was payment for the sins of humankind, but belief in both his death *plus* his resurrection is the means for salvation.

To the astonishment of both his followers and his enemies, Jesus rose from being dead, making him the only world leader who has claim to that feat. The resurrection of Jesus constitutes the most important proof of his deity. He was not just a tricky magician – Jesus was who he said he was.

Early on Sunday morning, as the new day was dawning, Mary Magdalene and the other Mary went out to visit the tomb.

Suddenly there was a great earthquake! For an angel of the Lord came down from heaven, rolled aside the stone, and sat on it. His face shone like lightning, and his clothing was as white as snow. The guards shook with fear when they saw him, and they fell into a dead faint.

Then the angel spoke to the women. "Don't be afraid!" he said. "I know you are looking for Jesus, who was crucified. He isn't here! He is risen from the dead, just as he said would happen. Come, see where his body was lying. And now, go quickly and tell his disciples that he has risen from the dead, and he is going ahead of you to Galilee. You will see him there. Remember what I have told you." Matthew 28:1-7

The moment a person believes that Jesus was God incarnate, who came to earth in the form of a man, who died on a cross to forgive mankind of their sins, and who was raised from being dead, that person is *born again* and receives the reward of eternal life.

Jesus appears to the disciples

Then the two from Emmaus told their story of how Jesus had appeared to them as they were walking along the road, and how they had recognized him as he was breaking the bread. And just as they were telling about it, Jesus himself was suddenly standing there among them. "Peace be with you," he said. But the whole group was startled and frightened, thinking they were seeing a ghost!

"Why are you frightened?" he asked. "Why are your hearts filled with doubt? Look at my hands. Look at my feet. You can see that it's really me. Touch me and make sure that I am not a ghost, because ghosts don't have bodies, as you see that I do." As he spoke, he showed them his hands and his feet.

Still they stood there in disbelief, filled with joy and wonder. Then he asked them, "Do you have anything here to eat?" They gave him a piece of broiled fish, and he ate it as they watched.

Then he said, "When I was with you before, I told you that everything written about me in the law of Moses and the prophets and in the Psalms must be fulfilled." Then he opened their minds to understand the Scriptures. And he said, "Yes, it was written long ago that the Messiah would suffer and die and rise from the dead on the third day. It was also written that this message would be proclaimed in the authority of his name to all the nations, beginning in Jerusalem: 'There is forgiveness of sins for all who repent.' You are witnesses of all these things.

"And now I will send the Holy Spirit, just as my Father promised. But stay here in the city until the Holy Spirit comes and fills you with power from heaven." Luke 24:35-49

The following passage was taken from 1 Corinthians, which many theologians believe to be the greatest book of the Bible.

I passed on to you what was most important and what had also been passed on to me. Christ died for our sins, just as the Scriptures said. He was buried, and he was raised from the dead on the third day, just as the Scriptures said. He was seen by Peter and then by the Twelve. After that, he was seen by more than 500 of his followers at one time, most of whom are still alive, though some have died. Then he was seen by James and later by all the apostles. 1 Corinthians 15:3-7

The many appearances of Jesus after his resurrection are evidence that he actually raised himself from being dead. Once convinced of the reality of Jesus' resurrection, his apostles lived their lives under the divine power of the Holy Spirit, telling people about God's simple plan of salvation. The apostles were so convinced of the *Good News* they were willing to suffer martyrdom so that those who believe may live eternally in Heaven. If they had not seen Jesus resurrected from being dead, it does not make sense that they would have been willing to live and die for a lie.

The resurrection is the cornerstone of the Christian faith. All other religions were founded by mortals whose end was the grave. We Christians take reassurance that God gives glorious victory over death to all who trust in Jesus' finished work on the Cross. It is sin that separates a person from God, but Jesus paid the price for the sin of mankind on the Cross, and his resurrection guarantees eternal life to all who believe.

Jesus' ascension

Then Jesus led them to Bethany, and lifting his hands to heaven, he blessed them. While he was blessing them, he left them and was taken up to heaven. Luke 24:50-51

I also pray that you will understand the incredible greatness of God's power for us who believe him. This is the same mighty power that raised Christ from the dead and seated him in the place of honor at God's right hand in the heavenly realms. Now he is far above any ruler or authority or power or leader or anything else—not only in this world but also in the world to come. God has put all things under the authority of Christ and has made him head over all things for the benefit of the church. And the church is his body; it is made full and complete by Christ, who fills all things everywhere with himself. Ephesians 1:19-23

Do not crucify Jesus again

Some Christian denominations teach that a Christian can lose their salvation – but this does not make sense. The Bible tells us the only sacrifice for sin is the shedding of blood. Consequently, if one can lose their salvation because of sin, the only way they can be saved again is by Jesus Christ shedding more of his precious Blood again on a cross.

> *For Christ did not enter into a holy place made with human hands, which was only a copy of the true one in heaven. He entered into heaven itself to appear now before God on our behalf. And he did not enter heaven to offer himself again and again, like the high priest here on earth who enters the Most Holy Place year after year with the blood of an animal. If that had been necessary, Christ would have had to die again and again, ever since the world began. But now, once for all time, he has appeared at the end of the age to remove sin by his own death as a sacrifice.* Hebrews 9:24-26

Do not ask Jesus to be crucified repeatedly so that you can be forgiven. Jesus' forgiveness was once and for all – including for you.

> *Jesus knew that his mission was now finished, and to fulfill Scripture he said, "I am thirsty." A jar of sour wine was sitting there, so they soaked a sponge in it, put it on a hyssop branch, and held it up to his lips. When Jesus had tasted it, he said, "It is finished!" Then he bowed his head and released his spirit.* John 19:28-30

Many scholars believe the phrase "It is finished," from that period of time meant "Paid in full." To argue that Christ's sacrifice was not payment in full could result in eternal punishment.

Repetitious note

If you are one who believes that salvation can be lost due to sinful behavior, ask yourself: What sin did Jesus' Blood not pay for? Answering that question should cure you once and forever.

Enjoy your gift of salvation. Instead of asking for forgiveness repeatedly, simply thank him for what he did, and then ask him how you can serve him. Serving Jesus is called *discipleship*, but it is not necessary for salvation. Jesus will answer you via the Holy Spirit, and he will be kind and gentle.

Don't forget to tell your friends!

But Jesus was so nice. Why did he have to die?

Jesus had to die because God's justice required atonement for sin from humanity, but God also knew humans were incapable of doing so sufficiently. Therefore, he developed a plan that would work. As his sacrifice for us, God became a man to sacrifice himself.

God's sacrifice of himself replaced the insufficient animal sacrifice of the Old Covenant. That is what Christians refer to as the *Good News.* Not only was it good for mankind, it was good news for the lambs.

Jesus' sacrifice eliminated the need for the cheap sacrifices, useless rituals, unnecessary customs, ineffective ceremonies, and futile atonements that were once necessary. God sacrificed himself, as a man named Jesus, so believers could spend eternity in Heaven.

> *"For God loved the world so much that he gave his one and only Son, so that everyone who believes in him will not perish but have eternal life. God sent his Son into the world not to judge the world, but to save the world through him."* John 3:16-17, Jesus' words

Salvation is by faith alone. The following passage destroys the notion that salvation includes works:

> *The old system under the law of Moses was only a shadow, a dim preview of the good things to come, not the good things themselves. The sacrifices under that system were repeated again and again, year after year, but they were never able to provide perfect cleansing for those who came to worship. If they could have provided perfect cleansing, the sacrifices would have stopped, for the worshipers would have been purified once for all time, and their feelings of guilt would have disappeared.*

> *But instead, those sacrifices actually reminded them of their sins year after year. For it is not possible for the blood of bulls and goats to take away sins.*
> Hebrews 10:1-4

Then, in Hebrews 10:11-14, we are told why Jesus' Blood was necessary:

> *Under the old covenant, the priest stands and ministers before the altar day after day, offering the same sacrifices again and again, which can never take away sins. But our High Priest offered himself to God as a single sacrifice for sins, good for all time. Then he sat down in the place of honor at God's right hand. There he waits until his enemies are humbled and made a footstool under his feet. For by that one offering he forever made perfect those who are being made holy.*

Because our High Priest (Jesus) offered himself, there is no need for further sacrifices.

> *And when sins have been forgiven, there is no need to offer any more sacrifices.* Hebrews 10:18

There are millions who still have not caught on

Sadly, you may be one of them. Yes, 2,000 years later there are many who claim to be Christians. Although they revere Jesus Christ, they still insist upon standing at the altar day after day offering sacrifices – this is blasphemy!

> *Yes, everything else is worthless when compared with the infinite value of knowing Christ Jesus my Lord. For his sake I have discarded everything else, counting it all as garbage, so that I could gain Christ and become one with him. I no longer count on my own righteousness through obeying the law; rather, I become righteous through faith in Christ. For God's way of making us right with himself depends on faith.* Philippians 3:8-9

So, who was responsible for Jesus death?

Maybe it was Pilate

The Roman governor of Palestine, Pilate, was the one who gave the approval for Jesus' execution to take place. So maybe Jesus' Blood is on his hands. However, Pilate offered to let Jesus go, when the crowd began to shout, "Crucify him."

> *Pilate saw that he wasn't getting anywhere and that a riot was developing. So he sent for a bowl of water and washed his hands before the crowd, saying, "I am innocent of this man's blood. The responsibility is yours!"* Matthew 27:24

That vindicates Pilate.

Maybe it was Pilate's soldiers

Perhaps we should blame the Roman soldiers who were the actual butchers. They were the ones who flogged him as the blood gushed from each new wound. And they were the ones who drove nails into his body to secure him to a cross. Yes, the soldiers certainly played a major role in it. But, if it was the soldiers, why did Jesus forgive them so easily?

> *Jesus said, "Father, forgive them, for they don't know what they are doing."*
> *And the soldiers gambled for his clothes by throwing dice.* Luke 23:34

I guess Jesus was right. After all, we cannot blame the man who pulls the switch on the electric chair for a crime, so we certainly cannot blame the soldiers for following orders.

If Jesus forgave them for brutalizing him and then gambling for his clothes, then at whom are we to point a finger? No, it was not the soldiers.

As the plot thickens, let us look for the killer elsewhere

If you stop and think about it, the Jews were the ones who insisted on the crucifixion. Jesus was not guilty of anything other than doing a little new-age (non-orthodox) preaching, but the Jews were relentless about getting him stopped. When Pilate washed his hands, it was the Jews who insisted on the shedding of blood.

> *And all the people yelled back, "We will take responsibility for his death—we*
> *and our children!"* Matthew 27:25

Close, but no cigar! The Jews may have played judge and jury, but it goes a lot deeper than that.

Could it have been you?

Jesus died for the sins of mankind, which includes you and me. We are the ones who need a Savior, so conceivably his Blood is on our hands. But that does not seem right because we were not there. We need what he provides, but we did not kill him.

Jesus' Father was ultimately responsible for Jesus' death

> *"For God loved the world so much that he gave his one and only Son, so that*
> *everyone who believes in him will not perish but have eternal life."* John 3:16,
> Jesus' words

In eternity past, God planned the date, time, and method for the execution of his only Son. Jesus' Blood is on his Father's hands.

> *At noon, darkness fell across the whole land until three o'clock. At about three o'clock, Jesus called out with a loud voice, "Eli, Eli, lema sabachthani?" which means "My God, my God, why have you abandoned me?"* Matthew 27:45-46

He said he is coming back

> *"And then at last, the sign that the Son of Man is coming will appear in the heavens, and there will be deep mourning among all the peoples of the earth. And they will see the Son of Man coming on the clouds of heaven with power and great glory. And he will send out his angels with the mighty blast of a trumpet, and they will gather his chosen ones from all over the world—from the farthest ends of the earth and heaven."* Matthew 24:30-31, Jesus' words

> *"When the Son of Man returns, it will be like it was in Noah's day. In those days before the flood, the people were enjoying banquets and parties and weddings right up to the time Noah entered his boat. People didn't realize what was going to happen until the flood came and swept them all away. That is the way it will be when the Son of Man comes."* Matthew 24:37-39, Jesus' words

> *"But when the Son of Man comes in his glory, and all the angels with him, then he will sit upon his glorious throne. All the nations will be gathered in his presence, and he will separate the people as a shepherd separates the sheep from the goats. He will place the sheep at his right hand and the goats at his left.*

> *"Then the King will say to those on his right, 'Come, you who are blessed by my Father, inherit the Kingdom prepared for you from the creation of the world.'"* Matthew 25:31-34, Jesus' words

When will this happen?

Unexpectedly! Will you be ready?

> *Now concerning how and when all this will happen, dear brothers and sisters, we don't really need to write you. For you know quite well that the day of the Lord's return will come unexpectedly, like a thief in the night. When people are saying, "Everything is peaceful and secure," then disaster will fall on them as suddenly as a pregnant woman's labor pains begin. And there will be no escape.* 1 Thessalonians 5:1-3

26

Jesus' Apostles

Jesus picked up twelve men from the bottom ranks of business and forged them into an organization that conquered the world.

Bruce Barton (1886-1967)

The definition of *apostle* is "one who has been sent." The definition of *disciple* is "a pupil or follower of any teacher." People occasionally confuse the two, but there is a distinct difference in Christianity. Jesus had many followers, but there were only a select few whom he anointed with Spiritual authority in his ministry. The apostles were both apostles and disciples, but the disciples were solely disciples. Contemporary theologians usually agree that apostleship no longer exists, but that all Christians should be disciples.

I am not going to elaborate on the nature and responsibility of each apostle, but I think it important that you are familiar with their names, and the price each paid to further Jesus' ministry. If you feel inclined to be a follower of Jesus, but you are afraid that what he may ask from you may cramp your style, then look at what these men did, not only for Jesus, but also ultimately for the world. Keep in mind they would not have done it had they not seen him alive after he was pronounced dead. They were not fools.

1. Peter was crucified upside down at Rome.
2. Andrew was bound to a cross from which he preached to his persecutors until he died.
3. James the Greater (son of Zebedee and older brother of the apostle John) was beheaded at Jerusalem.
4. John (son of Zebedee and the younger brother of the apostle James) miraculously escaped death after being put in a pot of boiling oil, was

banished to the Isle of Patmos, and was later celebrated at Ephesus. It was on Patmos that John wrote the divisive Book of Revelation to encourage believers to stay true to Jesus Christ and to give them hope of triumph.

5. Matthew suffered martyrdom by being slain with a sword at a distant city of Ethiopia.
6. Thomas died in the East Indies from a lance being run through his body.
7. James the Less (son of Alphaeus) was thrown from a lofty point of the temple, then beaten to death with a club.
8. Thaddaeus ("Lebbaeus" or "Jude") was shot to death with arrows.
9. Simon the Canaanite/Zealot was crucified in Britain.
10. Nathanael ("Bartholomew") was brutally whipped, crucified, and beheaded in Armenia.
11. Phillip was stoned and crucified in Phrygia.
12. Matthias was stoned to death and beheaded by the Jews in Jerusalem.
13. Paul, thought by most to be an apostle, was tortured in Rome, then beheaded by the Roman Emperor Nero.
14. Barnabas of the Gentiles was stoned to death at Salonica. I have placed his name with the apostles, purposely below Paul's name, because many scholars have considered him an apostle because of his constant travels with Paul. He is also sometimes thought to be the author of the book of Acts (rather than Luke) and the book of Hebrews.

Jesus originally chose 12 men, but he knew that one of his followers, Judas, would betray him. Following this betrayal, Judas hung himself.

It is also believed that perhaps there were other apostles that were not mentioned in the Bible.

27

Jesus said to love one another

It is wonderful how much time good people spend fighting the devil. If they would only expend the same amount of energy loving their fellow men, the devil would die in his own tracks of ennui.

Helen Keller (1880-1968)

Read the following statement by Jesus very carefully.

"If you love me, obey my commandments." John 14:15, Jesus' words

Legalistic Christians who want to make others think that Jesus is claiming we must obey the Ten Commandments to be saved from eternal punishment throw around this verse. Jesus was not referring to the Ten Commandments but to his two commands that summarize the 10. <u>It must be pointed out that Jesus did not say we could lose our salvation if we fail to obey his commands.</u>

Jesus' death fulfilled the law.

"Don't misunderstand why I have come. I did not come to abolish the law of Moses or the writings of the prophets. No, I came to accomplish their purpose." Matthew 5:17, Jesus' words

This passage makes it clear that Jesus' death on the Cross was the fulfillment of what man cannot do for himself, and that is to obey the Ten Commandments and to fulfill the law. So, Jesus summarized the 10 with two.

Jesus replied, "'You must love the Lord your God with all your heart, all your soul, and all your mind.' This is the first and greatest commandment. A second is equally important: 'Love your neighbor as yourself.' The entire law

and all the demands of the prophets are based on these two commandments."
Matthew 22:37-40

The following statement made by Jesus summarizes what he wants from us.

> *"So now I am giving you a new commandment: Love each other. Just as I have loved you, you should love each other. Your love for one another will prove to the world that you are my disciples."* John 13:34-35, Jesus' words

The Apostle Paul sums all of the commandments into one.

> *Owe nothing to anyone—except for your obligation to love one another. If you love your neighbor, you will fulfill the requirements of God's law. For the commandments say, "You must not commit adultery. You must not murder. You must not steal. You must not covet." These—and other such commandments—are summed up in this one commandment: "Love your neighbor as yourself." Love does no wrong to others, so love fulfills the requirements of God's law.* Romans 13:8-10

There are many legalistic Christians who insist other Christians follow the letter of the law, rather than the spirit of the law. They cannot handle the thought of Christianity being as simple as loving one another.

This from the Apostle Peter

> *Most important of all, continue to show deep love for each other, for love covers a multitude of sins.* 1 Peter 4:8

Jesus tells it best

NOTE: Before reading this, you should know that Samaritans were known as being nasty people. Although the Samaritans were half Jew, most Jewish people hated them. The Samaritans were not even allowed to enter the Temple. This makes it more remarkable that a Samaritan would help a Jewish priest.

> *Jesus replied with a story: "A Jewish man was traveling on a trip from Jerusalem to Jericho, and he was attacked by bandits. They stripped him of his clothes, beat him up, and left him half dead beside the road.*

> *"By chance a priest came along. But when he saw the man lying there, he crossed to the other side of the road and passed him by. A Temple assistant*

walked over and looked at him lying there, but he also passed by on the other side.

"Then a despised Samaritan came along, and when he saw the man, he felt compassion for him. Going over to him, the Samaritan soothed his wounds with olive oil and wine and bandaged them. Then he put the man on his own donkey and took him to an inn, where he took care of him. The next day he handed the innkeeper two silver coins, telling him, 'Take care of this man. If his bill runs higher than this, I'll pay you the next time I'm here.'

"Now which of these three would you say was a neighbor to the man who was attacked by bandits?" Jesus asked.

The man replied, "The one who showed him mercy."

Then Jesus said, "Yes, now go and do the same." Luke 10:30-37

Loving one another is not always easy

There are many things in Christianity that we cannot always do on our own. Loving one another is one of them. But when we cannot do it on our own, we must yield to the Holy Spirit who lives in us and through us.

But the Holy Spirit produces this kind of fruit in our lives: love, joy, peace, patience, kindness, goodness, faithfulness, gentleness, and self-control. There is no law against these things! Galatians 5:22-23

Allowing the Holy Spirit to control us is much more powerful than our carrying stone tablets with commandments written on them and insufficiently trying to obey them.

Attempting to love many people was a major problem when I first accepted Christ as my Savior. I felt guilty when I read Bible passages that insisted I love everyone. One day I told my wife, Loveda, about my guilt and her wisdom lifted a major burden from my shoulders. She explained that I could love someone without really liking him or her. The more I thought about it, the more I understood why Jesus died on the Cross. From that point, I allowed the Holy Spirit to look at my fellow man Spiritually, taking into consideration that they, too, are just human beings trying to get through what often is a very tough life. If that does not work, I try to visualize that person as a baby innocently and peacefully lying in their crib. I keep them very small and above suspicion in my visualization. Then I love them. I still may not like them so much, but I love them.

Here are some passages that may help you:

> *Share each other's burdens, and in this way obey the law of Christ. If you think you are too important to help someone, you are only fooling yourself. You are not that important.* Galatians 6:2-3

> *Therefore, whenever we have the opportunity, we should do good to everyone—especially to those in the family of faith.* Galatians 6:10

> *For God chose to save us through our Lord Jesus Christ, not to pour out his anger on us. Christ died for us so that, whether we are dead or alive when he returns, we can live with him forever. So encourage each other and build each other up, just as you are already doing.* 1 Thessalonians 5:9-11

> *Dear friends, I am not writing a new commandment for you; rather it is an old one you have had from the very beginning. This old commandment—to love one another—is the same message you heard before. Yet it is also new. Jesus lived the truth of this commandment, and you also are living it. For the darkness is disappearing, and the true light is already shining.*

> *If anyone claims, "I am living in the light," but hates a Christian brother or sister, that person is still living in darkness. Anyone who loves another brother or sister is living in the light and does not cause others to stumble. But anyone who hates another brother or sister is still living and walking in darkness. Such a person does not know the way to go, having been blinded by the darkness.* 1 John 2:7-11

28

Jesus has a job for you

You are a Christian because somebody cared. Now it's your turn.
Warren Wiersbe (born 1929)

The gift of eternal life by accepting Jesus Christ as Savior is the greatest information that a person can share with his or her fellow human. Christians have the authority and responsibility to tell people about God's simple plan of forgiveness by the shedding of Jesus' Blood.

This applies to you, too

The following passage outlines the missionary task given by Jesus to his apostles shortly before he ascended into Heaven.

> *Then the eleven disciples left for Galilee, going to the mountain where Jesus had told them to go. When they saw him, they worshiped him—but some of them doubted!*
>
> *Jesus came and told his disciples, "I have been given all authority in heaven and on earth. Therefore, go and make disciples of all the nations, baptizing them in the name of the Father and the Son and the Holy Spirit. Teach these new disciples to obey all the commands I have given you. And be sure of this: I am with you always, even to the end of the age."* Matthew 28:16-20

What you just read was the scene surrounding the spark that ignited a spiritual revolution that altered the course of history. Titled *The Great Commission*, it is the only reason that I have written this book. It is only by the power and the influence of the Holy Spirit that I had the desire or the fortitude to write it and the tenacity to finish it.

The Great Commission is the catalyst that has resulted in almost two billion people worldwide embracing the teachings of Christianity. Although this directive was given 2,000 years ago to 11 apostles, it is still applicable today. The proof of this is the fact that millions of Christians worldwide continue the ministry of these apostles. In addition to the apostles, Jesus sent out 72 disciples. He may have sent more who were not recorded in the Bible.

> *The Lord now chose seventy-two other disciples and sent them ahead in pairs to all the towns and places he planned to visit. These were his instructions to them: "The harvest is great, but the workers are few. So pray to the Lord who is in charge of the harvest; ask him to send more workers into his fields. Now go, and remember that I am sending you out as lambs among wolves."*
> Luke 10:1-3

We are ambassadors.

> *And all of this is a gift from God, who brought us back to himself through Christ. And God has given us this task of reconciling people to him. For God was in Christ, reconciling the world to himself, no longer counting people's sins against them. And he gave us this wonderful message of reconciliation. So we are Christ's ambassadors; God is making his appeal through us. We speak for Christ when we plead, "Come back to God!" For God made Christ, who never sinned, to be the offering for our sin, so that we could be made right with God through Christ.* 2 Corinthians 5:18-21

Now, it is your turn.

PART SIX
The Holy Spirit

Notes:

29

The Holy Spirit[5]

As the sun can be seen only by its own light,
so Christ can be known only by His own Spirit.

Robert Leighton (1611-1684)

Tragically, the Holy Spirit is not studied or discussed in many Christian churches. This omission prevents many Christians from accurately understanding their faith because it is the Holy Spirit who makes a person a Christian.

> *But you are not controlled by your sinful nature. You are controlled by the Spirit if you have the Spirit of God living in you. (And remember that those who do not have the Spirit of Christ living in them do not belong to him at all.)* Romans 8:9

The Apostle Paul's statement above makes it clear that a person must have the Holy Spirit living in them to be considered a Christian. Without the indwelling of the Holy Spirit, a person may be a Christian in name only. Millions believe they are Christians, but probably because of faulty teaching they are not. A person can attend church regularly, sing in the choir, offer money generously to his or her church, celebrate Christmas and Easter – but if the Spirit of God is absent, they are not Christians.

This chapter will introduce those who call themselves Christians but who lack the indwelling of the Holy Spirit to the spiritual experience that makes a person a genuine Christian. It will also educate unbelievers and hopefully will influence them to become Christians.

_____

5   There is repetition in this chapter, but the author feels that it was necessary for explaining the Holy Spirit and his role in the Trinity.

The triune nature of God

The Christian faith is built upon the fundamental belief that there is one God, but that he has revealed himself in three forms, commonly known as the triune nature of God (the Trinity). Those three forms are God (the Father), Jesus (the Son), and the Holy Spirit, all having the same power and authority.

<u>The Father, the Son, and the Holy Spirit are equal in rank</u>

Now, let us get into the meat of the matter. Although the Father is mentioned first, the Son second, and the Holy Spirit third, this does not indicate subordination within the Trinity in regard to substance or essence. The order of their names does not mean that each of the members of the Godhead is not equal or equally divine. For example, because the Father sent the Son, it does not mean that the Son is not equal to the Father in essence or divine nature. This is also true regarding the Holy Spirit.

Let us begin by pointing out some of the characteristics of the Holy Spirit, so that you will see this revelation is not merely a force or just the figment of a believer's imagination.

The Holy Spirit is mentioned on equal level with God.

> "Therefore, go and make disciples of all the nations, baptizing them in the name of the Father and the Son and the Holy Spirit." Matthew 28:19, Jesus' words

The Holy Spirit is referred to as a person by scripture.

> The Spirit of God, who raised Jesus from the dead, lives in you. And just as God raised Christ Jesus from the dead, he will give life to your mortal bodies by this same Spirit living within you. Romans 8:11

The Holy Spirit grieves.

> But they rebelled against him
>   and grieved his Holy Spirit.
> So he became their enemy
>   and fought against them. Isaiah 63:10

> And do not bring sorrow to God's Holy Spirit by the way you live. Remember, he has identified you as his own, guaranteeing that you will be saved on the day of redemption. Ephesians 4:30

The Holy Spirit loves.

> *Dear brothers and sisters, I urge you in the name of our Lord Jesus Christ to join in my struggle by praying to God for me. Do this because of your love for me, given to you by the Holy Spirit.* Romans 15:30

The Holy Spirit has a mind.

> *And the Father who knows all hearts knows what the Spirit is saying, for the Spirit pleads for us believers in harmony with God's own will.* Romans 8:27

The Holy Spirit speaks.

> *The Holy Spirit said to Philip, "Go over and walk along beside the carriage."* Acts 8:29

> *One day as these men were worshiping the Lord and fasting, the Holy Spirit said, "Dedicate Barnabas and Saul for the special work to which I have called them."* Acts 13:2

One can ascertain from the above that the Holy Spirit has very distinguishable characteristics.

The Holy Spirit is the conduit that connects Christians to Jesus

Once a person becomes a Christian, that person will need no intermediary between himself and God other than the Holy Spirit. No priest, minister, rabbi, or anyone or anything else is needed as a go-between. I am not saying these professions are not necessary for educational purposes, but no one is needed as negotiator in your communication with God.

People who are not Christians don't understand the Spirit, his power, or his influence.

> *But people who aren't spiritual can't receive these truths from God's Spirit. It all sounds foolish to them and they can't understand it, for only those who are spiritual can understand what the Spirit means. Those who are spiritual can evaluate all things, but they themselves cannot be evaluated by others. For,*

> > *"Who can know the Lord's thoughts?*
> > *Who knows enough to teach him?"*

> *But we understand these things, for we have the mind of Christ.*
> 1 Corinthians 2:14-16

Before Jesus left the earth, he promised his followers that the Father would send to them another helper. God honored this on the day of Pentecost when the Holy Spirit became God's power on Earth. The following are the words of Jesus:

> *"But now I am going away to the One who sent me, and not one of you is asking where I am going. Instead, you grieve because of what I've told you. But in fact, it is best for you that I go away, because if I don't, the Advocate won't come. If I do go away, then I will send him to you. And when he comes, he will convict the world of its sin, and of God's righteousness, and of the coming judgment. The world's sin is that it refuses to believe in me. Righteousness is available because I go to the Father, and you will see me no more. Judgment will come because the ruler of this world has already been judged.*
>
> *"There is so much more I want to tell you, but you can't bear it now. When the Spirit of truth comes, he will guide you into all truth. He will not speak on his own but will tell you what he has heard. He will tell you about the future. He will bring me glory by telling you whatever he receives from me. All that belongs to the Father is mine; this is why I said, 'The Spirit will tell you whatever he receives from me.'"* John 16:5-15, Jesus' words

This is referred to as *Holy Spirit baptism,* which took place on the day of Pentecost, seven weeks after Jesus' resurrection. This is the same baptism that has been saving the souls of believers ever since.

Holy Spirit baptism

It is the Spirit living in a Christian that provides eternal life in Heaven. Jesus said it best.

> *"Humans can reproduce only human life, but the Holy Spirit gives birth to spiritual life."* John 3:6, Jesus' words

John baptizes Jesus

Although Jesus was baptized in water, it was the baptism of the Holy Spirit that identified Jesus as a part of the Trinity and demonstrated to his followers their need for Spiritual baptism. The Spirit empowered Jesus for ministry, and it will empower the believer for his ministry.

After his baptism, as Jesus came up out of the water, the heavens were opened and he saw the Spirit of God descending like a dove and settling on him. And a voice from heaven said, "This is my dearly loved Son, who brings me great joy." Matthew 3:16-17

The symbol of the Holy Spirit is the dove.

You must also be Holy Spirit baptized (born again)

The term *born again* may be the most intimidating term in the Christian vernacular. It is the term used by Jesus to reveal the formula for eternal life.

> *There was a man named Nicodemus, a Jewish religious leader who was a Pharisee. After dark one evening, he came to speak with Jesus. "Rabbi," he said, "we all know that God has sent you to teach us. Your miraculous signs are evidence that God is with you."*
>
> *Jesus replied, "I tell you the truth, unless you are born again, you cannot see the Kingdom of God."*
>
> *"What do you mean?" exclaimed Nicodemus. "How can an old man go back into his mother's womb and be born again?"*
>
> *Jesus replied, "I assure you, no one can enter the Kingdom of God without being born of water and the Spirit. Humans can reproduce only human life, but the Holy Spirit gives birth to spiritual life. So don't be surprised when I say, 'You must be born again.' The wind blows wherever it wants. Just as you can hear the wind but can't tell where it comes from or where it is going, so you can't explain how people are born of the Spirit."* John 3:1-8

The directive you have just read should be the most important you will ever read.

> *But to all who believed him and accepted him, he gave the right to become children of God. They are reborn—not with a physical birth resulting from human passion or plan, but a birth that comes from God.* John 1:12-13
>
> *This means that anyone who belongs to Christ has become a new person. The old life is gone; a new life has begun!* 2 Corinthians 5:17
>
> *For you have been born again, but not to a life that will quickly end. Your new life will last forever because it comes from the eternal, living word of God.* 1 Peter 1:23

Being *born again* is where religion stops and a relationship begins

Being *born again* does not refer to becoming religious. It's meaning is quite the opposite. It is the Spiritual birth through faith that results in having a personal relationship with Jesus. Religion requires performance from the believer, versus faith in the Savior.

Judaism, Mormonism, Hinduism, Buddhism, Islam, and even certain forms of the Christian faith are examples of religions. Any organized group or institution with a belief system that embraces or dictates rules for salvation rather than God's grace is a religion. Of the 11 major religions of the world, 10 teach salvation through human effort. Christianity is the only belief system that only requires faith.

> *God saved you by his grace when you believed. And you can't take credit for this; it is a gift from God. Salvation is not a reward for the good things we have done, so none of us can boast about it.* Ephesians 2:8-9

The moment you believe, understand, and trust in the death, burial, and resurrection of Jesus Christ, you instantly become a part of Christ's body. If salvation was merely the forgiveness of sins without a change in behavior, we might think of it as a license to sin. However, immediately upon our accepting Jesus' finished work on the Cross as our only means for eternal life in Heaven, the Holy Spirit comes to live in us, and simultaneously we become a part of Jesus' body. I realize this sounds scary, but believe me, it is the Holy Spirit that gives you the comfort of knowing you are saved. The Holy Spirit is your comforter, so do not be afraid.

> *But the Comforter, which is the Holy Ghost, whom the Father will send in my name, he shall teach you all things, and bring all things to your remembrance, whatsoever I have said unto you.* John 14:26 (KJV)

When does it take place?

At the moment of belief. Immediately upon accepting Jesus as Savior, the Holy Spirit baptizes the believer.

It is all about the Spirit

When studying the New Testament, you will realize how important the Holy Spirit was in the early Church. That importance remains today.

Jesus came and told his disciples, "I have been given all authority in heaven and on earth. Therefore, go and make disciples of all the nations, baptizing them in the name of the Father and the Son and the Holy Spirit. Matthew 28:18-19

Then Peter said to them, "Repent, and let every one of you be baptized in the name of Jesus Christ for the remission of sins; and you shall receive the gift of the Holy Spirit." Acts 2:38 (KJV)

Even as Peter was saying these things, the Holy Spirit fell upon all who were listening to the message. The Jewish believers who came with Peter were amazed that the gift of the Holy Spirit had been poured out on the Gentiles, too. Acts 10:44-45

But you are not controlled by your sinful nature. You are controlled by the Spirit if you have the Spirit of God living in you. (And remember that those who do not have the Spirit of Christ living in them do not belong to him at all.) And Christ lives within you, so even though your body will die because of sin, the Spirit gives you life because you have been made right with God. The Spirit of God, who raised Jesus from the dead, lives in you. And just as God raised Christ Jesus from the dead, he will give life to your mortal bodies by this same Spirit living within you. Romans 8:9-11

Let me ask you this one question: Did you receive the Holy Spirit by obeying the law of Moses? Of course not! You received the Spirit because you believed the message you heard about Christ. How foolish can you be? After starting your Christian lives in the Spirit, why are you now trying to become perfect by your own human effort? Galatians 3:2-3

And all who have been united with Christ in baptism have put on Christ, like putting on new clothes. There is no longer Jew or Gentile, slave or free, male and female. For you are all one in Christ Jesus. Galatians 3:27-28

And now you Gentiles have also heard the truth, the Good News that God saves you. And when you believed in Christ, he identified you as his own by giving you the Holy Spirit, whom he promised long ago. The Spirit is God's guarantee that he will give us the inheritance he promised and that he has purchased us to be his own people. He did this so we would praise and glorify him. Ephesians 1:13-14

For you were buried with Christ when you were baptized. And with him you were raised to new life because you trusted the mighty power of God, who raised Christ from the dead. Colossians 2:12

He saved us, not because of the good things we did, but because of his mercy. He washed away our sins and gave us a new life through the Holy Spirit. He generously poured out the Spirit upon us because of what Jesus Christ our Savior did. He declared us not guilty because of his great kindness. And now we <u>know</u> that we will inherit eternal life. Titus 3:5-7 (NLT 1996)

Notice in the last passage, I have underlined the word *know*. It doesn't say *hope* or *guess*. When the Holy Spirit baptizes a person, he or she knows they have eternal life in Heaven. It is guaranteed.

Gifts of the Holy Spirit

Spiritual gifts are those that are believed to be bestowed upon Christians supernaturally by the Holy Spirit to strengthen the church:

There are different kinds of spiritual gifts, but the same Spirit is the source of them all. There are different kinds of service, but we serve the same Lord. God works in different ways, but it is the same God who does the work in all of us.

A spiritual gift is given to each of us so we can help each other. To one person the Spirit gives the ability to give wise advice; to another the same Spirit gives a message of special knowledge. The same Spirit gives great faith to another, and to someone else the one Spirit gives the gift of healing. He gives one person the power to perform miracles, and another the ability to prophesy. He gives someone else the ability to discern whether a message is from the Spirit of God or from another spirit. Still another person is given the ability to speak in unknown languages, while another is given the ability to interpret what is being said. It is the one and only Spirit who distributes all these gifts. He alone decides which gift each person should have.
1 Corinthians 12: 4-11

Although no one doubts the existence of the gifts of the Holy Spirit in early Christianity, many believe that their operation was limited to the early church, that they were evident for only a short time, and that they were only practiced by Jesus' followers to prove his divinity. Those who believe the gifts ceased argue that they stopped at the time of the completion of the last book of the New Testament or the death of the last apostle, and that the only source of knowledge needed after that are the Scriptures. This group is called *Cessationists*. Although some stand firm that there are no miracles or miracle workers today, there are different degrees of Cessationalism. Some feel God occasionally performs miracles or uses individuals to perform miracles, healings, and so forth.

Those who take the other side are referred to as *Continuationists* and are usually affiliated with the Charismatic movement, which includes Pentecostals, Apostolics, and some similar denominations. They believe the Spiritual gifts are still given by the Holy Spirit today.

The topic of Spiritual gifts is hotter than hot and is a major divider of Christ's body. Both sides use Bible passages to substantiate their opinion, and because there are so many variations of interpretations, I will not take a side. The purpose of this book is to provide the reader with the basics of Christianity, not to participate in the many ongoing interpretational battles.

Fear and a cause

Many fears are caused simply by a lack of knowledge. Hopefully, this book has helped enlighten you to clearly understand Christianity and the peace it brings an individual. However, I am going to go a step further and share with you what I consider to be a huge obstacle for some.

You have learned that it is the indwelling of the Holy Spirit that saves a person from eternal damnation. The term *born again* was once very intimidating to me because I was told that I would become a new creature as the result of a Holy Ghost living inside me. The mere mention of a Holy Ghost and being *born again* is frightening to many unsaved people, and causes them to resist listening to God's simple plan of salvation.

I have shared my pre-Christian fears with others who have not been born again and they admit that hearing these terms is also an obstacle for them. Few people welcome the thought of becoming a new creature because a ghost lives inside them. The Holy Spirit (the Holy Ghost) is probably the scariest part of Christianity because it is the least understood.

Most people are afraid to surrender their lives to Jesus, but when you include the indwelling of a ghost, it makes Christianity even less appealing. They are afraid they will become one of those fanatics at whom folks laugh, or they are afraid of losing control to a ghost.

The possibility of losing control to a ghost was a gigantic fear for me. This was especially true when I heard stories about church people who would holler, wave their arms, jump over pews, and roll down church aisles as a result of the Holy Ghost. Before I thoroughly understood this behavior, I went to one of these spirit-filled churches, but quickly exited. One guy was jerking around so much that his false teeth fell out.

Since becoming a Christian, I have never lost control, and my teeth are still intact. The indwelling of the Holy Spirit has been a great comfort to me and I find that my life is much more peaceful, I actually have more control. Rest assured, the Holy Spirit is a good guy. There are tens of millions of people who agree with me.

If you are not yet a Christian, I am sure you have other fears and objections about making the commitment, but I assure you that in my 30 years as an active Christian evangelist, I have never met one person who has regretted the choice of making Jesus Christ his or her Savior. His love will vaporize your fear.

How to know the Holy Spirit lives in you

Most Christians know they have been saved because they feel the presence of the Holy Spirit living in them. This is true particularly with Christians who were adults when they accepted Jesus as their Savior. With this mature group, their conversion to Christianity is usually accompanied by a unique change in behavior, which usually includes a passion to serve Jesus.

Sometimes adults question their salvation, particularly if they accepted Jesus as Savior in their youth. Young Christians are frequently led away from discipleship by new life experiences; however, if the young person was sincere in his or her proclamation of faith, their salvation is not lost. Having weak young flesh does not result in lost salvation. If a youth's acceptance of Jesus was sincere, he will never leave them.

For those of you who are unsure if you are saved, please allow God to reassure you that you were and still are. Take God's word for it.

> On the last day, the climax of the festival, Jesus stood and shouted to the crowds, "Anyone who is thirsty may come to me! Anyone who believes in me may come and drink! For the Scriptures declare, 'Rivers of living water will flow from his heart.'" (When he said "living water," he was speaking of the Spirit, who would be given to everyone believing in him. But the Spirit had not yet been given, because Jesus had not yet entered into his glory.)
> John 7:37-39

The indwelling of God's Spirit is not questionable if you believe Jesus was God incarnate, who came to earth in the form of a man, who died on a cross to forgive mankind for their sinful nature, and who rose from being dead to prove that he has overcome death. If you believe this, you are a Christian. As a Christian, the Holy Spirit has lived in you since your Christian proclamation. It is the Holy Spirit that lives in you and has constantly been with you that saves.

Backsliding adults

Most Christians occasionally relapse in moral behavior, but a Christian cannot backslide out of salvation. A Christian can only backslide in discipleship.

Do not compare yourself to Billy Graham or any other Christian. The Holy Spirit works differently in each individual's life. If you did backslide, it is because the Holy Spirit allowed it. Do not underestimate the power of the Spirit – if he wanted you to do something, you would have done it.

If you feel guilty for not serving God as consistently as you should, it is probably the Holy Spirit convicting you, so begin now.

The Apostle Paul's declaration

Do not compare yourself to the Apostle Paul either, but consider allowing Jesus to be a greater part of your life, as did Paul. After he had received God's Spirit, Paul described his new outlook on life.

> My old self has been crucified with Christ. It is no longer I who live, but Christ lives in me. So I live in this earthly body by trusting in the Son of God, who loved me and gave himself for me. Galatians 2:20

It's never too late

If you still question the Holy Spirit's indwelling, it is never too late to make the salvation proclamation again. Many people even chose to be water baptized a second time. Although water baptism does not save anyone, it is an outward expression of the inward confession you have made regarding Jesus as being your only means of eternal life in Heaven.

Listen to the Holy Spirit, and allow him to be the guiding force in your life. The Spirit will guide you into all truth and agitate your conscience. He will convict you as to what you should and should not do. Although the Holy Spirit may not present himself in a conspicuous way, he lives within all Christians, all of the time. He does not take coffee breaks, or go on vacation, or leave you when you sin – and you will sin.

Follow the wisdom of John the Baptist.

> *He must become greater and greater, and I must become less and less.* John 3:30

Although a Christian is in the world, he is not of the world. When the Holy Spirit indwells an individual, the Bible tells us he will control us.

> *Don't be drunk with wine, because that will ruin your life. Instead, be filled with the Holy Spirit,* Ephesians 5:18

Be cautious

If you seriously accepted Jesus as your Savior, the Bible says the Holy Spirit lives in you. Do not allow anyone to influence you regarding what you must do to prove you are a Christian. Christianity is not something you do; it is something Jesus Christ did for you.

Many people insist the evidence of the Holy Spirit living in them is that they speak an unknown language that very few, if any, understand. It is referred to as *tongues*, and was a gift given to Jesus' disciples to edify the original Church until the completed New Testament became available. The Apostle Paul declared in 1 Corinthians 13:8 that this gift would cease:

> *Prophecy and speaking in unknown languages and special knowledge will become useless. But love will last forever!*

Just because someone speaks in gibberish does not mean it is the Holy Spirit speaking through him or her. If I turn cartwheels, I can say it was the Holy Spirit working through me, and it may be. But unless it has a fruitful result, it was probably just me turning cartwheels. It makes people feel spiritual to do unusual things, and then they blame or credit the Holy Spirit.

Many Christians believe that praying in tongues is necessary. But do not feel bad if you are uncomfortable with this practice. God understands English.

If the gift of tongues does exist, a believer does not have to possess that particular gift to be a Spirit-filled Christian, says Paul.

> *All of you together are Christ's body, and each of you is a part of it. Here are some of the parts God has appointed for the church:*

first are apostles,
second are prophets,
third are teachers,
then those who do miracles,
those who have the gift of healing,
those who can help others,
those who have the gift of leadership,
those who speak in unknown languages.

Are we all apostles? Are we all prophets? Are we all teachers? Do we all have
the power to do miracles? Do we all have the gift of healing? Do we all have
the ability to speak in unknown languages? Do we all have the ability to
interpret unknown languages? Of course not! So you should earnestly desire
the most helpful gifts.

But now let me show you a way of life that is best of all.
1 Corinthians 12:27-31

Dear brothers and sisters, if I should come to you speaking in an unknown
language, how would that help you? But if I bring you a revelation or some
special knowledge or prophecy or teaching, that will be helpful. Even lifeless
instruments like the flute or the harp must play the notes clearly, or no one
will recognize the melody. 1 Corinthians 14:6-7

Paul claims there is something greater than any of the Holy Spirit gifts listed above,
and that is the choice to love!

If I could speak all the languages of earth and of angels, but didn't love
others, I would only be a noisy gong or a clanging cymbal. If I had the gift
of prophecy, and if I understood all of God's secret plans and possessed all
knowledge, and if I had such faith that I could move mountains, but didn't
love others, I would be nothing. If I gave everything I have to the poor and
even sacrificed my body, I could boast about it; but if I didn't love others, I
would have gained nothing. 1 Corinthians 13:1-3

There is nothing physical you must do to prove the Holy Spirit lives in you; just
believe.

"For God loved the world so much that he gave his one and only Son, so that
everyone who believes in him will not perish but have eternal life." John 3:16,
Jesus' words

Are you ready?

Right now, ask yourself this question: If I were to die this very moment, would I go to Heaven? If the answer is no, or if you are unsure, then it is time for you to be baptized in the Holy Spirit. Repeat and mean the following prayer.

> Dear God,
>
> I don't know much about religion, but I know I am in need of a Savior, and I believe with my heart that your Son Jesus is that Savior. At this very moment I trust that his shed Blood on the Cross was payment in full for every sin I have ever committed, every sin I am currently committing, and every sin I will ever commit. I pray this prayer in Jesus' holy name.
>
> Amen

According to God's Word, if you said this prayer with conviction, you have been born Spiritually, which means that you belong to Jesus Christ eternally. He will never leave you.

30

Discipleship is following the Spirit

Will power does not change men.
Time does not change men. Christ does.
Henry Drummond (1851-1897)

The purpose of this book is to clarify the simplicity of God's New Covenant. However, it is important to discuss the personal change and growth that usually occurs after a person is saved.

REMEMBER: There is a difference between being "saved" and being a "disciple."

The definition of *disciple* is "a pupil or follower of any teacher." A disciple should not be confused with an *apostle*, which means "one who was sent." *Christian discipleship* is the term used to describe the process by which Christians are equipped by the Holy Spirit to grow in the Lord Jesus Christ. This process requires the believer to respond to the Holy Spirit's guidance in everyday life.

Salvation is easy, but discipleship is a little tougher. Everything you do in the name of Jesus Christ should be done not for salvation, but as fruit from the Spirit – who lives in and through you.

Discipleship 101

Attempting to write one chapter to effectively and adequately describe Christian discipleship is as ineffectual as trying to write one chapter on how to sail around the world. Because I am an advocate of the KISS principle (Keep It Simple, Stupid), years ago I framed the Prayer of Saint Francis and placed it above my desk. It is very sweet, to the point, and it gives me a daily overview of how I should be living my life.

Although probably not written by Saint Francis himself, the poem is attributed to Saint Francis of Assisi, and it is believed to have first appeared in 1912 when it was printed in a small French magazine. The author could have been the publisher of that magazine, Father Bouquerel, but nobody knows for certain.

THE PRAYER OF SAINT FRANCIS

Lord, make me an instrument of your peace;
Where there is hatred, let me sow love;
Where there is injury, pardon;
Where there is doubt, faith;
Where there is despair, hope;
Where there is darkness, light;
And where there is sadness, joy.

O Divine Master, Grant that I may not seek
To be consoled as to console;
To be understood, as to understand;
To be loved, as to love;
For it is in giving that we receive;
It is in pardoning that we are pardoned,
And it is in dying that we are born to eternal life.

Amen

Put Jesus first

Then, calling the crowd to join his disciples, he said, "If any of you wants to be my follower, you must turn from your selfish ways, take up your cross, and follow me. Mark 8:34

The Cross is a representation of the transition from spiritual death to Spiritual life.

When we serve others we are serving God

Jesus called his followers to be servants of others. In fact, Jesus was humble enough to set the example.

But Jesus called them together and said, "You know that the rulers in this world lord it over their people, and officials flaunt their authority over those under them. But among you it will be different. Whoever wants to be a leader among you must be your servant, and whoever wants to be first among you must become your slave. For even the Son of Man came not to be served but to serve others and to give his life as a ransom for many." Matthew 20:25-28

To show others what genuine service means, he performed one of the most humbling examples – washing his disciples' feet.

So he got up from the table, took off his robe, wrapped a towel around his waist, and poured water into a basin. Then he began to wash the disciples' feet, drying them with the towel he had around him. John 13:4-5

After washing their feet, he put on his robe again and sat down and asked, "Do you understand what I was doing? You call me 'Teacher' and 'Lord,' and you are right, because that's what I am. And since I, your Lord and Teacher, have washed your feet, you ought to wash each other's feet. I have given you an example to follow. Do as I have done to you. I tell you the truth, slaves are not greater than their master. Nor is the messenger more important than the one who sends the message. Now that you know these things, God will bless you for doing them. John 13:12-17

If God is humble enough to wash others' feet, you can do anything to serve others. Some examples of how to serve others:

Share each other's burdens, and in this way obey the law of Christ. If you think you are too important to help someone, you are only fooling yourself. You are not that important. Galatians 6:2-3

We all love stuff, but it is just stuff. Not only do the following verses provide us with a suggestion on how we can find a little more peace while on earth, but they also remind us there are rewards in Heaven.

"Sell your possessions and give to those in need. This will store up treasure for you in heaven! And the purses of heaven never get old or develop holes. Your treasure will be safe; no thief can steal it and no moth can destroy it. Wherever your treasure is, there the desires of your heart will also be." Luke 12:33-34, Jesus' words

The following passage is Jesus' assurance that acts of kindness will have rewards.

Then he turned to his host. "When you put on a luncheon or a banquet," he said, "don't invite your friends, brothers, relatives, and rich neighbors. For they

will invite you back, and that will be your only reward. Instead, invite the poor, the crippled, the lame, and the blind. Then at the resurrection of the righteous, God will reward you for inviting those who could not repay you." Luke 14:12-14

Be meek in your giving, says Jesus:

"Watch out! Don't do your good deeds publicly, to be admired by others, for you will lose the reward from your Father in heaven. When you give to someone in need, don't do as the hypocrites do—blowing trumpets in the synagogues and streets to call attention to their acts of charity! I tell you the truth, they have received all the reward they will ever get. But when you give to someone in need, don't let your left hand know what your right hand is doing. Give your gifts in private, and your Father, who sees everything, will reward you." Matthew 6:1-4, Jesus' words

This list could go on and on. Hopefully, by now you have gotten the point.

Discipleship should be the fruit of thankfulness, not the yoke of guilt

Think about this: Jesus died on the Cross for every sin you have ever committed, every sin you are committing, and every sin you ever will commit. He loved you so much that he allowed doubters to crucify him on a cross, so that by your believing you can enjoy eternal life.

Do you feel like you want to do something in return to say thanks? Discipleship is the way.

Paul tells us how to live a new life in Jesus

So don't let anyone condemn you for what you eat or drink, or for not celebrating certain holy days or new moon ceremonies or Sabbaths. For these rules are only shadows of the reality yet to come. And Christ himself is that reality. Don't let anyone condemn you by insisting on pious self-denial or the worship of angels, saying they have had visions about these things. Their sinful minds have made them proud, and they are not connected to Christ, the head of the body. For he holds the whole body together with its joints and ligaments, and it grows as God nourishes it.

You have died with Christ, and he has set you free from the spiritual powers of this world. So why do you keep on following the rules of the world, such as, "Don't handle! Don't taste! Don't touch!"? Such rules are mere human

teachings about things that deteriorate as we use them. These rules may seem wise because they require strong devotion, pious self-denial, and severe bodily discipline. But they provide no help in conquering a person's evil desires.
Colossians 2:16-23

Paul continues:

Since you have been raised to new life with Christ, set your sights on the realities of heaven, where Christ sits in the place of honor at God's right hand. Think about the things of heaven, not the things of earth. For you died to this life, and your real life is hidden with Christ in God. And when Christ, who is your life, is revealed to the whole world, you will share in all his glory.

So put to death the sinful, earthly things lurking within you. Have nothing to do with sexual immorality, impurity, lust, and evil desires. Don't be greedy, for a greedy person is an idolater, worshiping the things of this world. Because of these sins, the anger of God is coming. You used to do these things when your life was still part of this world. But now is the time to get rid of anger, rage, malicious behavior, slander, and dirty language. Don't lie to each other, for you have stripped off your old sinful nature and all its wicked deeds. Put on your new nature, and be renewed as you learn to know your Creator and become like him. In this new life, it doesn't matter if you are a Jew or a Gentile, circumcised or uncircumcised, barbaric, uncivilized, slave, or free. Christ is all that matters, and he lives in all of us.

Since God chose you to be the holy people he loves, you must clothe yourselves with tenderhearted mercy, kindness, humility, gentleness, and patience. Make allowance for each other's faults, and forgive anyone who offends you. Remember, the Lord forgave you, so you must forgive others. Above all, clothe yourselves with love, which binds us all together in perfect harmony. And let the peace that comes from Christ rule in your hearts. For as members of one body you are called to live in peace. And always be thankful.

Let the message about Christ, in all its richness, fill your lives. Teach and counsel each other with all the wisdom he gives. Sing psalms and hymns and spiritual songs to God with thankful hearts. And whatever you do or say, do it as a representative of the Lord Jesus, giving thanks through him to God the Father. Colossians 3:1-17

First and foremost: Listen to and obey the Holy Spirit.

Notes:

31

The Holy Spirit saved me from Christian policemen

My purpose is not to attack those who mean well, but to warn new Christians of the pitfalls of following mentors, who are not qualified, and to caution you that there are some spiteful Christians who will attempt to put you into religious bondage. The Holy Spirit is kind and gentle, but sometimes people aren't.

Tim Finley (born 1946)

My deep dark hole

In 1980, I accepted Jesus Christ as my Savior. I knew little about the Christian faith, but I knew that I wanted to become a worthy follower of Christ. I had been attending a church, but I needed more Christian fellowship. I began to attend Bible studies, Christian men's groups, and other activities that were labeled Christian. I knew there were denominational differences, but I was unaware there was so much judgment and bigotry.

Although I was learning, much of it proved to be false teachings and manmade taboos constructed to seem like Biblical truths. Some of these came from well-meaning people, but even more came from overbearing Christian policemen, whom I refer to as *modern-day Pharisees*.

My quest to be a good Christian, coupled with my lack of Bible knowledge, made me very vulnerable. I was criticized for almost everything, from the translation of my study Bible to the food I ate. I was even censured for wearing such a worldly thing as aftershave. I assumed that because my critics were Christians, their opinions were Biblically accurate.

In an attempt to become pure, I began to modify my personality dramatically. I became acutely aware of every move I made so as not to do anything to offend God. I was on a journey to perfection, but I did not realize it would end up in darkness.

Increasingly, I realized how imperfect and immoral I was. Not only did I recognize my flaws, I considered myself despicable – so despicable that I thought it was impossible for God to love me. Although not suicidal, I was anxious, depressed, and immobile. My Christian brethren had contributed to my fear by assuring me that everything I did was offensive to God. I had learned that I was washed clean by the Blood of Jesus Christ, and I did not want to do anything to tarnish myself ever again.

This once happy-go-lucky, life-loving 34-year-old man checked into the psychiatric ward of Riverside Hospital in Columbus, Ohio. And I was relieved to be there, because I did not have to face my Christian brethren. At the facility, I did not have to hear how badly I was doing, and there were limited opportunities for me to get caught up in worldly endeavors. I was safe, although I did feel guilty for looking appreciatively at a few of the cute nurses.

Fortunately, I was not given any treatments because they could not find anything wrong with me. Although I sat around most of the time so as to not do anything immoral, I did make some beautiful leather belts and key chains, which I worked on daily in the therapy room.

There is a happy ending to this story, thanks to the Holy Spirit. Following two weeks of darkness, God spoke to me through the Holy Spirit. He told me that he alone was my counselor and my judge. The greatest thing he told me was that he loved me just the way I was created. I walked out of the hospital that day with a new attitude about myself and about God – and skepticism regarding demanding Christians.

God allowed me to see the dark side of religion, which is created by men and women. He enlightened me through the Holy Spirit to the fact that he did not send his Son to die on the Cross so that others could condemn me.

> *So now there is no condemnation for those who belong to Christ Jesus.*
> Romans 8:1

Those two weeks were truly a gift. They allowed me to comprehend the purpose of Christ's life, death, and resurrection. It is impossible to live a life bound by laws. I am free.

*For no one can ever be made right with God by doing what the law
commands. The law simply shows us how sinful we are.*

*But now God has shown us a way to be made right with him without keeping
the requirements of the law, as was promised in the writings of Moses and the
prophets long ago. We are made right with God by placing our faith in Jesus
Christ. And this is true for everyone who believes, no matter who we are.*
Romans 3:20-22

The passage you just read is why I am a Christian – hallelujah!

About modern-day Pharisees

Pharisees were a prominent and devout sect of Jews reputed to be experts in Jewish
law and traditions. They were the policemen of the Jewish faith.

The Christian police are those I referred to earlier as *modern-day Pharisees.* They
roam around Christendom stalking those who do not adhere to what they consider
legal. They load their guns with their favorite Bible passages and fire at those who do
not believe as they do, or who do not behave in ways they deem as Christian. They
appear to walk the walk and talk the talk – and they insist that other Christians walk
their same walk and talk their same talk. Tragically, to the novice Christian, they
seem to make sense.

Many are probably well meaning, but others are just plain mean, and they have undoubtedly scared millions of would-be Christians from Jesus through their overbearing demeanor. These legalistic promoters are quick to share every *shall not* and
must do they can conjure up. They convolute the *Good News* into bad news by attempting to add man-made Christian laws to the old Jewish laws, creating an unfor-
giving environment.

Christians should not be purveyors of guilt.

*For the Kingdom of God is not a matter of what we eat or drink, but of living
a life of goodness and peace and joy in the Holy Spirit. If you serve Christ
with this attitude, you will please God, and others will approve of you, too.
So then, let us aim for harmony in the church and try to build each other up.*
Romans 14:17-19

I am not suggesting that you stop listening to the teachings of other Christians,
but that you use discernment. Seek a Bible-believing church that does not have a

guilt-provoking pastor. Study the New Testament Bible with the assistance of the Holy Spirit. I definitely recommend reading the New Testament before delving into the Old Testament. But as you mature as a Christian, begin to study the Old Testament.

I have found many of the TV and radio pastors to be knowledgeable. Be careful: Do not allow legalists to place you in a *Procrustean Bed.*

A Procrustean Bed

In Greek mythology, Procrustes (*the stretcher*) was a bandit from Attica. He had his stronghold in the hills outside Eleusis where he had an iron bed into which he invited every passerby to lie down. If the guest proved too tall, he would amputate the excess length; if the victim was too short, he was stretched on the rack until he fit.

Nobody ever fit in the bed because it was secretly adjustable, and Procrustes would stretch or shrink it upon sizing his victims from afar. Procrustes continued his reign of terror until he was captured by Theseus, who "fitted" Procrustes to his own bed and cut off his head and feet. Because Theseus was a stout fellow, the bed had been set on the short position. A *Procrustean Bed* is an arbitrary standard to which exact conformity is forced.

A great percentage of self-righteous Christians foolishly attempt to use their flawed nature as the supreme model for all. Procrustes is a myth because his method was ludicrous. But unfortunately, those who utilize his methods are not astute enough to realize it divides the body of Christ. It also is in direct opposition to Christ's synergistic method – referred to in the Scriptures as *love* – which unites Christ's body.

Unfortunately, many of those who subscribe to the Procrustean method believe they are living the perfect Christian life. Their judgment of whether you fit into their family of Christians is determined by fitting into their mold, which has been cast from their own nature. Those who are more lenient will allow some wiggle room, but unless you fit perfectly, you are not of their caliber.

Mahatma Gandhi

Mahatma Gandhi is one of the most respected leaders of modern history. A Hindu, Gandhi nevertheless admired Jesus and often quoted from the *Sermon on the Mount*. Once when the missionary E. Stanley Jones met with Gandhi he asked, "Mr. Gandhi, though you quote the words of Christ often, why is it that you appear to so adamantly reject becoming his follower?"

Gandhi replied, "Oh, I don't reject your Christ. I love your Christ. It's just that so many of you Christians are so unlike your Christ."

Apparently, Gandhi's rejection of Christianity grew out of an incident that happened when he was a young man practicing law in South Africa. He had become attracted to the Christian faith, had studied the Bible and the teachings of Jesus, and was seriously exploring becoming a Christian. And so he decided to attend a church service. As he came up the steps of the large church where he intended to go, a white South African elder of the church barred his way at the door. "Where do you think you're going, *kaffir* (a disparaging term for a black person)?", the man asked Gandhi in a challenging manner.

Gandhi replied, "I'd like to attend worship here."

The church elder barked at him, "There's no room for *kaffirs* in this church. Leave here or I'll have my assistants throw you down the steps."

From that moment, Gandhi said he decided to adopt what good he found in Christianity, but would never again consider becoming a Christian if it meant being part of the church.

God permits non-conformity

It is ridiculous to demand that we must all think and act alike. Remember, not only do we each have the Holy Scriptures to guide us, but we also are given the Holy Spirit as our personal counselor.

> *"And I will ask the Father, and he will give you another Advocate, who will never leave you. <u>He is the Holy Spirit, who leads into all truth</u>. The world cannot receive him, because it isn't looking for him and doesn't recognize him. But you know him, because he lives with you now and later will be in you."* John 14:16-17, Jesus' words

> *But you have received the Holy Spirit, and he lives within you, <u>so you don't need anyone to teach you what is true</u>. For the Spirit teaches you everything you need to know, and what he teaches is true—it is not a lie. So just as he has taught you, remain in fellowship with Christ.* 1 John 2:27

> *"But when the Father sends the Advocate as my representative—that is, the Holy Spirit—<u>he will teach you everything and will remind you of everything I have told you.</u>*

> *I am leaving you with a gift—peace of mind and heart. And the peace I give is a gift the world cannot give. So don't be troubled or afraid."* John 14:26-27, Jesus' words

The underlined sections of the above passages are to emphasize that it is the Holy Spirit who teaches us truth, thus leading us to peace. Although we can learn from others, please listen intently to the Holy Spirit, who is gentle and peaceful.

> *But the Holy Spirit produces this kind of fruit in our lives: love, joy, peace, patience, kindness, goodness, faithfulness, gentleness, and self-control. There is no law against these things!* Galatians 5:22-23

Our personalities differ, just as our physical characteristics differ. No two of us have identical abilities, capabilities, or responsibilities – as created by God. Because of our differences, the Holy Spirit works differently and personally in each Christian.

It is our differences that make Christ's body synergetic. God chose many individual personalities to further his kingdom, from Adam to you, with many in between and many to follow. Jesus gave us the perfect example of a synergistic effect, evidenced by the growth of Christianity from a dozen mavericks to more than a billion people worldwide, including new mavericks like you and me.

No more bondage

The term *religion* comes from the Latin word *religare* meaning "to tie or bind." I will never again allow religious people to put me in bondage. I found freedom, balance, and guidance in the Holy Spirit. You do the same.

PART SEVEN

Miscellaneous

Notes:

32

Why I am not Jewish, Protestant, Catholic, Mormon, etc.

All religions are the same: religion is basically guilt, with different holidays.

Comedian Cathy Ladman

Christianity is not a religion

Prior to this book being published, I sent it to several theological professionals for their input. This chapter was the only one they said was negative, and they said this because they felt there was no need to be critical of counterfeit *religions*.

I prayed about this and the Lord told me that Martin Luther stepped on many toes when he revealed the truth, and although the truth may anger a few people, it will help many who are being misled.

> *"You can enter God's Kingdom only through the narrow gate. The highway to hell is broad, and its gate is very wide for the many who choose that way. But the gateway to life is very narrow and the road is difficult, and only a few ever find it."* Matthew 7:13-14, Jesus' words

Orthodox Christianity (Christianity as taught by the early Christian Church) is not a religion! The term religion is derived from the Latin word religare meaning "to tie or bind." Christianity is freedom from religion, as I will say over and over again in this book. Prior to Jesus, the Jewish faith had transformed from the simple faith of Abraham to a complicated system of laws and rituals. God sent his Son Jesus to simplify it again, once and for all. However, throughout the years people made it complicated again.

All of the faiths that are discussed in this chapter are religions because they bind the believer to rules of behavior to please God, or their god (there is only one God). If the adherent does not follow the rules, the result is guilt. Although I may not agree with their belief, I am not going to burn their books; I will try to educate them, and you, as to the truth through tutoring and via the influence of the Holy Spirit.

Christianity is the only world religion that is not a purveyor of guilt, but instead provides the believer with a divine source of forgiveness.

> *"For God loved the world so much that he gave his one and only Son, so that everyone who believes in him will not perish but have eternal life. God sent his Son into the world not to judge the world, but to save the world through him."* John 3:16-17, Jesus' words

In this chapter, a brief description of a few of the most recognized belief systems and religions is offered so that you may see the distinct difference between them and Biblical Christianity. Choose your faith carefully because the result is eternal.

Why I am not Jewish

I will start this chapter with Judaism because Judaism is one of the oldest monotheistic religions and is the foundation of and predecessor to Christianity.

Of all the religions that I have observed, I consider Judaism more of a family tradition than an actual, genuine faith. They refer to themselves as Jews and are convicted to not abandon the family tradition. Ask a Jew what their parents are and the answer will almost always be "Jewish."

The definition of a *Jew* is somewhat complicated. In a religious sense, the term refers to followers of Judaism, which means that anyone, regardless of nationality, race, and so forth, can refer to themselves as a Jew if they practice the Jewish tenets. Ethnically, it refers to the people who trace their maternal ancestry from the Biblical patriarch Abraham through his son, Isaac, and then through Isaac's son, Jacob.

Granted, there is a bloodline to consider, but the origin of that bloodline is recognized for their monotheistic belief in the God of Abraham, Isaac, and Jacob. However, there are many Jews who are atheists, so this desertion of a belief in God adds to the complication.

In fact, Christians revere the Biblical history of Judaism and faith in God more than a person who refers to himself or herself as a Jew. To be a Christian, one must believe in the Jewish God of Abraham, Isaac, and Jacob as the foundation of the Christian faith. The most important difference between Judaism and Christianity is that Christians accept the carpenter named Jesus, born 2,000 years ago, who claimed to be God incarnate, as the Jewish Messiah. Jews reject Jesus as the Messiah, and believe their Messiah is still to come.

Christianity is somewhat Judaism plus Christ. Most Jews will admit that the Christian Jesus existed, and that he was in fact a man with unusual characteristics, but they refuse to give in to the fact that he was the Messiah. They are so close to truth, yet so far away.

Most Jews with whom I have had the privilege of discussing their religious upbringing have told me there was little or no room for discussion. Most, if not all, teachings were hard and fast with absolutely no allowance for academic discourse. The children were trained to believe what the parents and grandparents believed.

The Apostle Paul (named Saul of Tarsus prior to being renamed Paul by God) was raised as a Jew and in adulthood developed into a hard-hearted Jewish Pharisee who hated Christians. He was responsible for the death of many Christians before he was transformed by a visit from Jesus on the road to Damascus, following Jesus' crucifixion. Most agree that Paul's Christian ministry had more influence on the growth of Christianity than anyone, anywhere, anytime. The following are his words to the Christians in Rome:

> Dear brothers and sisters, the longing of my heart and my prayer to God is for the people of Israel to be saved. I know what enthusiasm they have for God, but it is misdirected zeal. For they don't understand God's way of making people right with himself. Refusing to accept God's way, they cling to their own way of getting right with God by trying to keep the law. For Christ has already accomplished the purpose for which the law was given. As a result, all who believe in him are made right with God. Romans 10:1-4

Will Jews go to Heaven?

> But they rebelled against him
>   and grieved his Holy Spirit.
> So he became their enemy
>   and fought against them. Isaiah 63:10

Most of you know that Christianity is not in opposition to the Jewish faith, but that Christianity is actually an extension of Judaism. To be a Christian, one must also embrace the Jewish belief in the One Creator God. Although many Jews recognize Jesus as a Biblical character, many deny his deity, thus denying him as the fulfillment of the prophetic Jewish Messiah.

Many Christians and Jews believe that because the Scriptures refer to the Jews as God's chosen people, they will automatically be accepted into Heaven regardless of whether or not they accept Jesus as the Messiah. There are New Testament verses that renounce this assumption:

> *"And I tell you this, that many Gentiles will come from all over the world— from east and west—and sit down with Abraham, Isaac, and Jacob at the feast in the Kingdom of Heaven. But many Israelites—those for whom the Kingdom was prepared—will be thrown into outer darkness, where there will be weeping and gnashing of teeth."* Matthew 8:11-12, Jesus' words

> *"But everyone who denies me here on earth, I will also deny before my Father in heaven."* Matthew 10:33, Jesus' words

> *Jesus told him, "I am the way, the truth, and the life. No one can come to the Father except through me."* John 14:6

Keep in mind that many of the first Christians were Jews, and that the most prolific Jewish Christian in the history of Christianity was the Apostle Paul, who wrote more of the New Testament than anyone. Prior to his conversion from Judaism to Christianity, Paul was very active in persecuting Jewish followers of Jesus. But once he was a believer in Jesus, he spent his entire life spreading the *Good News* of salvation by faith. Paul, a Jew by birth, did this because he knew that Jesus was the only way, even for Jews.

To strengthen my personal belief and subsequent teaching that Jews must accept Jesus as their Savior, in addition to my studying the Scriptures, I contacted an international Jewish organization that focuses specifically on the conversion of Jews to Christianity. The following is their reply:

> Shalom, and thank you for your e-mail.

> With regard to your question about whether a Jew who does not know Christ will be lost, our answer would have to be "yes." We don't necessarily like believing this truth, because it means that many of our own loved ones are condemned, but the Bible does clearly say in Acts 4:12 that there is no other name under

heaven by which men can be saved. If we didn't believe that, the ministry of Jews for Jesus would not exist.

Nowhere does the Bible teach that Jews will be saved on the basis of their genealogy. Nor will they be saved on the basis of their religion (which denies Jesus) or good works. We'd all like to think that "good people" will somehow be exempted from the law of sin and death. But the Bible says there is no one good (Psalm 14:3), that we all have sinned (Romans 3:23), that "all our righteous acts are like filthy rags" (Isaiah 64:6), and that our only hope of salvation was Christ's death on the cross. To seek another way is to belittle His sacrifice. A person who claims to love God and yet rejects God's beloved Son (who is Himself God in the flesh) is worse than ungrateful. That person is condemned (John 3:16-18).

That makes things pretty concrete in terms of both Jews and Gentiles being lost if they don't know Jesus the Messiah. It also gives all the more urgency to our work, our prayers, and our need for people like you to stand with us as we proclaim the good news that Messiah has come, and His name is Y'shua (Jesus). Please do pray for our missionaries and the many people with whom they come in contact, that the seed we sow would fall on fertile ground and bear much fruit for the King – fruit that will not perish but last for eternity. And if you have not already done so, I hope you will sign up to receive the Jews for Jesus Newsletter.

Of course, none of us have the right to judge another's destiny, but as Christians we do have the responsibility to share our belief with those who do not know Jesus. So I have just shared with you what I have discovered.

If you are a Jew who has rejected Jesus as the Messiah, I suggest that you pray earnestly for God to reveal the truth to you – and he will.

Why I am not a Protestant

The term *Protestant* is derived from the Reformation, at which time those who opposed Catholicism were referred to as Protestants. Although I do not intellectually agree with most of the Catholic dogma, I do not consider myself a Protestant because I do not protest anyone. I may not agree, but I am offended by the term *protest*.

I am a Christian and I believe that term says all that needs to be said. I became a Christian the moment I accepted Jesus Christ as my Savior, at which time the Holy Spirit came to live in me permanently, as he always does when a person acknowledges Jesus as Savior.

I have found that most Protestants have no idea why the term *Protestant* is used or its origin. They know it means they are not Catholic, but that is the extent of their knowledge. I have tried to discuss Martin Luther (1483-1546) with hundreds of Protestants and they think I am referring to Martin Luther King, Jr. (1929-1968). If you are one of them, you have a lot to learn.

Many Americans refer to themselves as Protestant Christians because they were born in America and because they are not Catholic. That is about all they know about Protestantism or Christianity.

Why I am not a Roman Catholic

Many Catholics believe that theirs is the correct religion because of its longevity. Well, if longevity is the determining factor regarding truth, then Judaism wins the prize. Although Catholicism is 2,000 years old, Judaism has been in existence for 3,500 years.

The term *catholic* generally means "universal." When capitalized, it refers to the Catholic Church, a term first used in the early second century to describe the collective Christian Church. Catholicism is a broad term and applicable to several theologies and doctrines, but is generally used when referring to the Roman Catholic Church. When I use *Catholic* in this discussion, I am referring to the Roman Catholic Church or a member of that Church.

Just as with most Jews, most Catholics have told me there was little or no room for family discussions during their adolescence regarding any religions other than Catholicism. If there was discussion, it was only to stress that Catholicism was the only true religion. Teachings were also hard and fast with absolutely no allowance for academic discourse. Many Catholics egotistically refer to themselves as "Cradle Catholics," which is ignorantly admitting they were forced to believe what their parents believed. Some believe they actually have Catholic DNA.

The Catholic Church was established at a time in history when people needed extreme leadership, as there were no Bibles or modern means of communication. People did not have the opportunity of choice. Christianity was a new religion and the Catholic Church became the most powerful until the time of the Reformation, which is discussed in another portion of this book.

I really respect the devotion that dedicated Catholics demonstrate to their institution. A devoted Catholic usually attends mass regularly, respects the Catholic hierarchy, remains monogamous, does not participate in the murder of unborn children, is charitable, and tithes. I seriously considered joining the Catholic Church shortly following my acceptance of Jesus Christ as Savior because of the many admirable traits of its members.

I spent a lot of time studying what the Catholic Church teaches, which I compared to what the Bible teaches. I discovered there were too many inconsistencies, especially regarding how to get to Heaven. I had become a Christian because it seemed like a very uncomplicated plan that God had established after Jewish laws failed. However, Catholicism was as complicated as Judaism. Thankfully, I declined.

The Catholic Church also presented me with books other than the Holy Bible, which they instructed me to read, understand, and adhere to the teachings. I was told that although the Catholic Church reveres the Holy Bible as the Word of God, the church has also adopted the catechism, sacred tradition and the magisterium as additional authorities.

WARNING: Beware of any religion that claims to be of the Christian faith if they have a book, or books, that must accompany the Bible to defend their beliefs. The New and Old Testaments are all that are needed.

> *Let God's curse fall on anyone, including us or even an angel from heaven, who preaches a different kind of Good News than the one we preached to you.*
> Galatians 1:8

Apostolic succession

Apostolic succession is one of the pillars that the Catholic Church uses to claim they were the first and true Christian Church. They argue that the line of popes can be traced directly to the Apostle Peter, and that Peter was appointed by Jesus as the rock upon which the Christian Church would be built. However, Jesus was the rock upon which the Church was to be built.

Apostolic succession claims those individuals in the succession have inherited spiritual, ecclesiastical, and sacramental power and authorities bestowed to them by the apostles, who received their authority from Jesus Christ.

Contrary to what Catholics are taught, the papal office did not originate with Peter. The Bishop of Lyons (178-200) provided a list of the first 12 bishops of Rome, and Linus was the first. Peter's name does not appear. Paul, in writing to the Romans, greets many people by their names, but not Peter.

While discussing apostolic succession and the probability that it is a false belief, I must also inform you that there are other faiths that claim this succession – including the Eastern Orthodox Church, some Anglicans, and some Lutherans.

Most Protestants reject any succession of power based upon the fact that nowhere in Scripture did Jesus, the apostles, nor any other New Testament writer communicate any form of apostolic succession. In addition, nowhere in Scripture is Peter characterized as supreme over other apostles. Furthermore, nowhere are any of the 12 apostles documented as passing their Spiritual gifts and authority to anyone. Most Protestants stand firm that the authority of God is passed through the Holy Scriptures.

A trail of blood

Christian Rome has blood on its hands from the slaughtering of both Christians and Jews. In addition to those victims of the inquisition, the Huguenots, Albigenses, Waldenses, and other Christians were massacred, tortured, and burned at the stake by the hundreds of thousands, simply because they refused to align themselves with the Roman Catholic Church and its corruption and heretical dogmatic practices.

The victims of Roman Catholic torture were those Christians who attempted to follow the teachings of Christ and the apostles, independent of Rome – and for that crime they were imprisoned, tortured, and murdered. These horrendous acts were carried on for centuries in the name of Christ by the command of those who claimed to be the vicars of Christ. Although the Catholic Church has done much good, it also has left a trail of blood.

Vatican II

Vatican II was the Catholic Reformation instituted in 1965 by Pope John XXIII. Catholics can now eat meat on Friday, mass is given in English, nuns can choose their form of attire, and many other changes have taken place. Although Vatican II was a huge turning point for the Catholic Church, it was too little, too late. The ceaseless councils, committees, and subcommittees left some dazzled, but Catholics are still leaving the Church in droves.

The opulence and pomp displayed by the cardinals who attended Vatican II was disgusting. They arrived in very impressive black limousines whose license plates were engraved with the letters SCV (which stands for *Stato della Citta del Vaticano* and simply means "Vatican City State"). The rustling silk costumes of these powerful worldly leaders set them apart from their bodyguards and the common onlookers.

The glorification of the church's hierarchy definitely was not in sync with the style of Jesus, who rode into town on a donkey. His crown was made of thorns.

In an interview one nun said, "While I resent the hierarchy, I guess I came to think that, that isn't the church anyway. The real church exists in coming home after a fourteen-hour day, dragging your feet, coming in with a smile, and saying to a sister, 'Did you save me anything for supper?' That's the real church. The real church is helping the recovering alcoholic who had a slip. That's the real church. The real church is when you sneak some food out of the convent for some man standing there, who is on the run. You ask no questions. That's the real church."

Although the Catholic Church has done, and continues to do, many wonderful acts of benevolence worldwide, and although it has instilled Christian morality in millions, the Catholic Church must make major changes or it will cease to exist. Perhaps it is time for Vatican III.

Why I am not Mormon

I considered becoming a Mormon (The Church of Christ of Latter-Day Saints "LDS") until I realized they are not Christian. They claim the Christian name, but their beliefs are counter-Christian. In fact, although they profess to revere the New and Old Testaments, they have added a third book, *The Book of Mormon*; a fourth, *The Pearl of Great Price*; and even a fifth; *Doctrine and Covenant*.

WARNING: Beware of any religion that claims to be of the Christian faith if they have a book, or books, that must accompany the Bible to defend their beliefs. The New and Old Testaments are all that are needed.

> *Let God's curse fall on anyone, including us or even an angel from heaven, who preaches a different kind of Good News than the one we preached to you.*
> Galatians 1:8

I never knew much about Mormonism until many years ago when my wife, Loveda, and I became friends with a Mormon family in Columbus, Ohio. They were fine, hard-working, moral, and successful individuals. We were so impressed that we thought maybe there was something to Mormonism. We set out to learn more by asking them some questions regarding Mormonism.

Their answers were just what we wanted to hear, so we asked more questions – only these new questions were more specific. Of course these answers were also just right, except they kind of skirted the issue – sort of like when you ask a used car salesman a detailed technical question and he answers you with a lot of great things about the car, but never really answers your original question. Their answers were very appealing, but these fine people usually changed the subject somehow. Deception is the red flag that killed the deal for me. I lost tremendous respect for these folks because of this.

I wasn't going to allow their deception to stop me from being part of something that I could believe in, so I investigated Mormonism further. They call themselves Christians, and I suppose legally they are not breaking any laws by doing so. But their beliefs are *not* orthodox Christian.

I have outlined what I found in regard to their teachings. Although I do not guarantee its accuracy, I feel fairly confident I am close. If you ever feel the inclination to join their organization, please remember what I am about to tell you, if for no other reason than to protect yourself from being hoodwinked or becoming part of a cult.

Mormons believe that the god[6] of this universe is a being composed of flesh and blood who at one time lived on another planet (or in another galaxy) where, by following their rules, he became one of their many gods. He was then sent to this Earth to be our god, accompanied by his goddess wife.

This god produces spirit children who grow and mature, but whose spirit remains in Heaven waiting for a home here on Earth. When a baby is born here on Earth, that spirit, which was waiting in Heaven, enters the body of the new baby, but the memory of that spirit is masked. That is mankind, as we know it.

They also believe that because we are creatures of sin, we needed a savior god, so god came to earth, had sex with Mary and went home. Her child was Jesus. The Mormon's believe this was a plan worked out prior to the conception between this god and Jesus. They also believe that Jesus was a spiritual brother to Lucifer, who became jealous and rebelled, then convinced a large portion of the spirits in Heaven to side with him and oppose god.

Here is a big factor: They do not believe in the Trinity. They will lead you to believe they do until you back them into a corner, and then the truth prevails. Be very careful here!

_____

6   I sincerely apologize for not capitalizing the word 'god' in this section regarding Mormonism. This was done intentionally because I cannot think of the Mormon's god as being the God of Abraham, Isaac, and Jacob.

They also put a lot of faith in a man named Joseph Smith (1805-1844), who supposedly was called upon by god as a messenger. There were gold tablets involved, but these apparently were only seen by Mr. Smith and were lost somewhere along the way.

There are many, many differences within the Christian community that probably can be justified because historical records are just that – historical records. But most Christians have the same basic beliefs, and also an innate brotherhood as Christians. You may turn on a Christian radio station and hear ministers from various denominations preaching various doctrines, but you will not hear Mormons on those stations because they are not considered Christians, by Christians.

Why I am not a Seventh-Day Adventist

Most of the doctrines of Seventh-Day Adventists are based on the visions and writings of founder Ellen G. White (1827-1915). White claimed more than 2,000 visions, from which she produced some 100,000 handwritten pages of instructions. These have been published in about 50 different books. Many Adventists believe her writings to be their "source of authority" for interpretation of the Holy Scriptures.

WARNING: Beware of any religion that claims to be of the Christian faith if they have a book, or books, that must accompany the Bible to defend their beliefs. The New and Old Testaments are all that are needed.

> *Let God's curse fall on anyone, including us or even an angel from heaven,*
> *who preaches a different kind of Good News than the one we preached to you.*
> Galatians 1:8

According to White's teachings, Adventists believe the Saturday observance to be a prerequisite for being saved. They also believe in the vanishing of the wicked instead of the eternal Hell, which is mentioned in Mark, Luke, and especially in Matthew. Jesus himself mentions the reality of Hell a dozen times in the New Testament. Hell is also discussed many times in the Old Testament.

Many people do not want to accept the fact that a loving God would allow people to be damned eternally, although he made the provision for eternal life with him in Heaven. If one chooses to reject Jesus' death and resurrection, it is a decision they make – not one made for them. So in essence, we make the choice as to where we choose to spend eternity by either believing or rejecting.

Seventh-Day Adventists also believe that upon death they enter "soul sleep," a theory embraced by only a very few who interpret the Scriptures to say that after a person dies, his or her soul "sleeps" until the resurrection. In the Bible, the descriptions of "sleeping" following one's death do not literally imply sleep as we know it. The Bible is crystal clear that at the moment of a Christian's death, his or her soul is present with the Lord for eternity.

It is also the contention of Seventh-Day Adventists that, even though one is saved by grace, one can only remain in a state of grace by adhering to the Old Testament dietary and ceremonial laws, Saturday Sabbath observance, following the Ten Commandments, and tithing. These beliefs are clearly not those of orthodox evangelical Christians, who reject salvation by works.

> *And since it is through God's kindness, then it is not by their good works. For in that case, God's grace would not be what it really is—free and undeserved.*
> Romans 11:6

Giving credit where credit is due, some Seventh-Day Adventists believe the same as orthodox Christians except that worship should be on Saturday (which they believe to be the true Sabbath), instead of Sunday, as most other Christians.

Why I am not a Christian Scientist

Mary Baker Eddy (1821-1910) founded the Christian Science Church in 1879. The teachings are based on the Bible and her book, *Science and Health with Key to the Scriptures.*

WARNING: Beware of any religion that claims to be of the Christian faith if they have a book, or books, that must accompany the Bible to defend their beliefs. The New and Old Testaments are all that are needed.

> *Let God's curse fall on anyone, including us or even an angel from heaven, who preaches a different kind of Good News than the one we preached to you.*
> Galatians 1:8

Christian Science radically interprets the Holy Scriptures by teaching that every person is born flawless and without sin, and that humans have the innate spiritual nature of God. This is opposite to what orthodox Christians believe, which is that man is born sinful as the result of Adam's fall. Christian Scientists believe that because God is good, evils are the result of living apart from God.

Christian Scientists believe sin, disease, and death are merely physical and not a part of a person's spiritual nature. Church members generally substitute prayer for traditional medical care, often with the assistance of Christian Science practitioners.

Regarding the Trinity, Christian Scientists define the Father, Son, and Holy Spirit not as three persons in one, but as life, truth, and love – and include a rescue from every form of materiality that would try to alienate one from God. They refer to God as *Father-Mother, divine Love, or infinite Mind.*

They also believe that one works out his own salvation by following the course that wisdom dictates to him. However, they believe that Heaven and Hell are present states of one's mind, rather than future dwelling places. The number of people who believe in Christian Science is dropping.

Why I am not a Jehovah's Witness

According to Jehovah's Witness theology, God is a single person, not a Trinity, who does not know all things and is not everywhere. According to their doctrine, God created only Michael the Archangel – who they believe to be Jesus. They believe that Michael the Archangel (Jesus) created all "other things", including the universe, the Earth, Adam and Eve, and so forth.

When it came time for the Savior to be born, Michael the Archangel became a human, in the form of Jesus. When Jesus died, it was not on a cross but on a torture stake.

They believe Heaven is limited to the spirits of the 144,000 persons who work the hardest on Earth. They also believe there will be a great multitude who will live forever on Earth, which will be a paradise. In addition, they do not believe in Hell, and that those who are not of the Jehovah's Witness faith will merely cease to exist.

Jehovah's Witnesses refuse to vote, salute the flag, sing the "Star Spangled Banner," and celebrate birthdays or Christmas. They refuse blood transfusions and will not join the armed forces.

I once had a good friend who had been a hell-raiser in his younger days. In an effort to turn his life around, he became a Jehovah's Witness thinking it was a Christian religion. He enlisted his wife, his daughter, and her husband into the Jehovah's Witness church. Several years later, when he realized he had made a mistake, he and his wife left the Jehovah's Witnesses and joined an orthodox Christian church. As a result, he was never allowed to visit with his daughter and grandchildren again. It broke his heart. Jesus never shunned anyone, including his executioners.

Why I am not a Unitarian Universalist

In theology, *universalism* is the doctrine that all people will eventually be saved and go to Heaven when they die. *Unitarian* was a theological term applied in the 16th century to those who denied the doctrine of the Trinity. Almost all denominations of Christianity reject Unitarian Universalism as Christian.

A Unitarian Universalist is a community of religious (for the lack of a better term) persons whose beliefs and ethics are freely chosen and constantly evolving throughout their lives. In their churches (social halls) are humanists, nature worshippers, polytheists, those who affirm a personal god, agnostics, and even atheists – most of whom believe they have the liberty of deciding about God's nature as they please.

They believe in the oneness of reality and think of God as a unity rather than a trinity. They honor the ethical leadership of Jesus, but do not consider him to be their final religious authority, even though he made it clear that he had authority over all.

They rely on their own reason and personal understanding, while seeking the guidance and inspiration of the great pioneers of religious insight of many cultures and various traditions. A little of this, a touch of that, a handful of something else, mix it all together and you are off to the Promise Land, or wherever you have conjured up in your mind.

Their view of the Bible is that it is just one of many books containing profound insights, but it does not represent the ever-changing world. They pick out what sounds good and throw away what they do not want to hear. Heaven and Hell are states of mind created by human beings. Hell is created by injustice, violence, tyranny, and war. Heaven is created in compassion, mercy, liberty, and love.

Why I am not a Muslim

A *Muslim* is a follower of the Islamic religion. Nearly one-quarter of the world's population follow the religion that was revealed to the prophet Muhammad (570-632), 600 years after God was revealed in the form of a man named Jesus Christ. Muhammad died and is still dead, but Jesus Christ rose from being dead and is alive today.

Christianity and Islam have some similarities but significant differences. Both are monotheistic; however, Muslims reject the triune nature of God. Muslims believe Jesus existed, but was a mere prophet – not God incarnate.

Muslims believe paradise must be earned by keeping the five pillars of faith:

> *Shahada, Salat, Sawm, Zakat*, and *Hajj*, which translates to: confession of faith, prayer, fasting, alms, and the pilgrimage.

Christians believe that eternal life in Heaven is a gift for those who accept Jesus Christ as the propitiator for their sins.

Although there are similarities, only one can be the truth.

> *Jesus told him, "I am the way, the truth, and the life. No one can come to the Father except through me."* John 14:6

Warning

All of the quasi-Christian religions or faiths mentioned in this chapter have some Christian attachment, though the only one that is truthfully Christian is Protestant, because it embraces orthodoxy, although I do not like the term Protestant because it is confrontational. The others are counterfeit Christian. The Bible warns us they are dangerous:

> *Dear friends, do not believe everyone who claims to speak by the Spirit. You must test them to see if the spirit they have comes from God. For there are many false prophets in the world. This is how we know if they have the Spirit of God: If a person claiming to be a prophet acknowledges that Jesus Christ came in a real body, that person has the Spirit of God. But if someone claims to be a prophet and does not acknowledge the truth about Jesus, that person is not from God. Such a person has the spirit of the Antichrist, which you heard is coming into the world and indeed is already here.* 1 John 4:1-3

Hell is forever – don't go there!

A challenge

To those of you who belong to any of the aforementioned religions, I challenge you to say the following prayer, which separates Christians from the others. Say it with sincerity, and then see what happens.

Dear God,

I don't know much about Christianity, but I want to know the truth. If Jesus Christ was your Son and if he came to earth to die on the Cross, and then rose again so all those who believe can spend eternity with you, I am ready and willing to accept Jesus as my Savior.

Amen

33

Choosing a church

Once upon a time there was a fellow who was lost at sea, but after 25 years was discovered on a deserted island. Upon arrival the rescuers noticed three buildings, which were built side by side. They asked him why he had built three buildings, to which he replied, "The one in the middle is where I live; the one on the left is my church, and the one on the right is the church I used to attend."

A Funny Story

Nobody can say with authority that changing churches is right or wrong. It depends on several circumstances, which I will briefly discuss in this chapter. The Bible encourages us to have fellowship with one another.

What we are discussing in this chapter is the gathering of Christians for worship and fellowship.

> *All the believers devoted themselves to the apostles' teaching, and to fellowship, and to sharing in meals (including the Lord's Supper), and to prayer.* Acts 2:42

> *And let us not neglect our meeting together, as some people do, but encourage one another, especially now that the day of his return is drawing near.* Hebrews 10:25

These passages encourage Christians to congregate, but church attendance is not mandatory for eternal life in Heaven. Unfortunately, many good people attend church regularly thinking this will contribute to their salvation. Nothing could be farther from the truth. The only thing we can do to receive eternal life in Heaven is to trust in the finished work of Jesus Christ.

No perfect churches

I must warn you there are no perfect churches. And if you find one that you consider perfect, and they accept you as a member, it will not be perfect anymore. They are all made up of flawed folks. However, there are churches that teach more truth than others.

Christians must be careful about the church they become affiliated with, because not all churches teach the Biblical truth. For the purpose of increasing attendance, there is a trend to teach what people want to hear, rather than truth.

Another problem is that many pastors fail to interpret the Scriptures correctly. They may be outstanding orators, charismatic leaders, good businessmen, but if they have not been trained in a good Bible teaching school, they may be teaching you faulty doctrine.

Be careful of cults, religions, and denominations that sound real good – but whose authenticity fails when put to the test. The leaders sell the sizzle rather than the steak, which brings in the masses, but causes confusion. Be very careful.

Essential doctrine

The most important concern when choosing a church is to be certain their doctrine is Biblical.

> Not knowing the doctrines of the Bible, the child of God will be, even when sincere, 'tossed to and fro, and carried about with every wind of doctrine, by the slight of men, and cunning craftiness, whereby they lie in wait to deceive'; the many well-meaning believers who are drawn into modern cults and heresies being sufficient proof. On the other hand, the divine purpose is that the servant of Christ shall be fully equipped to 'preach the word; be instant in season, out of season; reprove, rebuke, exhort with all longsuffering and doctrine.'
> Lewis Sperry Chafer (1871-1952)

Example of doctrine

The following is the doctrine that we use in our ministry. We believe it to be Biblically grounded, and we are presenting it as an example of what we consider to be sound doctrine. Many churches word theirs differently, but please be sure their basic doctrine is correct.

We believe in the divine inspiration, truthfulness, and authority – without error in the original manuscripts – of both the Old Testament and New Testament Scriptures, in their entirety. We acknowledge that there are personal differences in Scriptural interpretations, and we respect the efforts and opinions of those who have earnestly searched and researched the texts seeking their true meanings.

We believe in one living God, the Father, eternally existent, Creator of the Heavens and Earth, who concerns himself in the affairs of men, and hears and answers prayers. He is manifested in three persons known as the Trinity: Father, Son, and Holy Spirit, equal in power and authority. The Holy Spirit bestows eternal life to all who come to him through Jesus Christ.

We believe the Lord Jesus Christ is the only begotten Son of God. Jesus is the second person of the Trinity, who was conceived by the Holy Spirit, who took on flesh, and dwelt on earth. Sinless and perfect, he was crucified, laid in a tomb, and rose on the third day. His resurrection demonstrated his divinity and power over life and death, thus he has the ability to give believers eternal life. We believe this was God's plan as a substitute blood sacrifice known as the New Covenant, and the only means for man's salvation. Jesus' shed Blood is God's gift to all those who accept it.

We believe Jesus Christ will return again to fulfill the rest of messianic prophecy.

We believe the Holy Spirit is the third person of the Trinity. We believe the Holy Spirit indwells every believer in Jesus Christ and that he is our personal counselor regarding matters of sin, righteousness, and truth. We believe the moment a person accepts Christ as his Savior, the Holy Spirit immediately indwells that believer, who is then born again, and sealed with the Holy Spirit. We believe that regeneration by the Holy Spirit is absolutely essential for the salvation of man.

We believe man is saved by undeserved mercy through faith, and nothing of man's efforts contributes to his salvation. We believe that one must be saved in order to obtain eternal life in Heaven. We believe a saved person has two births: one of the flesh and one of the Spirit, giving man both a flesh nature and a Spirit nature. The flesh nature is neither good nor righteous. The Spirit man does not commit any sin. This results in a war between the Spirit and the flesh that continues until physical death, or the return of the Lord.

We believe that God gave man free will to accept or reject the salvation he has provided. It is God's will that all would be saved and that none should perish. God foreknows, but does not predetermine any man to be condemned.

We believe when referring to *repentance* in salvation, it means "a change of mind from any idea that works or religion may save us." Salvation is the finished work of Christ, and nothing should be added to it.

We believe there are two final judgments awaiting mankind. One is for believers and is called the Bema Seat Judgment (Christ's Judgment). The other is for the unbeliever and is called the White Throne Judgment.

We believe one of Jesus' key teachings was to love one another. He displayed this by loving the outcasts and sinners. He also commanded us to love one another.

We believe in Spiritual gifts, and that love is the most spectacular and important gift. Without love other gifts are worthless.

We believe in water baptism as a public acknowledgement and symbol of one's faith and rebirth. Although recommended as a testimony to the world, it is not necessary for salvation.

We believe we all have a sinful nature that has been passed down to each human being by Adam and Eve. We believe that sin is any deliberate action, attitude, or thought that goes against God. People often think of sin as an obvious act such as murder, adultery, or theft. We believe that sin may include pride, envy, or worry. Sin can be something you should not have done (sins of commission) or something you should have done (sins of omission). We believe that being a Christian does not mean living a sin-free life, but it means living a life that is freed from the power of sin.

We believe that all true Christians have a personal relationship with Jesus Christ through the Holy Spirit, who is the Christian's personal counselor. Our personal convictions are conveyed upon us through that relationship.

We believe our newfound freedom does not mean we no longer sin, or no longer have the desire to sin, but it does mean that a process toward excellence has begun in each Christian. As we grow in our faith, our sin nature should become smaller, and our goal should be to become more Christ-like, as guided by the Holy Spirit. However, we must realize that we will never become divine or perfect. Christianity is a journey of highs and lows, strengths and weaknesses, triumphs and defeats.

We believe that because we are all sinners, we do not have the authority to stand in judgment of anyone.

<u>**We believe**</u> all believers are sent to be a blessing to the culture around them through a lifestyle that coincides with Jesus' teachings. The concept of being a missional people centers on the concept of Christians being called by the Holy Spirit to be an active part of the community, called to be a voice for those who have no voice, a friend to those who have no friends, and a family to those who have no family. This may take many evangelical forms, such as social activism, hospitality, acts of kindness and generosity, with a strong emphasis on verbal evangelism – not proselytizing.

<u>**We believe**</u> the world's sin is unbelief in Jesus Christ as the incarnate Son of God, the Jewish messiah, and the Savior of the world.

"The world's sin is that it refuses to believe in me." John 16:9, Jesus' words

Church government

<u>Episcopalian</u>

Using *episcopalian* in the context of church government is not referring to the Episcopalian Church. The word *episcopalian* comes from the New Testament Greek word *episcopos*, which is the word for bishop, or overseer. In this framework, the authority or pastoral leadership is empowered in one person who rules over one area – in some traditions called a diocese. The Anglican, Episcopal, and Methodist denominations use this form of government.

<u>Presbyterian</u>

This term, when referring to church government, is not to be confused with the Christian denomination Presbyterian. It is a local church government called the *presbyterian system* and is presided over by a body of elders (presbyters) who have authority over the local churches. Therefore, the authority is not rooted in one man.

<u>Congregational</u>

In the congregational system, bishops or presbyteries do not connect local congregations to one another by free or voluntary association. The government of the church is on the local level.

<u>The original Church</u>

The original (New Testament) Church had a central governing body of "apostles and elders" in Jerusalem. This body was possibly modeled after the 70-member Jewish

Sanhedrin, whose primary task was the preservation of doctrine and practice. Apostles, chosen by God and recognized by a body of believers, established the churches. Paul and other apostles ordained presbyters (elders) to preside over the church in each city or region.

Do not use these as criteria for choosing your church

➤ This is where your parents went. (Your family could have been wrong.)
➤ It is close to where you live.
➤ You like their music.
➤ They have nice potlucks on Sunday nights.
➤ Obtaining business contacts.
➤ You can dress casually.
➤ You can dress up and show off your clothes.
➤ They do not talk about sin.
➤ They do not talk about Hell.

The primary purpose of any church should be to teach attendees how to get to Heaven. Of course, getting to Heaven is easy, and students should be able to grasp the lesson of salvation easily – unless they are stubborn or have been brainwashed. Deprogramming someone may be futile, but for the sake of the individual it should be attempted, but with love.

> *Let your conversation be gracious and attractive so that you will have the right response for everyone.* Colossians 4:6

The second purpose of a church should be to teach the attendee how to obtain rewards in Heaven. This comes under the doctrine of discipleship, which takes a lifetime of learning and doing.

Ask!

You must ask your pastor, or the secretary, for a copy of the doctrine. Do not be embarrassed or timid about this because that is their job. Plus, if you drop anything in the offering, then you are paying their wages. You are entitled and expected to know what is in your church's doctrine. It is also in their best interest for you to know what they believe and teach at the outset, so that someday you do not realize you made the wrong choice and leave. No church wants revolving-door members.

> *I appeal to you, dear brothers and sisters, by the authority of our Lord Jesus Christ, to live in harmony with each other. Let there be no divisions in the*

church. Rather, be of one mind, united in thought and purpose. For some members of Chloe's household have told me about your quarrels, my dear brothers and sisters. Some of you are saying, "I am a follower of Paul." Others are saying, "I follow Apollos," or "I follow Peter," or "I follow only Christ."

Has Christ been divided into factions? Was I, Paul, crucified for you? Were any of you baptized in the name of Paul? Of course not! 1 Corinthians 1:10-13

 <u>**Notes:**</u>

34

Choosing and reading your Bible

*For the word of God is full of living
power. It is sharper than the sharpest knife,
cutting into our innermost thoughts and desires.
It exposes us for what we really are.*

Hebrews 4:12

Assume the Bible is trustworthy

The Holy Bible of the Christian faith is both the most criticized and loved book in history. The criticism results from a lack of knowledge regarding its contents. The Bible can be construed as confrontational because it reminds readers of their sins or causes them to question their beliefs, if other than Christian.

Throughout history, many historic authorities have tried to ban both the Bible and Christians. Many Christians have died defending this amazing book.

The Bible is the inspired word of God

Yes, mortals wrote the Bible, but God inspired it.

> *All Scripture is inspired by God and is useful to teach us what is true and to make us realize what is wrong in our lives. It corrects us when we are wrong and teaches us to do what is right. God uses it to prepare and equip his people to do every good work.* 2 Timothy 3:16-17

The Bible was composed and compiled by many individuals who were chosen by God, and they were inspired and instructed what to write by the Holy Spirit. The

Spirit uses it to reach the innermost parts of one's soul serving as the guide for developing character and morality. With the assistance of the Holy Spirit, the Bible instructs Christians how to live in the world, but not be of the world.

Sadly, many people criticize the Bible without any educational basis for their disapproval. The proof of the Bible's accuracy involves intellectual analysis, not feeble guesswork. There are two very compelling evidences that the Bible is trustworthy.

The first test

The first test is the reliability of the Holy Scriptures in predicting future events. The Old Testament contains hundreds of prophecies that have already come true, and dozens that are being revealed today. The Bible's ability to prophesize is the irrefutable evidence that differentiates it from all other books. The most important Old Testament prophecies, numbering about 200, are those of the coming Jewish Messiah. Specific details regarding Jesus' birth, life, death, and resurrection were prophesized centuries prior to his being born.

The second and most revealing test

The second test, which is the most revealing test of the reliability of the Bible, is the amazing power it has in affecting a person's life. Following the Bible's teaching is what demonstrates that it is alive, and it proves its integrity.

The Bible is the greatest book on psychology ever written. It reveals where mankind has come, why we are here, and where we will go after our death. If studied correctly, it eliminates all guilt, assists us in handling difficult times, and teaches us how to treat others.

However, it is not a book for those who cannot handle truth or confrontation.

History of the Bible

The Holy Bible, although written by men, is the inspired word of God. By now, you should have learned that God has three natures – the Father, the Son, and the Holy Spirit.

The Holy Spirit made the Bible possible, and now makes it understandable. The Spirit inspired its writing through human authors, prophets, editors, and so forth. The Spirit inspired its interpretation throughout the years, and the Spirit inspires us today when we study it.

The Bible has been translated into more than 2,000 languages. John Wycliffe completed the very first translation of the Bible into English in 1382. Today there are more versions available in English than any other language.

The KJV

The original Bible was written in Hebrew, Aramaic, and Greek. In January 1604, King James Charles Stuart of Scotland called the Hampton Court Conference in order to hear of things "pretended to be amiss" in the church. At this conference, Dr. John Reynolds, a Puritan, requested of the king a new translation of the Bible because those that were allowed during the reigns of Henry the VIII and Edward VI were corrupt.

In July 1604, the king appointed 54 men to the translation committee. These men were the best linguists and scholars in the world. Most of their work on the King James Bible formed the basis for our linguistic studies today. These men were not only world-class scholars – they were Christians who lived holy lives as deans and presidents of major universities such as Oxford, Cambridge, and Westminster.

In 1611, the Authorized King James Version (KJV) of the Bible was published, and it has become the best-selling book of all time. In modern times however many people will not read the King James Version because its old-fashioned language is difficult to understand and sometimes intimidating and confusing.

Some Christians insist the only perfect, flawless Bible is the King James Version, and that any other version is a fraud. This bigoted opinion advocated by the King James-Only Club (actually there is no such club) has caused splintering in Christ's Church because they are so very obstinate.

Folks such as me insist there have been advances in the translating process, providing us with easier-to-read, contemporary, and more accurate translations. I personally am convinced that the newer translations are an improvement over the King James Version, if for no other reason than they are reader friendly.

The purpose of the Bible

The Bible was written with two very different purposes in mind: the Spirit uses it to *reveal the purpose, vision, and love of God*, as well as to start, shape, and deepen faith in Christ. The Spirit made it to show how Christ renewed our relationship with God. It is the roadmap for developing strength of character from its examples. It patterns the moral values of your life in accordance with its narratives, and through the guidance of the Holy Spirit, who is guiding you. It instructs us how to live in the world, not be of the world, and it instructs how you can change the world.

The Scriptures tell us that the way God usually works is through humans. God even chose to become a human for us, in the person of Jesus. In a different way, the Spirit inspires each of us and reveals to us what Christ wants us to know.

The difference between the Old and New Testaments

The Old Testament

The Old Testament stories were preparing mankind for the New Testament stories by explaining in detail our creation and God's dealing with the nation of Israel. The Old Testament is composed of 39 books.

The New Testament

The New Testament contains the elements God wants us to know about Jesus and his Church. It is the result of 6,000 manuscripts discovered throughout history that maintain its integrity; it is divided among 27 books.

The first three books of the New Testament are Matthew, Mark, and Luke. These are referred to as *Synoptic Gospels*, which in Greek means, "a seeing together." These three gospels tell the story of Jesus from a similar point of view, often using the same stories and even the same words. The fourth Gospel, John, tells the story of Jesus from a radically different point of view and, because of this, is not considered a Synoptic Gospel.

The remainder of the New Testament contains letters written by apostles to Christians, Jews, and Gentiles. The Apostle Paul wrote 13 of the 27 books of the New Testament and about one-third of the total New Testament text. Paul has been a great influence in Christianity.

Bible translations – choosing the right one

My first piece of advice is this: Choose the one that you will read that uses words with which you are familiar! It should also be sufficiently easy for you to comprehend. However, it is imperative that you use a respected version. The fact that I primarily used the *New Living Translation* (2007 edition) to author this book makes it obvious that I respect both its accuracy and readability.

An example of a difficult to read Bible would be the King James, which is a very accurate Bible, but was written four centuries ago in *Elizabethan English*. Many of the words it uses are now obsolete or have changed meaning. Because it can be confusing to people, I do not generally recommend the King James Version.

Guidelines

Literal Translations: These translations of the Bible are word by word and are very accurate. While they are faithful to the original text, they can be somewhat clumsy when translated into English. Literal translations include the King James Version (KJV), the New King James Version (NKJV), the Revised Standard Version (RSV), the New Revised Standard Version (NRSV), and the New American Standard Bible (NASB).

Dynamic Translations: These are translated phrase-by-phrase, concept-by-concept, and thought-by-thought. They are still quite accurate but not as literal as the KJV, and they are usually much easier to understand. These include the Good News Bible, the New International Version (NIV), the Contemporary English Version (CEV), the New Living Translation (NLT), and many others. While the NIV is considered by many scholars to be the best dynamic translation, I prefer the NLT.

Paraphrases: These are very loose translations of the Bible, as they rearrange the information within each paragraph so it flows more smoothly. They should not be used for in-depth study. They include the Message, the Living Bible, the New Living Bible, and many others.

Wrong or Misleading Translations: These include the New World Translation of the Jehovah's Witnesses, the Holy Bible King James Version as produced by The Church of Jesus Christ of Latter-day Saints, and many other versions produced by cults.

The Bible can only be fully understood by a person who is indwelt by the Holy Spirit. The Holy Spirit will assist you in receiving the meaning he wants you to have at that point in time, no matter what translation you read.

Also, be sure to purchase a red-letter-edition Bible. In these Bibles, Jesus' words are presented in red, which brings the reader closer to the Savior.

Where to begin

If you ask 20 people where to begin reading the Bible, you will probably get 20 different answers. I will give you my opinion, based on what worked for me.

A mistake that many make is beginning with the Book of Genesis in the Old Testament. The Bible is not a book that can be easily read and understood if read cover to cover. To compound this problem, the new student often uses a King James Version. After about five minutes, the reader is totally confused and bored, so the Bible is placed back into the drawer from which it came.

I began reading the New Testament Book of Galatians in a very simple-to-read translation that was given to me by a Christian friend. My friend suggested beginning in the Book of Galatians because it was informative of what *not* to believe about Christianity. The writer of Galatians, Paul, was angry with the people of the Galatian Church because they were becoming slaves to the Law of Moses. Paul emphasizes in Galatians that Christ's death on the Cross freed them from laws. All of my life I was under the false impression that Christianity was a strict system of laws, and that those who obeyed them would go to Heaven and those who disobeyed them would go to Hell. When I finished reading the Book of Galatians, I was both astonished and freed from guilt.

If my memory serves me correctly, the next book I read was the Book of Romans, followed by Hebrews. At that point, I was able to begin to read the first four books of the New Testament because I understood why Jesus came to earth in the form of a man, why he died on the Cross, and why he rose from being dead. I wanted to know more and more about this God who freed me.

I first read the Book of John because it focused on the things Jesus claimed about himself. The Book of John is my favorite of the four Gospels.

I did not begin to read the Old Testament until about a year after I began the New Testament, and even then, I would only spend about 10 percent of my Bible study time in the Old Testament. That habit has been consistent throughout the years.

When starting to read the Old Testament, I would begin in Genesis because that describes how the world was created and how mankind became inherently sinful.

You will enjoy reading Psalms and Proverbs because they are wisdom-filled, and easy to read and understand.

Use it, use it, use it

Because your Bible is your guide to life, it should be used until the pages are so filled with underlines, highlights and notes that it needs to be retired and replaced with a new one that will be worn out again. Although the Bible is a holy book, it was created to be utilized.

Principle by principle, piece by piece

I do not want to imply that the Bible is like a puzzle, but it contains countless magnificent aspects that, when assembled, form a masterpiece. Each aspect is understood as the Holy Spirit rewards the reader with a formula for gaining wisdom – one principle at a time.

I have spoken with thousands of Christians who tell me each time they read the Bible – even if for only a few minutes – they discover something new that offers reassurance, direction, belief, stimulation, or encouragement. What seems complex at first eventually becomes understandable.

Although many passages seem redundant, you will eventually realize those repetitious topics are the things that God wants us to totally comprehend, understand, and put into practice. That is why he does it that way.

Study the Scriptures to grow in your relationship with Jesus Christ and not to win arguments, although this is difficult for those of us who enjoy a healthy debate.

> *Remind everyone about these things, and command them in God's presence to stop fighting over words. Such arguments are useless, and they can ruin those who hear them.*
>
> *Work hard so you can present yourself to God and receive his approval. Be a good worker, one who does not need to be ashamed and who correctly explains the word of truth. Avoid worthless, foolish talk that only leads to more godless behavior.* 2 Timothy 2:14-16

Should the Bible be read literally?

The human writers of the Bible were inspired by the Spirit to tell stories and histories, write poems and songs, and share visions with their readers for a particular time, for a particular reason. A good example of this is head coverings.

> *But a woman dishonors her head if she prays or prophesies without a covering on her head, for this is the same as shaving her head. Yes, if she refuses to wear a head covering, she should cut off all her hair! But since it is*

> *shameful for a woman to have her hair cut or her head shaved, she should wear a covering.* 1 Corinthians 11:5-6

This makes it very clear that a head covering should be worn in church. My female Amish friends not only cover their heads in church, but also when in public. There is nothing wrong with this head-covering observation, but many Christians would disagree with its necessity based on their particular interpretation of the Scriptures.

Correlation is the process of combining all the information from the Scriptures into a Christian belief system resulting in a lifestyle in agreement with what God desires for us individually and collectively.

We must be willing and able to identify the original meaning of the text and ascertain whether it's meaning is historical, literal, or cultural. In history, God spoke to a specific audience, to address a specific situation. The message was for that specific time, place, and situation. But there is also a universal dimension in the problems the original audience had to face and the solutions God gave them. We need to discover that timeless principle of the message. Look to your church, your commentaries, and to other Christians for interpretations, but first seek answers from the Holy Spirit.

The meaning of the Scriptures is revealed through the Holy Spirit, but in addition to his help, God also gave us one another. That is why it is so valuable to have the input from 2,000 years of church-going Christians and the billion Christians living throughout this planet.

Don't just read, study

One of the mistakes made by new Christians is that they read a few verses and misunderstand how they fit into the puzzle. You cannot take one or two verses and establish doctrine or begin to consider yourself a theologian. It takes years to understand many of the finer points of the Bible, and even those who have studied daily for decades usually disagree on some interpretations.

Each book of the Bible has it own unique purpose, as does each chapter, passage, verse, and word. It is vital to understand the big picture before a student can begin to dissect the details. Even the experts never really become experts. Identify situations in our world that are comparable to those faced by the Biblical audience. Think of a variety of contemporary applications to which the text might lead. Make the decision to apply those principles in your life.

Bible accessories

Depending on your budget, there are many aids that can be added to your library that will be of tremendous benefit as you spend the remainder of your life getting to know more and more about the Lord and his kingdom.

There are hundreds of translations of the Bible available and a variety of linguistic, philosophical, and ideological approaches have been used for each. Consequently, there are many words, verses, passages, concepts, and messages that require clarification. Although the Holy Spirit will assist the reader in finding answers, he has also provided tools, just as he provided us with the Bible. The following are a few that I believe to be invaluable. There are so many different brands that I am only giving the name of the tool, but you will have to decide for yourself which particular version fits your budget or your goal.

Bible Commentary: This is one of the most valuable tools because it has the ability to clarify the meaning of an entire book, section, passage, verse, or word. The Bible student must be careful that he or she does not misunderstand the meaning of what they are reading, and commentaries are a wonderful tool for clarification. Of course, the writer of each commentary is going to present his or her interpretation – so be careful that you obtain a brand that is reputable. There are many brands available, so ask your pastor for assistance in making your choice.

Parallel Bible: The Bible has been translated hundreds of times in the English language, as interpreted by the company and its staff that publishes a specific version. If the particular version you are reading has a passage or verse that is unclear, you can instantly compare what you are reading to the same verse or passage of another version by opening your parallel Bible to that same verse. Parallel Bibles will have multiple versions side by side. The same message may be understood more clearly and accurately by comparing. There are many brands available, so ask your pastor for assistance in making your choice.

Topical Bible: A wonderful tool for understanding the numerous subjects of the Bible is the Topical Bible, which presents all of the verses arranged by topic. For example, if the student wants to see all of the verses or passages regarding the subject of *salvation*, he or she can simply look up that word. Depending on the quality of the publication, the student will either see all of the verses, or at least be directed to the book, chapter and verse in which the verses/passages are found.

Bible Concordance: This is an alphabetical index of all of the words used in the Bible, with indications to enable the student to find all of the verses or passages where the words appear.

Internet Search Engines: Many of those tools listed above can be found on the Internet, plus much more. With the advent of the Internet, there is no excuse for Bible ignorance any longer.

Bible particulars

The Bible gets its name from a Greek word meaning "books." Its purpose is to reveal where we came from, why we are here, and where we will go after our last heartbeat. It is the source upon which much of Western civilization has been built.

The following are various particulars of the King James Version of the Old and New Testaments. The information was compiled from several sources and is presented for personal, not scholarly, information.

Old Testament

- Primary purpose: Pointing to the coming Messiah
- Books: 39
- Verses: approximately 23,000
- Chapters: 929
- Words: approximately 600,000
- First human author: Moses wrote the Hebrew Torah, as dictated by God. In Hebrew, *Torah* means, "the law." Another name for the Five Books of Moses is *Pentateuch*, which means "five scrolls."
- Language: Primarily Hebrew but translated into Greek about 200 BC, referred to as the Septuagint. The Latin word *Septuagint* is derived from the phrase "the translation of 70 interpreters."
- Commands: 613

New Testament

- Primary purpose: To reveal and revere the Messiah
- Books: 27
- Verses: approximately 8,000
- Chapters: 260
- Words: approximately 180,000

- Language: Greek (it is debated whether Jesus spoke Greek, Aramaic, or Hebrew)
- States: *"Don't ever let anyone call you 'Rabbi,' for you have only one teacher, and all of you are equal as brothers and sisters. And don't address anyone here on earth as 'Father,' for only God in heaven is your spiritual Father. And don't let anyone call you 'Teacher,' for you have only one teacher, the Messiah."* Matthew 23:8-10, Jesus' words
- States all Christians are priests: *And you living stones that God is building into his spiritual temple. What's more, you are his holy priests. Through the mediation of Jesus Christ, you offer spiritual sacrifices that please God.* 1 Peter 2:5
- States all Christians are saints: *To the church of God which is at Corinth, to those who are sanctified in Christ Jesus, called to be saints, with all who in every place call on the name of Jesus Christ our Lord, both theirs and ours:* 1 Corinthians 1:2 (NKJV)
- Speaks: The Bible refers only to Christ's Church. It does not mention the Catholic, Lutheran, Methodist, Presbyterian, etc., churches.
- Commands: 2

Old and New Testaments combined

- Inspired by: God
- Written by: people
- Number of promises given: 1,260
- Commands given: 6,468
- Predictions: 8,000
- Fulfilled prophecies: more than 3,000
- Unfulfilled prophecies: more than 3,000
- Number of times the words "God" or "Lord" appear: approximately 11,000

Notes:

35

Heaven yesterday, today, and tomorrow

*This is what the Lord says: "Heaven is my throne, and the earth is
my footstool. Could you build me a temple as good as that?
Could you build me such a resting place? My hands have
made both heaven and earth; they and everything
in them are mine. I, the Lord, have spoken!"*

Isaiah 66:1

Heaven is the dwelling place of God, and it is where those who accept Jesus Christ as Savior will spend eternity. The Scriptures tell us there is no sin, evil, tears, pain, or sorrow in Heaven.

I hope that by now you understand that most major religions believe in a heaven, but Christianity is the only major religion that believes a person can go there based on faith in Jesus as the Savior. Jesus' Blood was the ultimate and final sacrifice for all of mankind, and his resurrection proved that he had the power to overcome death.

Paradise – the original "sort of" Heaven

The Bible informs us that Heaven (although it was not really Heaven) started in the center of the Earth, but was moved following Jesus' death, and will be moved again following the millennium. The first, called *Paradise* or *Abraham's Bosom*, was located in the center of the Earth from the beginning of time, and is where Jesus went immediately after his death. Paradise was where all of the righteous people went prior to Jesus' death. That is also where the thief, who was crucified beside Jesus, went following his death. Remember, until the death of Jesus there was no remission of sins. Without the remission of sin, which comes with the acceptance of Jesus Christ and his sacrifice for us, there was no entrance into Heaven. The term *Abraham's Bosom* is still used by many to portray Heaven.

When an Old Testament righteous individual died, he went to *Paradise*, where he was held until Jesus died. Until that time, Satan had the keys to death and Hell, so everyone went into the center of the earth where the wicked were tormented, and the righteous were held without pain or suffering. There was a great gap between the two.

After Jesus died, he went into the center of the earth and took away the keys of death and Hell from Satan and brought out the righteous who were being held there. The Old Testament saints were saved from eternal damnation based on their faith in the coming messiah.

> *Then Jesus shouted out again, and he released his spirit. At that moment the curtain in the sanctuary of the Temple was torn in two, from top to bottom. The earth shook, rocks split apart, and tombs opened. The bodies of many godly men and women who had died were raised from the dead. They left the cemetery after Jesus' resurrection, went into the holy city of Jerusalem, and appeared to many people.* Matthew 27:50-53

It is only when Jesus gave his life for us on the Cross that a saint (all people become saints when we are saved) could enter the "new (*third*) Heaven," which is where we go following death.

Many people incorrectly believe Jesus went to the center of the earth to preach to those who were in Hell, but that is not what he did. Jesus did not preach to those in Hell who were being tormented because for them it was too late. Their fate and future was sealed. It was the saints being held prisoner that Jesus preached to when he went into the center of the earth.

Jesus gives us insight into this in Luke 16:19-26 as follows:

> *Jesus said, "There was a certain rich man who was splendidly clothed in purple and fine linen and who lived each day in luxury. At his gate lay a poor man named Lazarus who was covered with sores. As Lazarus lay there longing for scraps from the rich man's table, the dogs would come and lick his open sores.*
>
> *"Finally, the poor man died and was carried by the angels to be with Abraham. The rich man also died and was buried, and his soul went to the place of the dead. There, in torment, he saw Abraham in the far distance with Lazarus at his side.*

"The rich man shouted, 'Father Abraham, have some pity! Send Lazarus over here to dip the tip of his finger in water and cool my tongue. I am in anguish in these flames.'

"But Abraham said to him, 'Son, remember that during your lifetime you had everything you wanted, and Lazarus had nothing. So now he is here being comforted, and you are in anguish. And besides, there is a great chasm separating us. No one can cross over to you from here, and no one can cross over to us from there.'"

The "now" Heaven

If you are a Christian, and if you died this very moment, you would ascend to Heaven immediately. However, this is what theologians consider an intermediate Heaven. It is a transitional period and place between our past lives on earth and our future resurrection to eternity on the New Earth (the New Jerusalem). Please do not confuse this transitional period with the false doctrine of Purgatory!

NOTE: The definition of Purgatory in the Roman Catholic Encyclopedia is: *A place or condition of temporal punishment for those who, departing this life in God's grace, are, not entirely free from venial faults, or have not fully paid the satisfaction due to their transgressions.*

This sounds fair, except for one thing – Jesus Christ died for all of the sins of mankind on the Cross! He took all of the punishment we deserve. Stating that there is something we must do to pay for our transgressions is blasphemy. The belief in a place, or condition, in which a dead Christian must be "cleaned-up" is not Biblical. Claiming that a Christian must suffer for sins after death is contrary to everything the Bible says about salvation.

The concept of a place where the dead are imprisoned for cleansing originates from before Christ, when many people would pray to the gods for those who had died. Not only is this continued today in Catholicism, but it is also done in Mormonism and Judaism.

Any religion that claims to be Christian, yet teaches cleansing following death, totally misunderstands the totality and finality of Christ's death. Furthermore, any Christian belief system that teaches that anything must be done either while here on earth or after one's death does not understand that Christ died for all people and all sin.

I ask you this: Which sins didn't Jesus die for? If we must atone, suffer, sacrifice, or tithe for forgiveness, then we are boldly stating that Jesus' death, was not a perfect, complete, and sufficient sacrifice.

This "now Heaven" is where the physically deceased, but Spiritually alive (saved), went following Jesus' death and where those who are saved go immediately upon their physical death.

> *Yes, we are fully confident, and we would rather be away from these earthly bodies, for then we will be at home with the Lord.* 2 Corinthians 5:8

In that "now Heaven" we will await the time of Christ's second coming.

The following is a sketch of what most scholars consider the structure of the physical world, whose outer layer is the location of this Heaven.

- ➢ The lower sea of physical waters (our seas and oceans)
- ➢ The first heaven (the atmosphere)
- ➢ The second heaven (outer space)
- ➢ The sea of separation
- ➢ The third Heaven

The third Heaven (not to be confused with the final Heaven) is where someone goes if he or she dies before the second coming of Jesus. It is also the Heaven to which Paul was referring in 2 Corinthians, Chapter 12, verses 2-5:

> *I was caught up to the third heaven fourteen years ago. Whether I was in my body or out of my body, I don't know—only God knows. Yes, only God knows whether I was in my body or outside my body. But I do know that I was caught up to paradise and heard things so astounding that they cannot be expressed in words, things no human is allowed to tell.*
>
> *That experience is worth boasting about, but I'm not going to do it. I will boast only about my weaknesses.*

The Bible is much more explicit about the permanent Heaven than it is regarding this intermediate one, and most of what is believed is merely conjecture. Therefore, I am not going to dissect the Scriptures seeking nebulous specifications, as that is not the purpose of this book. There are many books available that explore this mystery vigorously, and I suggest you delve into this, but only after you become a more advanced student.

The New Jerusalem is yet to come

The New Jerusalem is where we will live eternally following all end time events. It is referred to in the Bible in several places:

"Look! I am creating new heavens and a new earth,
and no one will even think about the old ones anymore.
Be glad; rejoice forever in my creation!
And look! I will create Jerusalem as a place of happiness.
Her people will be a source of joy.
I will rejoice over Jerusalem
and delight in my people.
And the sound of weeping and crying
will be heard in it no more.

"No longer will babies die when only a few days old.
No longer will adults die before they have lived a full life.
No longer will people be considered old at one hundred!
Only the cursed will die that young!
In those days people will live in the houses they build
and eat the fruit of their own vineyards.
Unlike the past, invaders will not take their houses
and confiscate their vineyards.
For my people will live as long as trees,
and my chosen ones will have time to enjoy their hard-won gains.
They will not work in vain,
and their children will not be doomed to misfortune.
For they are people blessed by the Lord,
and their children, too, will be blessed.
I will answer them before they even call to me.
While they are still talking about their needs,
I will go ahead and answer their prayers!
The wolf and the lamb will feed together.
The lion will eat hay like a cow.
But the snakes will eat dust.
In those days no one will be hurt or destroyed on my holy mountain.
I, the Lord, have spoken!" Isaiah 65:17-25

Abraham was confidently looking forward to a city with eternal foundations,
a city designed and built by God. Hebrews 11:10

But they were looking for a better place, a heavenly homeland. That is why God is not ashamed to be called their God, for he has prepared a city for them. Hebrews 11:16

No, you have come to Mount Zion, to the city of the living God, the heavenly Jerusalem, and to countless thousands of angels in a joyful gathering. You have come to the assembly of God's firstborn children, whose names are written in heaven. You have come to God himself, who is the judge over all things. You have come to the spirits of the righteous ones in heaven who have now been made perfect. You have come to Jesus, the one who mediates the new covenant between God and people, and to the sprinkled blood, which speaks of forgiveness instead of crying out for vengeance like the blood of Abel. Hebrews 12:22-24

For this world is not our permanent home; we are looking forward to a home yet to come. Hebrews 13:14

Since everything around us is going to be destroyed like this, what holy and godly lives you should live, looking forward to the day of God and hurrying it along. On that day, he will set the heavens on fire, and the elements will melt away in the flames. But we are looking forward to the new heavens and new earth he has promised, a world filled with God's righteousness. 2 Peter 3:11-13

Frequently asked questions and answers

1. Will people who are married on earth be married in Heaven?

Regarding marriage in Heaven, the Scriptures answer this as follows:

Jesus replied, "Marriage is for people here on earth. But in the age to come, those worthy of being raised from the dead will neither marry nor be given in marriage. And they will never die again. In this respect they will be like angels. They are children of God and children of the resurrection. Luke 20:34-36

Another interesting verse follows:

"For when the dead rise, they will neither marry nor be given in marriage. In this respect they will be like the angels in heaven." Matthew 22:30, Jesus' words

This does not mean we will become angels, but it does mean we will be unmarried such as angels are unmarried. In fact, we will govern angels.

Don't you realize that we will judge angels? So you should surely be able to resolve ordinary disputes in this life. 1 Corinthians 6:3

2. Will we eat and drink in Heaven?

"And just as my Father has granted me a Kingdom, I now grant you the right to eat and drink at my table in my Kingdom. And you will sit on thrones, judging the twelve tribes of Israel." Luke 22:29, Jesus' words

3. Will we recognize one another?

Dear friends, we are already God's children, but he has not yet shown us what we will be like when Christ appears. But we do know that we will be like him, for we will see him as he really is. 1 John 3:2

The verses you just read give a little insight into what lies ahead. First, it is not comprehensible for us at this point. Second, we will be like him, so we will apparently be able to recognize each other, as he is all knowing.

In addition, Jesus called people by name, including Lazarus in the present Heaven; and Abraham, Isaac, and Jacob in the eternal Heaven. This indicates we will remain as the individuals we were while on earth – only as perfect beings. If you refer to the passage Luke 16:19-26, which is presented earlier in this chapter, you will notice that Abraham, Lazarus, and the rich man were all recognizable to one another.

4. Will we look like we did when we died?

This is still unknown, but Thomas Aquinas said he thought we would be the same age as Jesus when he died, which was 33. Also, it has been reported by some scientists that our DNA does not age beyond approximately 30 years, so this is in line with Aquinas. All speculation.

5. When will the judgment take place that determines our rewards in Heaven?

Opinions vary regarding this. Some people believe it will occur immediately upon death, while others believe it will happen between the time of our death and the second coming of Christ. There are others who think it will take place after the millennium.

6. Will the new Earth be a continuation of the Garden of Eden?

No. Many teach this, but the Garden was on the existing Earth and was the birthplace of sin. Eternity will be on a new Earth and it will be free of sin. We regard the Garden as defective, but we anticipate eternity as a perfect place.

7. Will we have emotions?

"God blesses you who are hungry now, for you will be satisfied.
God blesses you who weep now, for in due time you will laugh."
Luke 6:21, Jesus' words

8. Because we will have emotions, won't we be unhappy because some of our loved ones went to Hell?

That is a very good question, with a very clear answer. Although you may not be able to comprehend it now, at that time, you will have a clear understanding why God allows certain things to happen. The perfection of this new Earth is so beyond our understanding, there are certain things we must accept in faith.

You must also remember, God does not send anyone to Hell. It is a choice the individual makes regarding his own destiny. This is also a good reason for you to witness today to those you hope will be with you in eternity!

9. One of the most frequently asked questions about Heaven is whether our deceased pets will be there?

As a Christian evangelist, one of the most frequent questions that I am asked is if people's pets will go to Heaven? I have read several books on the subject and the commentaries of more than 60 pastors from many denominations, and they all state emphatically that the Bible is clear our pets will be in Heaven.

I do not mind telling you, I have a lump in my throat and a tear in my eye while writing this. I am so excited that I will someday be reunited with Lassie, Laddie, Buck, Babe, Blonde Beau, Beau, Hanna, Rocky, Chief, Mt.

Airy Jill, Little Sugarplum, Chuckler, Super Gyp, and a bunch more. My pets have been a major part of my life, and those that are gone are sorely missed.

If I have ever counted on the Holy Spirit to give me a definite affirmation, it is now. He says, "Yes Tim, you will definitely be reunited with all of your critters."

10. Last, but certainly not least, won't Heaven get boring?

Again, we are thinking with our minuscule intellects. Most people with whom I discuss Heaven are concerned they will love it at first, but after a while will become bored. Golfers say they will get tired of hitting holes-in-one every day, and although bowlers strive for a perfect 300, they wonder if, after a few of them, they might welcome a split just for the challenge. By now, you probably know my sport is horseracing, but I will admit winning a race every day would not bore me.

Chances are you have at least a little faith in God, and if you are going to Heaven, it is because of your faith. So why would you believe that what he has in store for you is boring? After all, without God there would be no laughter, no joy, no beautiful sunrises or sunsets, no succulent lobster, no yellow roses, no diamonds, or any of those other masterpieces.

For you will not leave my soul among the dead
  or allow your holy one to rot in the grave.
You will show me the way of life,
  granting me the joy of your presence
  and the pleasures of living with you forever. Psalm 16:10-11

Notes:

36

Change hearts – not laws

Create in me a clean heart, O God.
Renew a loyal spirit within me.

Psalm 51:10

You have been around long enough to know that more laws and more policemen do not have the force to bring an end to evil. Morals, self-control, kindness, and love for one another cannot be legislated.

So, what is the answer? It is as plain as the nose on your face. Whether we want to change the neighborhood or change the world, we must first change the hearts of the people in it.

Unfortunately, we live in a society where most individuals either have no idea how to do that, do not have the time, or just do not care. For those of us who have Christian hearts, we know the answer.

> *This means that anyone who belongs to Christ has become a new person. The old life is gone; a new life has begun!* 2 Corinthians 5:17

I am sure there are many ways of changing people. However, I will share with you the method I have seen that is superior to them all. The reason I was so impressed with its results is that it took place in a maximum-security prison, where the hardened hearts of inmates were made new again. My involvement was the result of an urging from the Holy Spirit – perhaps so I could share this miraculous experience with you.

As an evangelist, I felt a tug to become involved with a prison ministry, but I had no idea how to get started. So, I typed the words "prison ministry" into my favorite search engine and miraculously up popped Kairos Prison Ministry. I say miraculously because as I read about Kairos, I discovered it was an offshoot of the Cursillo movement, via de Christo, Emmaus, Fourth Day Movement, Street Weekend, and so forth. The Cursillo and its counterparts are a spiritual weekend retreat designed to bring the attendee closer to Christ and to provide the desire and knowledge to evangelize his personal relationship with the Savior. Although Cursillo is a Catholic movement, I consider it to be ecumenical. I attended this three-day adventure with reluctance in 1980, and it was the most dramatic, life-changing event of my life. Consequently, I was very excited to see this concept was being utilized in prisons.

The Cursillo was the experience that advanced my understanding of grace. It was the Cursillo experience that set me free from the bondages of religion, guilt, and social pressures. The more I read about Kairos, the more forceful the Spiritual tug became, so I joined Kairos without apprehension. The word *kairos* in Greek means, "God's special time," and it was just that.

My mission took place a few years ago in a maximum-security prison here in Florida. I was a neophyte, but there were three-dozen Kairos team members who helped indoctrinate me, as well as several others like me. Following 12 weeks of humble training, we put on our best behavior and our army went behind prison walls for three powerful days of sharing our personal testimonies with about 30 of the toughest guys around. One of the primary rules of Kairos is that we leave our masks of pride and superiority outside the prison walls.

> *When I first came to you, dear brothers and sisters, I didn't use lofty words and impressive wisdom to tell you God's secret plan. For I decided that while I was with you I would forget everything except Jesus Christ, the one who was crucified. I came to you in weakness—timid and trembling. And my message and my preaching were very plain. Rather than using clever and persuasive speeches, I relied only on the power of the Holy Spirit. I did this so you would trust not in human wisdom but in the power of God.* 1 Corinthians 2:1-5

It is not the task of Kairos to change the moral behavior of the participants, because that is the job of the Holy Spirit – who does it well. The efforts of us mortals are so miniscule to the power of him. We do our job, and he does his.

I will not go into detail about Kairos' methods, but I will share two things. First, we did not beat them over the heads with Bibles, telling them they would burn in Hell if they did not repent. Second, we transformed their hearts by opening ours. Jesus referred to it simply as love. We did not attempt to denominationally proselytize anyone, which would have been foolish. Our team members came from a wide array of Christian faiths, so we majored on the majors. The beauty of it was that we worked together in one body – the body of Jesus Christ – to accomplish our prescribed mission. Thanks to the Holy Spirit and the time of a few men, our mission was accomplished. Of the total six-dozen men who attended the Kairos event, both missionaries and inmates, all hearts were softened.

In 1976, a Cursillo movement in Union Correctional Institution, a maximum-security institution in Rayford, Florida, preceded the ministry of Kairos. Today, Kairos has 363 ministries in 31 states, and 422 ministries worldwide. These ministries, in Australia, Canada, Costa Rica, Dominican Republic, Honduras, Nicaragua, Peru, South Africa, and the United Kingdom (including Northern Ireland), employ a total of only 11 people. Approximately 200,000 prison inmates have reaped the benefits of the hundreds of thousands of Christian individuals who have volunteered to follow Jesus' teaching to love one another.

When referring to medium to maximum-security prisons, statistics show that approximately 90 percent of inmates presently incarcerated will eventually return to society, and that 86 percent of them will end up back in prison. Studies also indicate *miraculously* that only 15 percent of those who experience a Kairos weekend will ever go back. Changing hearts works!

The Holy Spirit succeeds when cops, courts, and confinement fail. Government-imposed laws are a joke compared to what Jesus can do. The Apostle Paul said it best:

> *Clearly, you are a letter from Christ showing the result of our ministry among you. This "letter" is written not with pen and ink, but with the Spirit of the living God. It is carved not on tablets of stone, but on human hearts.*
> 2 Corinthians 3:3

Notes:

37

Historic people you should meet

*No eulogy is due to him who simply
does his duty and nothing more.*

Saint Augustine (354-430)

The Christian faith has thousands of years of history, going back to Genesis 1:1 when Jesus created all that we see, touch, feel, love, like, dislike, and tolerate. Although Jesus foreknew that mankind would disappoint him, he also knew that he would love us – transgressions and all.

In eternity past, Jesus had a plan that would reveal our sinful nature by giving us laws that we could not keep. He then demonstrated his love by dying on a cross to forgive us, and rose from being dead to confirm that he had power over death. His covenant was that if we would believe what I have just told you, we could spend eternity with him in a place called Heaven.

Throughout the centuries, from the beginning of creation, many people have been instrumental in Jesus' plan. Most were good people, but a few also had evil characteristics. As a Christian, you should be familiar with some who were a part of God's plan.

There have been so many that it would take an entire series of books to give the biographies of them all. Therefore, we have chosen those we believe were most important to the birth, growth, and problems within Christianity. Many that you will meet were disgusting humans, but as Christians, we must try to acquire the same attitude Jesus had when he asked his Father God to forgive his executioners.

*Jesus said, "Father, forgive them, for they don't know what they are doing."
And the soldiers gambled for his clothes by throwing dice.* Luke 23:34

That is hard to believe, but true!

In chronological order

NOTE: Rather than putting the names in alphabetical order, they have been placed in chronological order so that you may be able to understand how they each fit into the era, rather than merely recognizing them by name.

The Hebrew and King James timeline of the Bible (Old Testament) are approximately 250 years apart, so the timelines offered in this chapter are approximate. They are presented so that you may have some idea where each person fits into the historical picture.

The Creation stage to Jesus' birth

In the beginning God created the heavens and the earth. Genesis 1:1

The Hebrew word for God – *Elohim* – is plural, which contributes to the belief that God has three natures, known as: the Father, the Son, and the Holy Spirit. The Spirit of God is mentioned in Genesis 1:2. Later in Genesis, God states that he will create people in "our" image, which many believe is the basis for the Triune nature of God.

Angels: It is impossible to establish when angels were created because they were in existence before the world was formed. They were created outside of time, and all remain in existence today. Following is a very short biography of three considered to be the majors:

1. Lucifer/Satan: Satan, (meaning "the accuser") is an angel who fell from Heaven and attacks the people of God. It is predicted that he, along with other fallen angels, will eventually be thrown into the Lake of Fire.

2. Gabriel: an archangel who acts on God's behalf as a messenger.

3. Michael: an archangel who served as guardian over the heavenly battles related to Israel.

Abraham (about 1812 BC — 1637 BC): known as the first monotheistic human, and father of Judaism, Islam, and Christianity. *Abram* means "high father," but God changed his name to *Abraham*, which in Hebrew means "the father of many nations." At the call of God, he left his idolatrous kindred and moved to Haran, in Mesopotamia, with his father; his wife, Sarai; his brother, Nahor; and his nephew,

Lot. Abram, with a large household of probably a thousand souls, entered on a migratory life and dwelt in tents. Moving from place to place for convenience of water and pasturage, he was driven by a famine into Egypt. Returning to Canaan rich in flocks and herds, he left Lot to dwell in the fertile valley of the lower Jordan.

Abraham is one of the most remarkable people in Scripture. He is revered for his simple and unwavering monotheistic faith. Believers, including Muslims as well as Jews and Christians, refer to Abraham as "the father of the faithful."

Abraham was a Hebrew, but he was not an Israelite, nor a Jew. The word Hebrew is first mentioned in Genesis 14:13, where Abraham is called Abram the Hebrew. Because Abraham was called a Hebrew, his descendants were also given that designation, including the descendants of Ishmael, who are the Arabs of today. But by common usage, this designation is applied only to those of the nation of Israel.

The promise of a son being yet unfulfilled, Sarai gave Abraham (when Abraham was 86 years old) her maid, Hagar, as a concubine for the purpose of bearing him a child. Hagar's son was named Ishmael at the direction of the Lord.

Thirteen years later, three men, who were messengers of God, approached Abraham's tent, and one of them predicted that Sarai would give birth to a child. It was about this time that Sarai's name was changed to Sarah.

After this, Abraham journeyed south to Gerah, where Sarah gave birth to their son, Isaac. Soon after Isaac was born, Sarah began to treat Hagar and Ishmael harshly, so Hagar took Ishmael to seek a new home.

God put the faith of Abraham to test by commanding him to sacrifice Isaac upon Mount Moriah. Moments before the sacrifice, his uplifted hand was arrested by the angel of God, and a ram, which was entangled in a thicket nearby, was seized and offered instead. 12 years later Sarah died. Abraham married Keturah and had six sons, each one the founder of a distinct people in Arabia. At the age of 175, full of years and honor, Abraham died and was buried by his sons in the same tomb with Sarah.

Most people regard Abraham as the first Jew, and technically he was, because he was the seed of Judaism through his circumcision covenant with God, known as the *Abrahamic Covenant*. Circumcision is a religious ritual that first defined Abraham as a Jew and the procedure of circumcision still remains as the introduction of every Jewish male to his faith. It is a spiritual link with God that can never be removed and is a declaration of Jewishness on the organ by which future generations are created.

When Abram was ninety-nine years old, the Lord appeared to him and said, "I am El-Shaddai—'God Almighty.' Serve me faithfully and live a blameless life. I will make a covenant with you, by which I will guarantee to give you countless descendants."

At this, Abram fell face down on the ground. Then God said to him, "This is my covenant with you: I will make you the father of a multitude of nations! What's more, I am changing your name. It will no longer be Abram. Instead, you will be called Abraham, for you will be the father of many nations. I will make you extremely fruitful. Your descendants will become many nations, and kings will be among them!

"I will confirm my covenant with you and your descendants after you, from generation to generation. This is the everlasting covenant: I will always be your God and the God of your descendants after you. And I will give the entire land of Canaan, where you now live as a foreigner, to you and your descendants. It will be their possession forever, and I will be their God."

Then God said to Abraham, "Your responsibility is to obey the terms of the covenant. You and all your descendants have this continual responsibility. This is the covenant that you and your descendants must keep: Each male among you must be circumcised. You must cut off the flesh of your foreskin as a sign of the covenant between me and you. From generation to generation, every male child must be circumcised on the eighth day after his birth. This applies not only to members of your family but also to the servants born in your household and the foreign-born servants whom you have purchased. All must be circumcised. Your bodies will bear the mark of my everlasting covenant. Any male who fails to be circumcised will be cut off from the covenant family for breaking the covenant." Genesis 17:1-14

However, he could not be referred to as a Jew because that term did not exist until Judah. The patriarchal genealogy that follows Abraham is, Isaac, Jacob, and then Judah (one of Jacob's 12 sons who formed the 12 tribes of Israel). The first Israelite was Jacob, the grandson of Abraham, whose name was changed by God to Israel.

Sarah/Sarai (about 1677 BC – 1540 BC): wife of Bible patriarch Abraham and mother of Isaac. Sarah's name was originally *Sarai*, but later changed to *Sarah* (meaning princess) by God. Sarah was one of the matriarchs of Judaism.

Ishmael (about 1726 BC – 1589 BC): the first child (a son) of Abraham and the child of Hagar, the Egyptian handmaid to Abraham's wife Sarah. In Hebrew *Ishmael* means "God has harkened."

Believing she was too mature to bear children, Sarah offered Hagar in order that Abraham might have a child. Hagar gave birth to Ishmael when Abraham was 86 years old. Miraculously, 14 years later, Sarah bore Isaac, the second son born of Abraham.

Sarah became very jealous of Ishmael and Hagar, so she demanded that Abraham send them away. Abraham was upset, but the Lord told him to do as Sarah had requested, because Isaac was to be the heir of Abraham and inherit the promises that God had made to Abraham and his offspring.

God also promised Abraham that he would make Ishmael into a nation. Hagar and Ishmael left Abraham and lived in the wilderness. God blessed Ishmael and he became the father of 12 sons, and they became the founders of the 12 tribes that bore their names: Nebaioth, Kedar, Abdeel, Mibsam, Mishma, Dumah, Massa, Hadad, Tema, Jetur, Naphish and Kedmah. These tribes were scattered across the land. The Bible and Islamic tradition agree that Ishmael became the leader of the Middle East. According to the Qur'an, the Abrahamic covenant – including the title to the land of Israel – was passed to the Arabs through Ishmael. Ishmael died at the age of 137.

Isaac (about 1712 BC – 1532 BC): the second son of Abraham, who was born when Abraham was about 100 years of age, and Abraham's wife, Sarah, was well beyond child-bearing age. In Hebrew *Isaac* means "he laughs or will laugh."

> *Then God said to Abraham, "Regarding Sarai, your wife—her name will no longer be Sarai. From now on her name will be Sarah. And I will bless her and give you a son from her! Yes, I will bless her richly, and she will become the mother of many nations. Kings of nations will be among her descendants."*
>
> *Then Abraham bowed down to the ground, but he laughed to himself in disbelief. "How could I become a father at the age of 100?" he thought. "And how can Sarah have a baby when she is ninety years old?" So Abraham said to God, "May Ishmael live under your special blessing!"*
>
> *But God replied, "No—Sarah, your wife, will give birth to a son for you. You will name him Isaac, and I will confirm my covenant with him and his descendants as an everlasting covenant. As for Ishmael, I will bless him also, just as you have asked. I will make him extremely fruitful and multiply his descendants. He will become the father of twelve princes, and I will make him a great nation. But my covenant will be confirmed with Isaac, who will be born to you and Sarah about this time next year." When God had finished speaking, he left Abraham.*

> *On that very day Abraham took his son, Ishmael, and every male in his household, including those born there and those he had bought. Then he circumcised them, cutting off their foreskins, just as God had told him. Abraham was ninety-nine years old when he was circumcised, and Ishmael, his son, was thirteen. Both Abraham and his son, Ishmael, were circumcised on that same day, along with all the other men and boys of the household, whether they were born there or bought as servants. All were circumcised with him.* Genesis 17:15-27

Isaac was Abraham's second son. His first was Ishmael, who he fathered as the result of an arrangement suggested by Sarah because she believed she was too old to bear children. Shortly following Isaac's birth, Sarah became very jealous of Ishmael and Hagar, and demanded that Abraham send them away.

When Isaac was a teenager, Abraham was given a command by God to take Isaac up a mountain and sacrifice him. This story is oftentimes compared to God sacrificing his Son Jesus. Immediately before Abraham was to sacrifice Isaac, God stopped him, as it was only a test of Abraham's faith.

When Isaac was 40 years old he married his cousin, Rebekah, and they bore twin sons, Esau and Jacob.

Esau: It was said that Esau was the first-born and stronger than his twin, Jacob. He was the favorite of their father, Isaac, because he was a fine hunter and loved being out and about the countryside.

Jacob: As stated in the 2007 NLT: "Jacob lived up to his name, which means *he grasps the heel* (figuratively, 'he deceives'). He grabbed Esau's heel at birth, and by the time he left home, he had also grabbed his brother's birthright and blessing." God later changed Jacob's name to Israel.

Rebekah, his mother, favored Jacob and together they planned to deceive Isaac into giving his patriarchal blessing to Jacob instead of Esau, the first-born. Jacob fathered 12 sons, who are known as the progenitors of the 12 tribes of Israel. The Jews are of the tribe of Judah. The Jews believe the land of Israel belongs to them as a result of God's covenant, with its promises to Abraham that this land would be theirs through the lineage of Abraham, Isaac, and Jacob.

Moses (about 1525 BC – 1405 BC): the Old Testament patriarch who delivered the Israelites from Egyptian slavery and led them to the Promised Land. Also, Moses received and delivered the Ten Commandments, known as the Old Testament Law, to the Israelites.

Joseph: husband of Mary and stepfather to Jesus.

Following the physical birth of Jesus Christ

The physical birth of Jesus Christ is the act of God coming to Earth in the form of a man.

> *This is how Jesus the Messiah was born. His mother, Mary, was engaged to be married to Joseph. But before the marriage took place, while she was still a virgin, she became pregnant through the power of the Holy Spirit.* Matthew 1:18

NOTE: Many of the people mentioned in the first part of this section may have been born before Jesus' physical birth, but they are not mentioned in the Old Testament, so have been presented in this section.

John the Baptist: the "forerunner of Jesus." The birth of John preceded the birth of Jesus by six months, but his biography is being placed in this section because he was first recognized in the New Testament. Many believe John the Baptist and Jesus were cousins. He lived by himself in the wilderness, eating locusts and wild honey. His garment was woven of camel's hair.

The core of his preaching was to prepare people for the coming of Jesus Christ. He denounced the Sadducees and Pharisees as a "generation of vipers," and warned them of the foolishness of placing importance in governmental privileges. His doctrine and manner of life provoked the entire south of Palestine, and the people from all parts flocked to the banks of the Jordan, where he was. There he baptized thousands. Jesus came from Galilee to Jordan to be baptized of John.

John's public ministry lasted about six months, but was suddenly ended by being cast into prison by Herod, whom he had admonished for the sin of taking the wife of his brother. Herod gave instructions to an officer of his guard to execute John in prison, and John's head was brought to the adulteress as a prize.

Mary: five women named Mary are mentioned in the New Testament:

1. Mary, the mother of Jesus and wife of Joseph
2. Mary Magdalene
3. Mary, the wife of Cleophas, and mother of James the Less and Joses
4. Mary, the sister of Lazarus
5. Mary, the mother of Mark, the evangelist

Mary, the mother of Jesus and wife of Joseph: the wife of Joseph and the mother of Jesus is commonly referred to as the "Virgin Mary," but that term does not appear in Scripture. Little is known of her personal history, but she was of the tribe of Judah and the lineage of David. She was connected by marriage with Elizabeth, the mother of John the Baptist.

After the beginning of Jesus' ministry, Mary's presence in Scripture is minute. She was present at the marriage in Cana, and a year and a half after this, we find her at Capernaum.

> *Then Jesus' mother and brothers came to see him. They stood outside and sent word for him to come out and talk with them. There was a crowd sitting around Jesus, and someone said, "Your mother and your brothers are outside asking for you."*
>
> *Jesus replied, "Who is my mother? Who are my brothers?" Then he looked at those around him and said, "Look, these are my mother and brothers. Anyone who does God's will is my brother and sister and mother."*
> Mark 3:31-35

The next time we find her is at the Cross accompanied by her sister, Mary, who was the wife of Cleophas; Mary Magdalene; Salome; and other women. The next and last time we are aware of her presence is in the Upper Room after Jesus' ascension. The time and manner of her death are unknown.

Magdalene, Mary: one of Jesus' most dedicated followers. It is believed she came from Magdala, hence the name. The Bible tells us Jesus cast seven devils from her. She was present during the closing hours of Jesus' agony on the Cross, and she remained by the Cross until the body was taken down and placed in the tomb. Mary, along with Salome and Mary, the mother of James, brought sweet spices for the anointing of Jesus' body. Very early the next morning, she came to the tomb and found it empty. There she saw two angels sitting at the head and foot of where Jesus had been laid. One angel asked her why she was crying, and she told him it was because someone had taken Jesus' body. She glanced over her shoulder and saw someone she thought was the gardener. To her surprise, it was the resurrected Jesus. Jesus told her not to touch him, for he had not yet ascended to his father.

This was the last incident in the Gospels regarding Mary of Magdala; however, it is believed she was among the group of women, including Jesus' mother, who joined the apostles in the Upper Room in Jerusalem following Jesus' ascension.

Mary of Bethany: sister to Lazarus, and sometimes also thought to be Mary Magdalene, Mary of Bethany (sister of Martha and Lazarus), and the unnamed repentant woman who anointed Jesus' feet are sometimes thought to be the same woman. From this, plus the statement that Jesus had cast seven demons out of her, has risen the tradition that she had been a prostitute before she met Jesus.

Caesar: the title of Roman emperors after Julius Caesar (100 BC – 44 BC). In the New Testament, this title is given to various emperors as sovereigns of Judea without their accompanying proper names. The last of these was Nero (15 AD – 68 AD), but the name was retained by his successors as a title belonging to the imperial dignity.

Pilate, Pontius: the Roman procurator who sentenced Jesus to death.

Lazarus: the brother of Martha and Mary of Bethany, who was raised from the dead by Jesus.

Apostle Paul (about 5AD – 67 AD): known as the Great Apostle Paul, he is revered by countless Christians as the greatest Christian who ever lived. Paul was a hardhearted Jewish Pharisee (named Saul of Tarsus prior to being renamed Paul by God) who hated Christians before being transformed by a visit from Jesus on the road to Damascus, following Jesus' resurrection. There is no evidence that Paul ever met Jesus before this.

Saul was a Roman tax collector, and it is believed he was responsible for the killing of many Christians before his conversion.

Known as the "apostle to the Gentiles," Paul's epistles form the bulk of the New Testament, and most agree that his ministry had more influence on the growth of Christianity than anyone, anywhere, anytime. It is believed that Paul was beheaded during the reign of the Roman Emporer Nero.

Sabellius: a third-century priest and theologian who most likely taught in Rome.

Arius (about 256 AD – 336 AD): a popular preacher from Libia who taught during the time of the early Church, considered a heretic by most, and advocated that there is only one God. Therefore, belief in the full diety of Christ would mean the Father and Son (Jesus) were two separate Gods. He believed that Jesus was something like a super-angel. (Note: This is similar to what Jehovah's Witnesses believe, which is one of the reasons Christians do not recognize Jehovah's Witnesses as Christians.) Arius' teaching spread quickly, and the church began to divide over this opinion.

Constantine I (about 272 AD – 337 AD): ruled a large portion of the Roman Empire from 306 until his death. As the first Christian Emperor, he led in the ending of the persecution of Christians. Throughout his rule, Constantine supported the church financially, built churches, and promoted Christians to high-ranking offices.

In approximately 313 AD, the new Roman Emperor, Constantine had a very realistic vision consisting of a fiery red cross and on that cross was written, "By this thou shalt conquer." Constantine interpreted the dream that he should give up paganism and become a Christian.

Thus, he called a council and the first Hierarchy was formed. Consequently, Christ was dethroned as the head of the church in favor of Constantine. This is considered as the beginnings of what is now the Catholic Church.

Because of the adoption of baptismal regeneration, Constantine, not being a Christian yet, was in a quandary: "If I am saved from my sins by baptism, what is to become of my sins which I may commit after I am baptized?" He finally decided to unite with the Christians and put off baptism until just before his death. This doubt of baptismal regeneration continues to be debated even in present times.

Athanasius (about 293 AD – 373 AD): pope of Alexandria and noted Egyptian leader during the era of Constantine's reign. He taught and defended the belief that God, Jesus, and the Holy Spirit are of a triune nature known as the Trinity. His view was adopted at the Council of Nicea as the official belief of the Christian Church, and remains that way today.

Saint Jerome (about 347 AD – 420 AD): Catholic priest known for translating the Bible into Latin for the Catholic Church.

Pelagius (about 354 AD – 418 AD): a teacher in Rome, though he was British by birth. Most churches have had a streak of *Pelagianism* (which derives its name from Pelagius and is indicative of Pelagius' teachings) running through their theologies at some point in time. Pelagius taught that humans could, by their own efforts, refrain from sinning and thus be capable of saving themselves. Pelagius believed that a person is born with the same purity as Adam when he was first created, thus denying the doctrine that we have inherited a sinful nature from Adam's original sin. This meant that God gave us the capacity to adhere to his commands; hence, God's grace is only for attracting individuals to him.

Saint Augustine (about 354 AD – 430 AD): "Augustine of Hippo" was a Christian saint, philosopher, and theologian whose writings were very influential in Western

Christianity. He was born in Tagaste, a little town in the then-flourishing Roman province of Numidia (now Algeria). Augustine's father was a pagan, but his mother was a Christian.

In Augustine's younger years, he lived a hedonistic lifestyle. He had a 13-year affair with a young woman who gave birth to his son, Adeodatus. It was during this period that he uttered his renowned prayer, "Grant me chastity and continence, but not yet."

One day he heard about two men who had become Christians and became very ashamed of himself. He cried to his friend Alipius, "What are we doing? Unlearned people are taking Heaven by force, while we, with all our knowledge, are so cowardly that we keep rolling around in the mud of our sins!"

Augustine became a Christian and was baptized in 387, devoting the remainder of his life to serving God as a priest, a bishop, and one of the greatest saints who ever lived.

Wycliffe, John (about 1320 AD – 1384 AD): An English theologian and dissident of the Catholic Church who felt that all people should have access to the Bible. Therefore, he began a translation from the Latin Vulgate into English, known as the Wycliffe Bible. Because of his criticism of the Catholic Church, he was persecuted, and his body was exhumed and burned by the Catholic Church 44 years after his death.

Hus, John/Jan (about 1369 AD – 1415 AD): a Czech priest in the 1400s. He was a religious thinker and reformer in what is now the Czech Republic. His reform movement was based on the teachings of John Wycliffe, and his followers became known as *Hussites*. He was excommunicated from the Catholic Church in 1411 and burned at the stake with Wycliffe's manuscript Bibles used as kindling. Although his ministry was short-lived, he was a key predecessor to the Reformation efforts, as Martin Luther was influenced by Hus' teachings.

Luther, Martin (about 1483 AD – 1586 AD): a German-born monk, theologian, and church reformer he is often considered the founder of *Protestantism*. From 1510 to 1520, Luther lectured on the Psalms and the books of Hebrews, Romans, and Galatians. While studying these, he began to realize that salvation is a gift of God's grace, only attainable through faith in Jesus as the Messiah.

Luther began an attempt to reform the Roman Catholic Church, particularly involving the teaching and sale of indulgences. Another of his major conflicts was the church's buying and selling church positions, and the corruption in the church's hierarchy, even reaching the position of the pope. On October 31, 1517, in what is now Germany, Luther nailed his *Ninety-Five Theses* to the door of the Wittenberg Castle Church.

In 1521, church leaders denounced Luther for his rebellions and placed him on trial at the Diet of Worms. He was found guilty and placed under the emperor's ban, which was a harsh sentence that threatened his life. Luther escaped sentencing and took refuge with a friend, at which time he began to translate the Bible from the original Greek and Hebrew to German. He made the translation so people could read the Scriptures for themselves, enabling them to make doctrinal decisions for themselves.

On June 13, 1525, Luther married Katharina von Bora, one of a group of 12 nuns he had helped escape from the Nimbschen Cistercian Convent. They had six children.

Zwingli, Ulrich/Huldrych (about 1484 AD – 1531 AD): a leader of the Reformation in Switzerland. Unlike Martin Luther, who searched the Scriptures seeking forgiveness for sins, Zwingli's interest in the Bible was intellectual questioning. In an era when priests were not familiar with the Scriptures, Zwingli studied the Bible and taught from its contents.

Zwingli was so enthralled with the New Testament that he used the Rhine River as an illustration in his preaching by stating, "For God's sake, do not put yourself at odds with the Word of God. For truly it will persist as surely as the Rhine follows its course. One can perhaps dam it up for awhile, but it is impossible to stop it."

Struggling with many of the traditional Catholic customs, Zwingli secretly married in 1522, but in 1524 wedded his wife publicly, insisting that priests had the right to marry.

In 1525, Zwingli challenged the belief in transubstantiation, and along with others abolished the mass, but he retained the Lord's Supper as a symbolic gesture. In 1529, Zwingli and Luther met at Marburg, and although they agreed on 14 revised points of doctrine, they could not agree on the doctrine of Christ in the Eucharist. Luther insisted in Christ's literal presence.

Two years later Zwingli died in battle defending Zurich against Catholic forces, and Zurich remained Protestant.

Tyndale, William (about 1494 AD – 1536 AD): Protestant reformer and scholar who translated the Bible into the early modern English of his day. Tyndale's life ended when he was strangled and burned at the stake by the Roman Catholic authorities for alleged heresy. His project was completed by his assistants, John Rogers and Miles Coverdale, in 1535. It is known as the Coverdale Bible.

Tyndale's was the first English translation to work directly from Hebrew and Greek texts, and the first to take advantage of the new medium of print, which allowed for wide distribution. Tyndale's work was included in the King James Version of the Bible.

Calvin, John (about 1509 AD – 1564 AD): born in France, and influenced by Martin Luther. Calvin's teachings are still prominent today in many denominations, and he is probably revered mostly for his position known as *unconditional election,* an interpretation of the Scriptures that people are saved by grace alone, but that God must be the one who takes the initiative for salvation. In other words, no person has the free will to choose God, and God controls the eternal destiny of the world by imposing irresistible grace only to those individuals he chooses to be part of his Kingdom.

Calvin's premise began when he was 25 and it continued throughout his lifetime. He was a very strict individual and had high Christian expectations of himself and others. He was the founder of the *Reformed Church*, which was the second major Protestant movement, known as *Calvinism,* following *Lutheranism.* This includes denominations such as Presbyterians, Reformed Churches, and many Baptist churches. Many Christians are Calvinists and do not know it.

John Calvin actually believed and taught that the Roman Catholic Church was a false church that needed to be replaced, not just reformed. There are varying degrees of Calvinism.

Most Calvinists believe salvation cannot be lost because God presents an irresistible calling that cannot be resisted. Calvinists also believe that good works are demonstrated as the evidence of being saved, and that if good works are not present; the individual may not actually be saved.

Although Calvin was in agreement with Luther on most interpretations of the Scriptures, he did not agree with Luther that the body and blood of Christ are spiritually present in the bread and wine that is served in the Eucharist (Communion).

Calvin's best-known work is *Institutes of the Christian Religion.*

Calvin's chief opponent was Jacobus Arminius. The feud over the interpretations of certain Scriptures remains in Christendom today.

Arminius, Jacobus (about 1559 AD – 1609 AD): Dutch theologian and founder of an anti-Calvinist Reformed theology and known for his free-will approach to Christianity, which became opposite to the irresistible grace of his mentor, John Calvin. Arminius was born slightly before John Calvin died and was actually taught by Calvin's son-in-law. Arminius was a Calvinist until he was forced to defend his beliefs to someone who objected to the Calvinistic view. This caused Arminius to reject his Calvinistic background and to proceed to modify Calvinism.

Arminius' theological views stirred up controversy in Holland, and his followers faced persecution from Calvinists. 200 pastors lost their posts, statesman John van Olden Barnveldt was beheaded, and Hugo Grotius was imprisoned for life (although he escaped two years later).

Arminius' theology is still taught today. *Arminianism* is predicated on the belief that people are able of either accepting or rejecting salvation without any influence from God, and that it is a choice made by the individual involving free will. Many Christians are Arminians and do not realize it.

There are degrees of Arminianism, but strong adherents believe that Jesus Christ died for everyone and that his death paid for all the sins of mankind from the beginning of time. Of course, because this is a free-will choice, an individual has the option of rejecting Jesus as Savior, as many do. Many Arminians also believe that people can lose salvation if they chose to live a life of sin, or if they backslide into a life that is not obedient to what Christ requests. The chief writing of Arminius is *Examination of Perkins' Pamphlet.*

Know, John (about 1514 AD – 1572 AD): a leader of the Protestant Reformation and Scottish clergyman who brought reform to the church in Scotland.

Pascal, Blaise (about 1623 AD – 1662 AD): French mathematician, physicist, philosopher, and religious philosopher who composed *Pascal's Wager.* The Wager insists that it is a better *bet* to believe that God exists than to not believe.

Edwards, Jonathan (about 1703 AD – 1758 AD): a preacher, theologian, and missionary to Native Americans. Edwards is recognized as one of America's most important theologians. He was very influential in teaching Reformed theology, which was the Lutheran theological movement that protested Catholicism. Edwards was also active in bringing about the First Great Awakening.

Wesley, John (about 1703 AD – 1791 AD): a Church of England theologian, Wesley was the founder, along with his brother, Charles, of the Methodist movement.

Objecting to George Whitefield's Calvinism, Wesley embraced the Arminian doctrines that were prevalent in the 18th century Church of England.

Whitefield, George (about 1714 AD – 1770 AD): an Anglican Protestant minister who helped spread the teachings of the Great Awakening in Britain and in the British North American colonies. He traveled through all of the American colonies and drew large crowds, and was possibly the most famous preacher in Britain and America in the 18th century.

Finney, Charles (about 1792 AD – 1875 AD): a leader in the Second Great Awakening. Finney studied to become a licensed minister in the Presbyterian Church, although he had many differences of beliefs regarding the doctrines of Presbyterianism. These differences are credited with Finney making many changes to the Old School Presbyterian theology.

Spurgeon, Charles (about 1834 AD – 1892 AD): recognized as the "Prince of Preachers." Spurgeon was a motivating force in the Reformed Baptist tradition, defending the Church in agreement with the 1689 London Baptist Confession of Faith, which was in opposition to the liberal theology tendencies that were being accepted. It is estimated that Spurgeon preached to 10 million people, and would preach in many locations on a weekly basis.

Moody, Dwight L. (about 1837 AD – 1899 AD): Moody's name is still prevalent in Christian circles today. Although not an eloquent speaker, he was able to win many souls to the Lord. As the founder of the Moody Church, the Moody Bible Institute, and Moody Publishers, he is still a strong force in the world of Christians.

Sunday, William "Billy" (about 1862 AD – 1935 AD): an American baseball player who became the most celebrated and influential American evangelist during the first two decades of the 20th century. Converted to evangelical Christianity in the 1880's, Sunday left baseball for Christian ministry by becoming an evangelist in the Midwest. He was so outstanding that he became the nation's most famous evangelist with his down-to-earth, but very enthusiastic, style. Sunday held widely reported revivals in America's largest cities, which attracted the largest crowds of any evangelist before the beginning of the electronic sound system.

McPherson, Aimee Semple (about 1890 AD – 1944 AD): a Christian evangelist from Los Angeles during the 1920's and 1930's. Also known as "Sister Aimee," she was the founder of the Foursquare Church, and led the way in the use of radio to spread the Word.

Notes:

38

Important events in the history of Christianity[7]

The history of Christianity, therefore, must be of concern to all who are interested in the record of man and particularly to all who seek to understand the contemporary human scene.

Kenneth Scott Latourette (1884-1968)

BC stands for "Before Christ", and is an abbreviation used for dating years prior to the birth of Jesus.

AD stands for "Anno Domini", which is Latin for *year of our Lord*. It represents the era in time from the birth of Jesus Christ.

CE stands for "Christian Era" and is another designation for "AD", which is considered to be a Christian conception of time. However, people that are not of a Christian persuasion refer it as: "Common Era" or "Current Era."

God created all things

According to the Holy Scriptures, Jesus was God in the flesh, and he created all things. Jesus always was, is, and always will be. His story begins in Genesis 1:1, as follows:

> *In the beginning God created the heavens and the earth.*

---

7   Most of the dates shown in this chapter are approximations. This chapter is only to give you an overview of the historic occurrences in Christian history. It was not trouble-free.

The Bible teaches that the Father is God, Jesus is God, and the Holy Spirit is God. This is referred to as the triune nature of God.

The first man to sin

The first man to walk upon this earth was Adam. All of mankind has been, or is, of the lineage of Adam. A woman, Eve, was formed from a rib in Adam's chest, to be Adam's mate. These two individuals walked with God, talked with God, and lived together with God in a perfect garden paradise called Eden.

Unfortunately for all of humankind, Adam and Eve disobeyed God, which is known as *original sin*, and the immediate effect was that they died spiritually. As a result, sin entered the entire human race, and this is referred to as *imputed sin. Impute* means "to attribute a fault or misconduct to another." Because of imputed sin, everyone after Adam and Eve was born a sinner.

Countless Biblical scholars have attempted to calculate the age of the world using the Scriptures and the approximate ages of the Old Testament patriarchs and their families. Estimates run from 6,000 to 11,000 years. The exact year of creation remains God's secret.

Judaism began about 2,000 years before Jesus was physically born

Abraham is the father of Judaism, Islam, and Christianity. His name was *Abram*, which means "high father." Later, God changed his name to *Abraham*, which in Hebrew means "the father of many nations."

Abraham was a Hebrew, but he was neither an Israelite nor a Jew. The word *Hebrew* is first mentioned in Genesis 14:13, where Abraham is called Abram the Hebrew. His descendants were also given that designation, including the descendants of Ishmael, who are the Arabs of today. But by common usage, this designation is applied only to those of the nation of Israel.

Although considered the Father of the Faithful, Abraham was not an Israelite. The first Israelite was Jacob, the grandson of Abraham, whose name was changed by God to Israel. God is known as *the God of Abraham, Isaac, and Jacob.*

Approximately 1500 BC

About 500 years following the foundation of the Israelites, when they left Egypt God gave them the Ten Commandments by using Moses as God's spokesman. The Ten

Commandments were just the beginning of God's given laws. Following the Ten Commandments, there were 603 additional laws that the Jews were to obey in order to gain favor with God.

Throughout the centuries many non-Israelites adopted the God, of the Israelites as their God and the faith grew.

Because God is infinitely holy and righteous, he wants his human creation to be just as holy and righteous. The punishment for breaking God's laws is death and separation from God in a place known as *Eternal Hell*. To keep from going to Hell, we sinners needed a way to become righteous.

God came to earth in the form of a man – BC becomes AD

Jesus, the original Christian, was born to Mary and Joseph approximately 2,000 years ago in a stable in the town of Bethlehem.

The foundation of Christianity began with Judaism. Because it was impossible for the Israelites to keep all of God's laws, the blood of lambs was commonly used for sacrifices to God for temporary cleansing. But God, in his infinite wisdom, presented a new plan that would end this practice forever. His name was Jesus, and he was the ultimate and final *Sacrificial Lamb*.

The earliest Christians were Jews who were converted by Christ himself as disciples. These disciples then became apostles because they were sent into the world by Jesus Christ to preach the *Good News of salvation by grace through faith*. Apostle means "one who has been sent."

It is accurate to state that Christianity had its roots in Judaism because the Old Testament laid the foundation for a coming Jewish Messiah.

> *Then Jesus told her, "I am the Messiah!"* John 4:26

AD 30

Jesus began his ministry, which lasted three years.

AD 33

Jesus Christ was crucified on a hill called Golgotha, outside Jerusalem. His body was laid in a borrowed tomb by Roman soldiers and then sealed. Jesus arose from the dead three days later and appeared to his disciples several times during the next 40 days. After 40 days, Jesus ascended into Heaven.

Pentecost is a Jewish festival commemorating the giving of the Torah and the harvest of the Firstfruits. It was no coincidence that the Christian Church officially began on this day.

> *"So let everyone in Israel know for certain that God has made this Jesus, whom you crucified, to be both Lord and Messiah!"* Acts 2:36

The 12 apostles, Jesus' mother and Jesus' family, and many of his disciples gathered together in Jerusalem to celebrate this holiday. While they were praying, a sound like that of a rushing wind filled the house and tongues of fire descended and rested over each of their heads. This was the outpouring of the Holy Spirit on human flesh, promised by God through the prophet Joel. The disciples were suddenly empowered to proclaim the gospel of the risen Christ. They went out into the streets of Jerusalem and began preaching to the crowds gathered for the festival. Not only did the disciples preach with boldness and vigor, but also by a miracle of the Holy Spirit, they spoke in the native languages of the people present, many of whom had come from all corners of the Roman Empire. This created a sensation. The Apostle Peter seized the moment and addressed the crowd, preaching to them about Jesus' death and resurrection for the forgiveness of sins. The result was that about 3,000 people became Christians that day.

Pentecost marks the birth of the Christian Church by the power of the Holy Spirit. *Pentecost* means "50th day," and is celebrated on the seventh Sunday after Easter. Although many American Christians do not celebrate Pentecost, many European churches consider it a celebration.

AD 30 to 70 were the formative years

Although the first Christians were mostly Jewish or Jewish converts, the Gentiles were also hungrily accepting Jesus as the Jewish Messiah. Accusations that the Jews had murdered their own Messiah enraged many Jewish leaders, who began to put a brutal end to this heresy. The greatest example of an enraged Jewish leader was Saul of Tarsus, a Roman tax collector, who is considered by many to be the greatest Christian who ever lived following his conversion to Christianity.

Saul was renamed Paul after being transformed by a visit from Jesus on the road to Damascus following Jesus' resurrection. There is no evidence that Paul ever met

Jesus before this date. It is believed he was responsible for the killing of many Christians before his conversion. Paul's epistles form the bulk of the New Testament, and most agree his ministry had more influence on the growth of Christianity than anyone, anywhere, anytime. It is believed that Paul was beheaded during the reign of the Roman Emporer Nero.

Although Jesus was executed by Rome at an early age, his ministry would have a massive impact on the Roman Empire. The resurrected Jesus commanded the apostles to spread his teachings worldwide. Following Jesus' death, his Good News message of eternal life and hope was spread throughout the Mediterranean region. This was known as the *Apostolic* or *Primitive Church*. Many of the New Testament books were written during this period.

By the late first and early second centuries, a hierarchy began to emerge. This structure was based on the doctrine of Apostolic Succession, in which, the ritual of laying on of hands, a bishop became the spiritual successor of the previous bishop in a line tracing back to the apostles themselves. Other positions of authority were also established.

AD 64 to 312 was the development period

The growth of Christianity continued, but it was plagued by dissention, destruction, torture, and execution. There was significant persecution of Christians at the hands of Roman authorities. Nero ordered that the Apostles Peter and Paul be put to death sometime between AD 64 and 67.

In the first century, Jewish rebels weakened the Roman authority, but the Romans captured Jerusalem and destroyed the Jewish Temple in AD 70. The Romans embraced gods such as Jupiter and Mars for the purpose of gaining blessings from these gods. They wanted nothing to do with Christianity.

The Jews fled from Jerusalem and scattered throughout the vast Roman Empire. But during this same time period, Christianity spread rapidly throughout the Roman Empire and to many other countries.

Although there were problems, Christianity was receiving a reputation of being a faith like none other before. *The Letter to Diognetus*, the work of an unknown author, was one of the most powerful and useful writings in early Christian history that defended its continuation. Written in about 130, it describes Christians to the Romans as follows:

Christians are indistinguishable from other men either by nationality, language or customs. They do not inhabit separate cities of their own, or speak a strange dialect, or follow some outlandish way of life. Their teaching is not based upon reveries inspired by the curiosity of men. Unlike some other people they champion no purely human doctrine. With regard to dress, food, and manner of life in general, they follow the customs of whatever city they happen to be living in, whether it is Greek or foreign. And yet there is something extraordinary about their lives. They live in their own countries as though they were only passing through. They play their full role as citizens, but labor under all the disabilities of aliens. Any country can be their homeland, but for them their homeland, wherever it may be, is a foreign country. Like others, they marry and have children, but they do not expose them. They share their meals, but not their wives. They live in the flesh, but they are not governed by the desires of the flesh. They pass their days upon earth, but they are citizens of heaven. Obedient to the laws, they yet live on a level that transcends the law.

Christians love all men, but all men persecute them. Condemned because they are not understood, they are put to death, but raised to live again. They live in poverty, but enrich many; they are totally destitute, but possess an abundance of everything. They suffer dishonor, but that is their glory. They are defamed, but vindicated. A blessing is their answer to abuse, deference their response to insult. For the good they do they receive the punishment of malefactors, but even then they rejoice, as though receiving the gift of life. They are attacked by the Jews as aliens, they are persecuted by the Greeks, yet no one can explain the reason for this hatred.

To speak in general terms, we may say that the Christian is to the world what the soul is to the body. As the soul is present in every part of the body, while remaining distinct from it, so Christians are found in all the cities of the world, but cannot be identified with the world. As the visible body contains the invisible soul, so Christians are seen living in the world, but their religious life remains unseen. The body hates the soul and wars against it, not because of any injury the soul has done it, but because of the restriction the soul places on its pleasures. Similarly, the world hates the Christians, not because they have done it any wrong, but because they are opposed to its enjoyments.

Christians love those who hate them just as the soul loves the body and all its members despite the body's hatred. It is by the soul, enclosed within the body, that the body is held together, and similarly, it is by the Christians, detained in the world as in a prison, that the world is held together. The soul, though immortal, has a mortal dwelling place; and Christians also live for a time amidst perishable things, while awaiting the freedom from change and decay that will be theirs in heaven. As the soul benefits from the deprivation of food and drink, so Christians flourish under persecution. Such is the Christian's lofty and divinely appointed function, from which he is not permitted to excuse himself.

Christians in Rome experienced horrific persecution. The most terrible period was between 186 and 312, when Roman emperors tortured and executed Christians. In 303, Diocletian (236-316) ordered a persecution of Christians, which was the last and greatest in the Roman Empire.

AD 301 was the turning point

In 301, Armenia became the first country to accept Christianity as a state religion. Christianity spread east to Asia and throughout the Roman Empire, in spite of resistance by the Roman emperors until its legalization by Emperor Constantine in 313.

AD 313 celebrated the legalization of Christianity

Constantine I (272-337) ruled a large portion of the Roman Empire from 306 until his death. He was the first Roman emperor to convert to Christianity. He issued the Edict of Milan in 313, which proclaimed religious tolerance. Constantine feared that the serious disagreements regarding the natures of God the Father, Jesus, and the Holy Spirit within the church would also cause disorder within the Empire.

Emperor Constantine legalized Christianity in the Roman Empire, officially ending persecution. Crucifixion was eliminated and replaced with public hangings, which had been the accepted Roman punishment for capital crimes.

The term *Catholic Church* was first used in the early 2nd century to describe the collective Christian Church. Catholicism is a broad term and applicable to several theologies and doctrines, but Christianity became the official religion of the Roman Empire. Bishops were given positions of admiration in the Roman government. By AD 400, the terms *Roman* and *Catholic* were synonymous.

On March 7, 321, Sunday was declared the official day of rest. Businesses were ordered closed to observe this day. Gladiator games were eliminated shortly thereafter.

Constantine supported the Church financially, built churches, and promoted Christians to high-ranking offices. He also organized the Council of Nicea, held in 325, which was the first *ecumenical* (meaning to seek to achieve worldwide unity among religions through greater cooperation and improved understanding) council that hosted approximately 275 attendees. It was here that the *Nicean Creed* was developed, but it was improved and sanctioned at the First Council of Constantinople in 359. Many Christians have accepted it as doctrinal. The final form of the Nicean Creed is as follows:

> We believe in one God, the Father, the Almighty, maker of heaven and earth, of all that is seen and unseen.
>
> We believe in one Lord, Jesus Christ, the only Son of God, light from light, true God from true God, begotten, not made, of one Being with the Father: through him all things were made. For us and for our salvation he came down from heaven, was incarnate of the Holy Spirit and the Virgin Mary and became truly human. For our sake he was crucified under Pontius Pilate; he suffered death and was buried. On the third day he rose again in accordance with the Scriptures; he ascended into heaven and is seated at the right hand of the Father. He will come again in glory to judge the living and the dead, and his kingdom will have no end.
>
> We believe in the Holy Spirit, the Lord, the giver of life, who proceeds from the Father (and the Son), who with the Father and the Son is worshipped and glorified, who has spoken through the prophets. We believe in one holy catholic and apostolic Church. We acknowledge one baptism for the forgiveness of sins. We look for the resurrection of the dead, and the life of the world to come.
>
> Amen

One of the primary problems of the original Church was the disagreement regarding the nature of God. There were many theories, some of which are still believed today, but the primary three were:

> **Modalism:** Also known as *Sabellianism,* and/or *Oneness theology,* this belief is probably the most common theological error concerning the nature of God. Present-day groups that hold to forms of this error are the United Pentecostal and United Apostolic Churches. A noteable modern adherent of modalism is T. D. Jakes.
>
> In denial of the Trinity, modalism states that God is a singular person who has revealed himself in three forms. Modalists consider God as singular, who first

manifested himself as the Father, second as Jesus, and third as the Holy Spirit; but that all are seperate entities of the same God.

These modes are consecutive and never simultaneous. In other words, the Father, the Son, and the Holy Spirit never all exist at the same time, only one after another. Modalists believe that God revealed himself as Father in the Old Testament, as the Son in Jesus during Christ's ministry on earth, and now as the Holy Spirit after Christ's ascension, thus denying the distinctiveness of the three persons in the Trinity.

In addition, Modalism maintains that water baptism is necessary for salvation and that it must be done with the formula "In Jesus' name" rather than "In the name of the Father, the Son, and the Holy Spirit."

Speaking in tongues is considered a necessary manifestation of the indwelling of the Holy Spirit, and that it is possible to lose one's salvation.

Arianism: This view advocates there is only one God. Therefore, belief in the full diety of Christ would mean the Father and Son (Jesus) were two separate Gods. They believe that Jesus was something like a super-angel. Jehovah's Witnesses are the best example of a church with the Arian belief. Many think the Mormon Church's belief also fits into this category, although Mormons believe the universe has multiple gods.

Trinitarianism is a view that believes in the triune nature of God. God (the Father), Jesus Christ (the Son), and the Holy Spirit (the Counselor) are one. It was adopted as the official belief of Christians, and is still considered to be one of the fundamental foundations of Christianity as pronounced in the Nicean Creed.

Until the reign of Constantine, Christians had been persecuted, but beginning with Roman Catholicism this appeared to reverse itself. Some emperors encouraged pagans to become Christians to avoid persecution.

It was during this time that various church councils were formed to determine official church doctrine, and as the Roman Empire became weaker, the Roman Catholic Church became more powerful. The Church claimed to have apostolic authority over all Christian churches and the Bishop of Rome began to call himself *pope*, meaning "the Father."

This was the beginning of an era referred to as the Dark Ages.

AD 450 to 1000 were The Dark Ages

The Dark Ages are considered the early part of the Middle Ages, referring to the 500 years following the fall of Rome in about AD 450 and continuing until about 1000. Because there was no longer an authority to protect the citizens, Rome and other cities deteriorated when barbarians invaded from northern and central Europe.

The Dark Ages period saw growth in the power of the Christian Church, although much of the growth was developed through monasticism. Many zealous Christians sought to separate themselves from the masses by living in monasteries.

Benedict of Nursia became the driving force behind European monasticism by organizing monasteries and implementing rules. Benedict gave monasticism a permanent place in Western Europe that is still in effect today.

AD 1054 – the Eastern Orthodox Church broke all ties

For centuries, the Western and Eastern Churches had been growing apart. Tensions were evident because what had once been a single church was slowly separating into two. The bishop of Rome (or the pope) excommunicated the patriarch of Constantinople (the leader of the Eastern Church) after the patriarch closed the Western-oriented churches in his area. The event is later known as *The Great Schism*, which led to the Roman Catholic Church and the Greek Orthodox Church becoming two separate entities.

AD 1095 to 1291 – Christian Crusades

A series of seven military conflicts, which were attempts by Christians to reclaim land in the Middle East that had been conquered by Muslim/Arabs, the crusades were brutal and evil. Many people were forced to convert to Christianity.

AD 1517 – The Protestant Reformation

The Protestant Reformation was a movement that began in Europe in 1517, prompted by a Catholic monk named Martin Luther (1483-1546).

Unable to find personal peace by adhering to the dictates of the Roman Catholic Church, Luther dedicated himself to do good works to please God and serve others through prayer for their souls – yet personal peace with God was absent. He devoted himself to fasts, flagellations, long hours in prayer and pilgrimages, and continuous confession. The more he struggled to please God, the more he became depressed by his sinfulness.

While painstakingly studying the Holy Scriptures, Luther began to understand that salvation is a gift of God's grace, only attainable through faith in Jesus as the Messiah. This study convinced him that the Roman Catholic Church had neglected several basic truths. To Luther, the most important of these was the doctrine of forgiveness through Christ's death on the Cross that brought him peace with God.

Luther began an attempt to reform the Roman Catholic Church. His summation of the Gospel was "by Christ alone, through faith alone, by grace alone." He did not believe the Catholic Church was a false church, but felt it must reform errors in church doctrine. This was the beginning of a faith revolution known as the Reformation. On October 31, 1517, in now what is Germany, Luther nailed his *Ninety-Five Theses* to the door of the Wittenberg Castle Church. This was the beginning of Protestantism (from the word *protest*).

Luther's actions were the catalyst that motivated many western Christians who were troubled by the Church's false doctrines and malpractices. Two major contentions were the selling of indulgences by the church, and buying and selling church positions.

Luther's forerunners were scholars such as John Wycliffe and John Hus. Other reformers rapidly followed, such as Ulrich Zwingli and John Calvin. Additional issues of contention were the teaching of Purgatory, devotion to Mary, the intercession of and devotion to saints, most of the sacraments, mandatory celibacy of clergy, and the authority of a pope.

It was from this reformation that many Protestant denominations began. The first was Lutheranism. As the Reformation developed in Germany, various groups in other parts of Europe also began to break away from the Catholic Church.

Reformed Christianity developed in Switzerland based on the teachings of Ulrich Zwingli and John Calvin. When it spread to Scotland under John Knox, the Reformed faith became Presbyterianism. Switzerland was also the origin of the Anabaptists, spiritual ancestors of today's Amish, Mennonites, Quakers, and Baptists. Anglicanism was established in 1534 when England's King Henry VIII left and denied the authority of the pope. This later became Episcopalianism in America. Methodism, based on the teachings of John Wesley, also has its derivation in Anglicanism.

Martin Luther initially hoped to maintain the unity of a reformed Catholic Church, but Pope Leo X excommunicated him in 1520. He was also made an outlaw of the

Holy Roman Empire at the national assembly known as the Diet of Worms, which was a meeting in the Rhineland city of Worms in 1521.

Combat and separation were not the only results of the Protestant Reformation that Luther launched. At the same time, the Protestant Reformation stimulated a deep religious spirituality in Protestant countries including Germany, Scandinavia, England, Scotland, and the Netherlands. Most importantly, the Reformation placed new emphasis on the importance of adhering to the Bible as the definitive source of theology.

AD 1545 to 1563 – Council of Trent

To combat the Protestant Reformation, the Roman Catholic Church initiated the *Counter-Reformation*, also known as the *Catholic Reformation.*

The term "Counter-Reformation" is used primarily by Protestants to describe the changes made by the Catholic Church as a reaction to the Protestant Reformation. However, Catholics prefer to use the term "Catholic Reformation" because they argue they were not reacting to the Protestant Reformation, but instead, were making changes they deemed as timely.

Whichever term is used, it was a period of Catholic revival held in the mid-1500s that addressed contentious issues such as corrupt bishops and priests, indulgences, and other matters that had been revealed through the Protestant Reformation.

The Council of Trent rejected many of the allegations and upheld the basic doctrine of the Roman Catholic Church. The council maintained its position on "salvation by grace through faith plus works," which was not in accordance with Protestant belief.

The council condemned anyone who claimed sacraments were not necessary for salvation. It also upheld the belief in transubstantiation, which claims that the bread and wine used in the Eucharist (Communion) is changed into the literal body and blood of Christ.

Although the basic tenets of the Roman Catholic Church remained unchanged, there were some changes made primarily in the areas of integrity of the administration.

There are still extreme differences between the Roman Catholic Church and Christian denominations that subscribe to the firmness of the *Five Solas,* which are five Latin phrases that emerged during the Protestant Reformation summarizing the reformer's basic beliefs. These are in contradiction to what was/is taught by the Roman Catholic Church:

1. *Sola Scriptura* (by Scripture alone): belief that the Bible is the only inspired and authoritative Word of God. It is the only source for Christian doctrine and is accessible to all.
2. *Sola Fide* (by faith alone): belief that God declares us righteous only by our faith, and there is no need for good works.
3. *Sola Gratia* (by grace alone): belief that salvation comes by God's grace through faith, and there is no need for good works.
4. *Solus Christus* (Christ alone): belief that Christ is the only mediator between God and man, and that no mediator is necessary.
5. *Soli Deo Gloria* (glory to God alone): belief that all glory is to be given to God for the salvation of man, because salvation is accomplished solely through his will.

I recently had a good Catholic friend tell me he thought the Roman Catholic Church was the true church because of their longevity. My reply to him was that if longevity was the determining factor for truth, then the traditional Jewish faith should negate Christianity, and that Jesus was not the Messiah. My friend walked away.

Martin Luther, by studying the Scriptures, rediscovered what the original Church had taught and over time had been convoluted by the tradition of men. Even following Luther's revelation, many misled individuals have deviated from the simple truth that we are saved only by grace through faith in Jesus Christ. This can be found in the Bible, which has complete authority. All glory is to be given to God, and we can give thanks to him directly, needing no other mediator. That's the *Good News*!

Great Awakenings: refers primarily to four specific periods of Christian revivals. The dates are approximations.

The First Great Awakening (1730s – 1760s) was a Calvinistic movement of revivals led by Jonathan Edwards and George Whitefield, who preached that salvation was only an act of God and that humans did not possess the free will to accept or reject salvation. They taught that God chooses those he wants saved and uses irresistible grace to woo them. Accompanying that Calvinistic belief is the statement that once a person is saved, salvation cannot be lost.

The Second Great Awakening (1800s – 1830s) began when Yale theology professor Nathaniel Taylor challenged Calvinism by advocating an Arminian position that mankind has the freedom to accept or reject Jesus as Savior. He also advocated that mankind has the free will to make good and bad moral choices, including those that can cause salvation to be lost.

The Third Great Awakening (1850s – 1900s) encouraged Christian activism by addressing social issues as new denominations of Christianity emerged. The Protestant mainline churches were growing rapidly in numbers while building colleges and universities. Although this Third Awakening was somewhat interrupted by the American Civil War, the war also stimulated revivals.

The Fourth Great Awakening (1960s – today) is an awakening that, in my opinion, has not ended. The Christian landscape has changed dramatically since the 1960s as the system of communication has become super-sophisticated. People are beginning to do their own research through newly published books, radio, television, and the Internet. This is resulting in individuals becoming more sophisticated in areas of creationism, homosexual reasons and rights, abortion, and Bible knowledge. The traditional church is dying as mega-church pastors shed their robes for blue jeans and golf shirts. Home churches are bursting up like popcorn, and women are being recognized as capable spiritual leaders. "Born again" Christians are finally coming out of the closet.

Glossary of Theological Terms[8]

This glossary has been included in anticipation of your continuing study of the New and Old Testaments, as well as the history of Judaism and Christianity. Please keep this book nearby as a tool for your growth. Also, many of the terms that appear here are part of very complex theological theories and have only been included to give you a starting point to become more learned. We strongly recommend that you become familiar with the terms, but that you investigate the meanings through theological books and the Internet.

The terms in this glossary are defined as learned by the author of this book, and have not been cited from any specific source. Although the author believes them to be correct, it is suggested that the theological student refer to specialized sources, such as *Vine's Expository Dictionary of Old and New Testament Words*, or other dictionaries that are compiled for the scholar.

AD: Anno Domini, Latin for "year of our Lord," represents the era from the birth of Jesus Christ onward.

Abiding in Christ: to live in harmony with the Lord by keeping his commandments.

Abomination: something that brings out great dislike.

Abraham's bosom: means to enjoy happiness and rest in Paradise.

Absolution: the remission of guilt and penalty for sin by a priest, following confession.

---

8 Note: When a subject is complex, you may be directed to another term or name within this glossary. There were a number of names, terms, or places that needed elaborate description or explanation because of their importance or complexity. In these cases you will be directed to "also see" the additional names or terms.

Abyss: a bottomless pit – such as Hell.

Adam: the first created human.

Adoration: the act of adoring.

Advent: the period beginning four Sundays before Christmas and observed by some Christians as a season of prayer and fasting in preparation for Christ's second coming. This began in the early church.

Adventism: the doctrine that the second coming of Christ and the end of the world, or age, is near.

Agape: unconditional love.

Age of accountability: the stage of a youth's maturity at which Christians believe God will hold a person accountable for his or her acceptance, or rejection, of Jesus Christ as Savior. Most Christians believe if a youngster dies before this age, they will go to Heaven, but following this age, if they have not accepted Jesus as Savior, they will not be accepted as a *child of God* (a "child of God" is a person who has been born again).

Agnostic: one who believes it is impossible to know if God exists.

Allegory: a story, picture, or play that is fictional, but is presented to illustrate a deeper sense. An example could be the Biblical story of the Garden of Eden. Some believe this to be an allegory, although others interpret it literally.

Altruism: concern for the welfare of others.

Amen: "so be it."

Anabaptist: a member of a radical movement of the 16th-century Reformation who viewed water baptism solely as an external witness to a believer's profession of faith. Anabaptists are still alive and well and continue to believe water baptism is not necessary for salvation. They reject infant baptism, believe in the separation of church from state, and some believe in the shunning of non-believers. Believing in the simplicity of life, a modern example would be the Mennonites.

Angel: the original word, both in Hebrew and Greek, means "messenger." The general term is applied to an assembly of intelligent beings, who surround God and are his messengers or agents to the world. Angels also support the well-being of individuals. According to the Scriptures, they were created long before our present world. Whether pure spirits, or having spiritual bodies, they have no body as we perceive it and are without gender.

The Bible represents them as exceedingly numerous and remarkable in strength. However, we are not to put trust in them, pay them adoration, or pray in their name. Though Scriptures do not state that each individual has a personal guardian angel, it does teach that the angels minister to each and every Christian. Those angels who are considered fallen, by having rebelled against God, are called *angels of Satan*, who are destined to be cast into Hell and reserved unto judgment. Angels are believed to never die.

Angel of the Lord: another term used for Jesus.

Annihilationism: the belief that when the unsaved person dies, that person simply ceases to exist, rather than going to Heaven, Hell, or somewhere else. An annihilationist does not believe that a loving God would allow someone to suffer eternally in Hell. Annihalationism has absolutely no Scriptural basis. Although the belief seems pleasant, it is a man-made idea. However, annihilationists do believe saved people go to Heaven, so they are half-right.

Anointing: the act of consecration by the application of oil, used in consecrating sacred objects or persons, and as preparation for death or in completing the effectiveness of baptism. (also see *consecrate*)

Antichrist: the person who rules the world and opposes God during the last days.

Antinomian: a member of the Christian sect who believes that it is faith alone that is necessary for salvation. (also see *Free grace theology*)

Apocalypse: the last book of the New Testament, also called the Revelation of Saint John the Divine.

Apocalyptical: anything viewed as a prophetic revelation.

Apocrypha: a group of books accepted by Roman Catholics as part of the Bible, but rejected by Christians. (also see *Septuagint*)

Apollos: a friend of Paul who was a valuable helper to him in Corinth. Martin Luther and other scholars have proposed that Apollos is the author of the Book of Hebrews.

Apologetics: referring to the study and practice of demonstrating the truth of Christianity.

Apostle: one who has been sent.

Apostolic legates: those appointed under the authority of an apostle who wrote for them.

Apostolic succession: within some Christian denominations refers to a doctrine asserting that there have been chosen successors of the 12 Apostles, from the 1st century to the present day. Apostolic succession claims those individuals in the succession have inherited Spiritual, ecclesiastical, and sacramental powers and authorities bestowed in them by the apostles, who received their authority from Jesus Christ.

The main advocates of this thinking are the Roman Catholic Church, the Eastern Orthodox churches, some Anglicans, and some Lutherans. A case in point is that the Roman Catholic Church sees Peter as the leader of the Apostles and believes that he later became the first bishop of Rome. Furthermore, they believe that all Roman bishops who followed Peter were/are accepted as the authority in all doctrinal matters.

Most Protestants reject any succession of power based upon the fact that nowhere in Scripture did Jesus, the apostles, nor any other New Testament writer indicate any form of this. In addition, nowhere in the Bible is Peter characterized as supreme over other apostles, nor are any of the 12 Apostles documented as passing their Spiritual gifts and authority to anyone. Most Protestants stand firm that the authority of God is passed by way of the Holy Scriptures.

Aramaic: the language used for nearly all of southwestern Asia after about 300 B.C.

Archangel: an angel of the highest order.

Arianism: the doctrines of Arius, who denied that Jesus was of the same substance as God and held instead that he was only the highest of created beings. Most Christian churches see this view as heretical.

Armageddon: the last battle between good and evil on the plains near Mount Megiddo in Israel.

Ascension: the ascent Christ made into Heaven; celebrated on Ascension Day, the 40th day after Easter.

Atheist: one who does not believe that God exists.

Atonement: the compensation for a loss. When used to describe Christ's death on the Cross, atonement means that his shed blood was the propitiation (a gesture of reconciliation to gain or regain the favor of someone or something) for the sin of mankind. God offers the invitation to all, but only those who respond in faith receive Spiritual birth.

BC: "Before Christ"; an abbreviation used for dating years prior to the birth of Jesus.

Backsliding: abandoning one's discipleship.

Baptism (fire): some interpret the baptism of fire as referring to the day of Pentecost, when the Holy Spirit was sent from Heaven. A more acknowledged interpretation is that the baptism of fire refers to judgment for the damned.

Baptism (infant): The Bible makes it very clear that it is Spiritual baptism that saves, which results from a mature person accepting Jesus Christ as Savior. It is impossible for an infant to make a mature decision, so the mere sprinkling of water on an infant, or dunking that child, adds nothing to the eternal destiny of that person. Infant baptism is not a Biblical practice. The Bible does not record any infants being baptized.

If Christian parents wish to dedicate their child to Christ, then a baby dedication is appropriate, but it still does not affect the destiny of that child as an adult.

Baptism (Spiritual): describes the movement of the Holy Spirit into the new believer, which takes place at the exact time of salvation. A minority of Christians believes this baptism occurs sometime following salvation; however, this is not the common interpretation.

Baptism (water): a Christian symbol proclaiming one's Spiritual regeneration. Via the use of water and the recital of words, the recipient expresses his or her outward declaration of an inward affirmation of Jesus Christ as their personal Savior. This practice is not necessary for salvation, but is well-regarded.

Beatitude: supreme blessedness or happiness.

Beatitudes: nine declarations of blessedness made by Jesus at the *Sermon on the Mount* appearing in Matthew 5:3-11.

Believer: a Christian.

Beget: to father, or to cause to exist.

Bethlehem: Generally believed to be the birthplace of Jesus, although debated by some historians. Meaning "house of bread," it is located five miles south of Jerusalem.

Bible commentary: a Bible that contains interpretations of verses.

Bigot: a person of strong conviction or prejudice, especially in religion, race, or politics, who is intolerant of those who differ with him.

Birthright: entitlements usually bestowed upon the firstborn son, particularly involving an inheritance.

Bishop: a high-ranking Christian clergyman. In modern churches, a bishop is usually in charge of a church or diocese; regarded as having received the highest ordination in unbroken succession from the Apostles in some churches.

Blasphemy: exhibiting disrespect for God.

Blood of Christ: the final sacrifice needed by mankind for the atonement of one's sins if an individual trusts in Jesus' sacrificial death for his salvation.

Blood of the Lamb: the *Blood of Christ*. Before the incarnation, lambs and other animals were sacrificed as payment for sins. However, Jesus' Blood replaced that of the animals.

Body of Christ: the Christian Church.

Book of Life (Lamb's Book of Life): there are many references to the Book of Life throughout the Scriptures, beginning with Exodus 32:32-33:

> *"But now, if you will only forgive their sin—but if not, erase my name from the record you have written!"*
>
> *But the Lord replied to Moses, "No, I will erase the name of everyone who has sinned against me."*

And, ending in Revelation 21:27:

> *Nothing evil will be allowed to enter, nor anyone who practices shameful idolatry and dishonesty—but only those whose names are written in the Lamb's Book of Life.*

(also see *Judgment Seat of Christ*)

Born again: "born from above." The new birth enjoyed by a Christian upon his conversion and regeneration. When born as humans, we are born from a physical mother. When born of the Spirit, we are born into the body of Jesus Christ, referred to as the Church. It is only following one's Spiritual birth that an individual is entitled to the free gift of eternal life in Heaven, which is made available by the finished work of Christ. (also see *Finished work of Jesus Christ*)

Bread of life: the Spiritual food needed by man. Without the bread of life, man cannot live Spiritually. Just as physically, man needs to eat in order to live, the bread of life gives nourishment for the soul. Unless one eats from the bread of life, he faces eternal death.

Bride of Christ: the Christian Church is the bride, and Jesus Christ is the bridegroom.

Byzantine Empire: the term used since the 16th century to describe the Greek-speaking Roman Empire of the Middle Ages, ruled from Constantinople. It is also known as the Eastern Roman Empire. Many consider Constantine I to be the first Byzantine Emperor.

CE: refers to a period of time known as the *Christian Era* and is another designation for AD. It is considered to be a Christian concept of time; however, people who are not of a religious persuasion prefer to use *Common Era* or *Current Era*.

Caesar: the title assumed by the Roman emperors after Julius Caesar. In the New Testament, this title is given to various emperors as sovereigns of Judea without their accompanying distinctive proper names. The last of these was Nero, but the name was retained by his successors as a title belonging to the imperial dignity.

Calvary: the hill outside Jerusalem where Jesus was crucified. It is also known as *Golgotha*, a Hebrew word meaning "place of the skull." The name Golgotha is derived from the Aramaic word *gulgulta*, but later translated into the Latin word for skull, *calvaria*, which was later converted into the English word Calvary.

Canaan: son of Ham and grandson of Noah. (also see *Canaanite*)

Canaanites: the descendants of Canaan. Their first habitation was in the land of Canaan, where they multiplied extremely, acquired great riches by trade and war, and sent out colonies throughout the islands and coasts of the Mediterranean. When the measure of their idolatries and abominations was completed, God delivered their country into the hands of the Israelites, who conquered it under Joshua's leadership.

The extermination of these tribes, however, was never fully carried out, and even after the return from captivity survivors of five of the Canaanite tribes were still found in the land. The name *Canaanite* is also sometimes used to designate the non-Israelite inhabitants of the land in general.

Canonize: to approve as being within the body of officially established rules, such as the books contained in the Bible. In order to be canonized, books have to meet the criteria for inclusion.

Capernaum: a city on the northern shore of the Sea of Galilee and the heart of Jesus' ministry.

Carnal: of the flesh; worldly.

Catechism: a manual or oral instruction for moral and religious instruction.

Catholicism: is a broad term and applicable to several theologies and doctrines, but is generally used referring to the Roman Catholic Church. The word *catholic* generally means "universal." When capitalized it refers to the Catholic Church. The term *Catholic Church* was first used in the early 2nd century to describe the collective Christian Church.

In 313 AD, the Roman Emperor Constantine had a conversion experience, which led to legalizing Christianity in the Roman Empire. In the early centuries of legal Christianity, it was uncommon for Christian priests or bishops to hold more than one religious or secular office. Usually the priest or bishop was a religious adviser to the government official, who may or may not have been Christian. Roman Catholic bishops were given positions of honor within the Roman government and even though it rapidly became the prevailing religion in the empire, it was not the only existing religion. It was after the empire began to disintegrate that Christian officials assumed governmental roles in the vacuum left by the broken Roman government.

Until the reign of Constantine, Christians had been persecuted, but beginning with Roman Catholicism this persecution diminished. However, some emperors encouraged pagans to become Christians to avoid persecution and some actively supported peaceful evangelism and apologetics.

During this era infant water baptism was introduced to wash away original sin, and that ritual is still practiced today, although not considered adequate. Christians (a person must be born again to be considered a Christian) consider water baptism to be an outward expression of an inward confession.

Also, during this time, various church councils were formed to determine official church doctrine. As the Roman Empire became weaker, the Roman Catholic Church became more powerful. The Church claimed to have apostolic authority over all Christian churches and the Bishop of Rome began to call himself *pope*, meaning "the Father." In 1054, the Eastern Orthodox Church broke all ties. (also see *Apostolic succession*)

The Roman Catholic Church was dominant until the 16th century, when a Catholic monk named Martin Luther was unable to find personal peace by adhering to the dictates of the church. Martin dedicated himself to do good deeds to please God and to serve others, yet inner-peace with God evaded him. He devoted himself to fasts, flagellations, lengthy hours in prayer, and constant confession. The more he struggled to please God, the more aware he became of his sinfulness.

While painstakingly studying the Holy Scriptures, Luther began to discover, comprehend, and appreciate that salvation is a gift of God's grace, only attainable through faith in Jesus as the Messiah. This study convinced him that the Roman Catholic Church had lost sight of several central truths. To Luther, the most important of these was the doctrine of forgiveness via Christ's death on the Cross, which brought him peace with God.

Luther began an attempt to reform the Roman Catholic Church. His summation of the Gospel was "by Christ alone, through faith alone, by grace alone." Luther was adamant the Catholic Church needed to reform its doctrine because it erred in many ways. This was the beginning of a faith transformation known as the Reformation. On October 31, 1517, in what is now Germany, Luther nailed his *Ninety-Five Theses* to the door of the Wittenberg Castle Church. This was the inauguration of Protestantism (from the verb *protest*).

The official position of the Roman Catholic Church is that a person must believe in Jesus Christ, be baptized, receive the Eucharist, partake in other sacraments, and obey the scores of dictates of the Roman Catholic Church. Furthermore, the Roman Catholic Church teaches that a person never really has the complete assurance he or she will go to Heaven until given the *Last Rites*. This has the effect of keeping its members in bondage until the moment of their death.

Although the Catholic Church reveres the Holy Bible as the word of God, the church has also adopted the *Catechism*, *Sacred Tradition*, and the *Magisterium of the Church* as additional authorities.

WARNING: Beware of any religion that claims to be of the Christian faith if it has a book, or books, that must accompany the Bible to defend its beliefs. The New and Old Testaments are all that are needed.

*Let God's curse fall on anyone, including us or even an angel from heaven,
who preaches a different kind of Good News than the one we preached to you.*
Galatians 1:8

Charismatic: derived from *charisma,* the Greek word for "gift." This term is used to describe Christians who believe some Christians are given supernatural gifts, such as prophecy and speaking in tongues.

Chasten: to punish.

Cheap grace: grace without discipleship, although grace is not cheap because it was paid for with the Blood of Jesus. (also see *Grace*)

Christen: to baptize into a Christian church, usually referring to infant baptism.

Christendom: the worldwide community of Christians.

Christian: a term that was first used in Antioch; now used everywhere to describe those who trust in Jesus' death, burial, and resurrection as their only means for salvation.

Christianity: the Christian belief that is founded on the teachings of Jesus.

Christology: the study of Christ's person and qualities.

Chronology: the science that deals with measuring time by regular divisions and assigns to events their proper dates.

Communion: See *Lord's Supper.*

Concordance: an alphabetical index of the principal words in a book, citing the passages in which they occur.

Conditional election: a controversial Arminian belief in Christian theology believing that God accepts only those who have faith in Christ as their Savior. This belief emphasizes the importance of a person's free will; however, God has known from the time of creation who would come to him. Many of those who embrace this belief also believe that salvation can be lost.

This Arminian position is in contrast to the Calvinist doctrine of *unconditional election,* which is the belief that before God created the world, he chose to save some people according to his own purposes – apart from any condition related to that person's behavior. (also see *Unconditional election*)

Confirmation: the rite by which persons are inducted into the church.

Consecrate: to set apart as sacred certain persons, animals, places, objects, or times.

Consubstantiation: the belief that Christ's body and Blood are spiritually "present" during the Eucharist (communion). The word *present* is somewhat confusing because this does not mean the body and Blood of Christ are literally *present within* the bread and wine, but *alongside*. This concept is the belief of many Protestants and is not to be confused with *transubstantiation*. (also see *Transubstantiation*)

Corinth: ancient Greece's most important trade city, where the Apostle Paul established a thriving church.

Covenant: agreement. In Christianity, it usually refers to the *Old Covenant*, which was obeying laws and making sacrifices; and/or the *New Covenant*, which is Jesus.

Creed: an authoritative formula or summary of the essential articles of a faith.

Crucifixion: the method of execution used by the Romans by nailing a prisoner to a cross.

Cult: in Christianity, a religion regarded as unorthodox or Satanic.

Damascus: a celebrated metropolis of Syria, first mentioned in Genesis. Damascus is now probably the oldest city on the globe. It is located in a beautiful and fertile plain 130 miles northeast of Jerusalem.

After various changes in government, Syria was invaded by the Romans in 64 BC. Damascus became the seat of the government of the province. In AD 37, Aretas, the king of Arabia, became master of Damascus, having driven back Herod Antipas. Damascus is memorable because Paul was on his way there when he had his conversion experience.

David: second king of Israel, ancestor of Jesus Christ, and writer of numerous Psalms.

Deacon: minister or servant.

Dead Sea Scrolls: 500 scrolls and scroll fragments discovered accidentally in 1947 by a shepherd in a series of caves along the Dead Sea. Considered the most significant discovery in many centuries, these scrolls, written between 250 BC and AD 68, provide amazing insights into the practices and beliefs of the Qumran Community, Jews who had close ties with the early Christians. Although the scrolls are Jewish and not Christian, they have assisted scholars in reconstructing the history of Israel and the Holy Land between 300 BC and AD 135.

Deist: one who believes in a god who exerts no influence on men or the world he created.

Denomination: an organized group of religious congregations.

Devotional: a book filled with daily readings that Christians use as a Bible reading supplement.

Disciple: a follower of Jesus Christ.

Dispensationalism: a system of theology based upon what we understand happened in the past in relation to what was recorded in the Scriptures, and what we anticipate will happen in the future based on the prophetic writings. This system sees God working with man in different ways during different dispensations or time periods. While dispensations are not ages, we tend to see them now as ages as we look back on specific time periods when they were in force.

Most traditional Dispensationalists recognize seven distinct dispensations.

1. Innocence – Adam
2. Conscience – After man sinned, up to the flood
3. Government – After the flood, man allowed to eat meat, death penalty instituted
4. Promise – Abraham through Moses and the giving of the Law
5. Law – Moses to the Cross
6. Grace – The Cross to the millennial kingdom
7. Millennial Kingdom – A 1,000-year reign of Christ on earth centered in Jerusalem

While not everyone needs to agree on this breakdown, the Dispensationalist's view is that God is working with man in a progressive way. At each stage, man has failed to be obedient to the responsibilities set forth by God.

While opponents will point out that Dispensationalism is relatively new as a system of theology, evidence exists from the early church writers that there was clearly an understanding that God dealt with his people differently in progressive dispensations, and that Israel wasn't seen as replaced by the Church. (also see *Replacement Theology*)

Doctrine: the principle or position of a belief system.

Doctrine of Illumination: the Holy Spirit's work in enabling the believer to understand the truths of Scripture and how the passages apply to the reader/believer. The text usually quoted to support this belief is 1 Corinthians 2:14-15:

> *But people who aren't spiritual can't receive these truths from God's Spirit. It all sounds foolish to them and they can't understand it, for only those who are spiritual can understand what the Spirit means. Those who are spiritual can evaluate all things, but they themselves cannot be evaluated by others.*

Doctrine of Inspiration: belief that the Bible is the inspired word of God, evidenced by its moral teachings plus the prophecies about the future and their fulfillment. The text usually quoted to support this belief is 2 Timothy 3:16-17:

> *All Scripture is inspired by God and is useful to teach us what is true and to make us realize what is wrong in our lives. It corrects us when we are wrong and teaches us to do what is right. God uses it to prepare and equip his people to do every good work.*

Docetism: one of many theories that began in the early Church regarding the nature of Jesus Christ. This theory maintained that he was a totally divine being who only appeared to be human. From that, many went further to claim that he didn't really suffer a crucifixion because it was just an illusion.

Dogma: a system of doctrines proclaimed true by a religious sect.

Doxology: from the Greek terms *doxa,* meaning "glory," and *logos,* meaning "word" or "speaking." Among Christian traditions, a doxology is typically a sung expression of praise to the Holy Trinity.

Dying to self: a very widely used term in Christendom meaning to relinquish all that one has to follow Jesus.

Easter: a festival in the Christian Church commemorating the Resurrection of Christ, celebrated on the first Sunday following the full moon that occurs around March 21.

Easy beliefism: the idea that more than belief and trust in Jesus Christ is needed to be saved. It is often used as a derogatory remark towards Christians who lack discipleship.

Ebonitism: one of the many theories that began in the early church regarding the nature of Jesus Christ. It maintained that Jesus was a human being, not at all divine, and that he was given certain gifts by God's Spirit that set him apart from other people – similar to Moses. Because of the God-given gifts, Jesus was deemed the Messiah or Christ, but that meant only that God chose him, not that he was savior of all humankind. The Law of Moses was still what counted with God. The church rejected this idea as early as AD 120.

Ecclesiastical: pertaining to a church, especially as an organized institution.

Ecumenical: seeking to achieve worldwide unity among religions through greater cooperation and improved understanding.

Elder: one of the governing officers of the church, often having pastoral or teaching functions.

End times: events surrounding the Second Coming of Christ.

Epiphany: a sudden, clear appearance of the intrinsic properties or meaning of something. In Christianity, it is referring to Jesus, the carpenter, revealing himself as the Christ.

Episcopal: a church that is governed by bishops.

Epistle: one of the letters written by an apostle and included in the New Testament.

Eschatology: the branch of theology that is concerned with the end times. Derived from the Greek words *eschatos* meaning "last" and *logy* meaning "the study of." There are various opinions among Christian theologians based on conflicting Biblical interpretations, but following are the three most popular:

Amillennialism: Amillennialists do not believe in a literal "1,000-year theocratic reign" upon Earth. They deny any future restoration of Israel to any particular blessing. This view is very broadly accepted by a wide cross section of Christendom. The amillennialist view is accepted among many Catholics and some Protestants.

Post-Millennialism: Post-millennialists usually hold to the literal 1,000-year period, but some consider it just to mean a long period of time. They also believe that the millennium has already begun and that the forces of Satan will gradually be defeated by the expansion of God's kingdom. Many post-millennialists are *preterists*, which means that many of the end-time prophecies have been fulfilled.

Pre-Millennialism: The belief that Jesus will literally be on earth for his 1,000-year reign. It is called pre-millennialism because the system holds that Jesus will physically appear prior to the beginning of the millennium.

Esoteric: knowledge limited to a small group of people.

Essenes: a Jewish religious sect not actually mentioned in the Bible but described by Josephus, Philo, and mentioned in the Dead Sea Scrolls. Most members lived communal, celibate lives. They observed Jewish law very strictly and they practiced ceremonial baptisms. Essenes were apocalyptic, and they opposed Temple priesthood.

Eternal life: unending reward and glory for those who trust Jesus Christ as Savior.

Eternal death: unending penalty for those who reject Jesus Christ as Savior.

Eternal security: the work of God that guarantees salvation is received from God and it cannot be lost or taken away.

Etymology: analysis of the origin and development of a word by tracing its development from its earliest use.

Eucharist: See *Lord's Supper*.

Evangelical: a Christian who believes one is saved (worthy of eternal life in Heaven) only by grace through faith. An evangelical believes good deeds are a person's way of thanking God for the Blood of Jesus, but have no effect on one's salvation. This is referred to as the *Good News* or *Gospel of Jesus Christ.* Evangelicals generally believe one must be "born again" to receive eternal life in Heaven.

Evangelist: one who preaches, teaches, and shares the Gospel of Jesus Christ – salvation by grace through faith. 2 Corinthians 5:18 tells us that God "...has given to us the task of reconciling people to him" (winning the lost to Christ).

Evil One: Satan.

Existentialism: philosophical movement emphasizing individual existence, freedom, and choice.

Fable: a fictitious, legendary story intended to enforce a useful truth.

Faith: belief that does not rest on logical proof or material evidence. In religion, it is belief and trust in God and the doctrines expressed in the Scriptures or other sacred works.

> *Faith is the confidence that what we hope for will actually happen; it gives us assurance about things we cannot see.* Hebrews 11:1

Fall of man: the result of the original sin of Adam and Eve.

Filled with the Spirit: a term that is used frequently by Charismatics to describe their experience of speaking in tongues, healings, and other gifts they claim are the manifestation of the Holy Spirit.

Finished work of Jesus Christ: When Jesus said, *"It is finished,"* he was saying that through his sacrificial death on the Cross, the sins of every person were paid for – thus making eternal life in Heaven possible for those who trust Jesus Christ as Savior.

Everyone who places his or her faith in the finished work of Jesus Christ, including his resurrection, receives this gift, which is neither earned nor deserved, but which is freely given to us by a gracious God.

First fruits: first sheaf of harvested grain given to God.

Five Crowns: although eternal life in Heaven is a gift, the rewards we receive are earned while we are here on Earth. This doctrine pertains to the future rewards for the Christian discussed in the New Testament of the Bible. They are not available to us now, but we will receive them after Christ's return. The Bible tells us some things about the crowns, but not everything. A big part of the rewards will be the surprise of finding out everything about our new life, and the privileges that go with it.

1. *The Incorruptible Crown*: Received for running the race. This crown will never be destroyed. We will be immortal, and so will this crown. *See 1 Corinthians 9:25*
2. *The Crown of Rejoicing*: This is the soul-winner's crown. When he does return, our earthly, mortal bodies will be changed to be like his – immortal and glorious. *See 1 Thessalonians 2:19*
3. *The Crown of Righteousness*: This crown will be given on the day of Christ's return to those who have lived their lives anticipating this day. *See 2 Timothy 4:8*
4. *The Crown of Glory*: Happy is the person who endures trials, tribulations, and temptations. For when he is proved, he will receive the crown of life. This crown will be given to those instructing others in God's Word. *See 1 Peter 5:4*
5. *The Crown of Life*: This is sometimes termed the "martyr's crown." It is for those who suffer for the cause of Christ. Christ gives this crown, like the others, personally. *See Revelation 2:10*

Five Solas: five Latin phrases that emerged during the Protestant Reformation that summarize the Reformer's basic beliefs. These are in contradiction to what is taught by the Roman Catholic Church:

1. *Sola Scriptura* ("by Scripture alone"): belief that the Bible is the only inspired and authoritative Word of God. It is the only source for Christian doctrine and is accessible to all.
2. *Sola Fide* ("by faith alone"): belief that God declares us righteous only by our faith, and there is no need for good works.
3. *Sola Gratia* ("by grace alone"): belief that salvation comes by God's grace through faith, and there is no need for good works.
4. *Solus Christus* ("Christ alone"): belief that Christ is the only mediator between God and man, and that no human mediator is necessary.
5. *Soli Deo Gloria* ("glory to God alone"): belief that all glory is to be given to God for mans salvation, because salvation is accomplished solely through his will.

Free from bondage: free from depending on *adhering to laws* for salvation.

Free grace theology (antinomianism): belief system that states that faith and trust alone in the finished work of Jesus Christ is all that is necessary for salvation. The most frequent attack on salvation by grace alone is that this belief system encourages sin. Salvation by grace alone is not to be misconstrued as a license to sin, because when a person is saved, the Holy Spirit comes into that individual as counselor.

> *But you are not controlled by your sinful nature. You are controlled by the Spirit if you have the Spirit of God living in you. (And remember that those who do not have the Spirit of Christ living in them do not belong to him at all.)* Romans 8:9

> *So now there is no condemnation for those who belong to Christ Jesus. And because you belong to him, the power of the life-giving Spirit has freed you from the power of sin that leads to death. The law of Moses was unable to save us because of the weakness of our sinful nature. So God did what the law could not do. He sent his own Son in a body like the bodies we sinners have. And in that body God declared an end to sin's control over us by giving his Son as a sacrifice for our sins. He did this so that the just requirement of the law would be fully satisfied for us, who no longer follow our sinful nature but instead follow the Spirit.* Romans 8:1-4

> *Let me ask you this one question: Did you receive the Holy Spirit by obeying the law of Moses? Of course not! You received the Spirit because you believed the message you heard about Christ. How foolish can you be? After starting your Christian lives in the Spirit, why are you now trying to become perfect by your own human effort?* Galatians 3:2-3

The opposing position is called *Lordship salvation*, which is the teaching that to be saved a person must not only trust Jesus as Savior, but also accept the Lord as his authority evidenced by good works. In other words, Jesus cannot be considered a person's Savior without simultaneously being Lord of that person's life, and that good works are necessary to confirm salvation. (also see *Galatianism*)

Free will: the ability of an individual to make his own decisions without God's intervention. This term is frequently used regarding man's ability to either accept or reject Jesus Christ as Savior. (also see *Conditional election*)

Free-will offering: an offering that is voluntary out of love, rather than one that is expected or ordered, such as the Old Testament law of tithing. (also see *Tithing*)

Free worship: a non-traditional, non-structured form of worship services that proponents consider a more flexible approach that appeals to the needs of congregations because it is more in line with the historical ministry of Jesus and the early church. (also see *Liturgy*)

Fundamentalism: any religious inclination that firmly embraces its basic principles. Christian fundamentalism believes the original manuscripts of the Bible are perfect, and that the resulting Bibles are correct, although subject to interpretation.

Gabriel: an archangel who acts on God's behalf.

Galatianism: the belief that Christians must add works to their faith to be saved.

Galilee: the most northern of the three provinces of Palestine; Galilee was the home of Jesus before his ministry.

Gap theory: the view that God created a fully functional Earth with all animals, including the dinosaurs and other creatures we know only from the fossil record, then something happened to destroy the Earth completely, and it became void. God then re-created the Earth in its paradise form, as further described in Genesis. The gap is presumed to be between Genesis 1:1 and 1:2.

Those who embrace this theory do so to resolve the claim of modern scientists that the earth is billions of years old. Even some Christians accept this as a possibility, although there are many disputes within Christendom.

Gehenna: originally a deep, narrow glen to the south of Jerusalem, where the idolatrous Jews offered their children in sacrifice to Molech (the fire god). This valley afterward became the common receptacle for all the refuse of the city. Here, the dead bodies of animals and of criminals and all kinds of filth were cast and consumed by fire, which was always burning. Gehenna became the representation of the place of everlasting destruction.

Gentile: a person who is not Jewish.

Gethsemane: the garden, presumably of olives, where Jesus went for prayer prior to his betrayal and arrest, which also took place in this garden.

Gnosis: knowledge of spiritual truth held by ancient Gnostics.

God incarnate: God becoming the human known as Jesus Christ.

Golden calf: a molten image of a calf, which the idolatrous Israelites formed at Sinai. This symbol was borrowed from the custom of the Egyptians. It was destroyed at the command of Moses.

Golgotha: See *Calvary*.

Good deeds: things people do to please God.

Gospel: translation of the Latin word *evangelium* referring to the *Good News* of salvation by grace through faith – made possible through the death, burial, and resurrection of Jesus Christ.

Gospels: the first four books of the New Testament: Matthew, Mark, Luke, and John.

Grace: receiving something that is undeserved. From a Christian perspective, grace is what God shows to humans by offering salvation through the death, burial, and resurrection of Jesus Christ. Although free to the recipient, it is costly because the price was the shed Blood of Jesus Christ. (also see *Cheap Grace*)

Great Commission, The: the instruction of the resurrected Jesus to his disciples that they spread his teachings to all the nations of the world. The commission from Jesus has been interpreted by evangelical Christians as meaning that his followers have the responsibility to go, teach, and baptize. It has become a tenet that emphasizes missional work and evangelism. Although the command was initially given directly only to Christ's Eleven Apostles, many Christians have interpreted the commission as a directive to all Christians of every time and place. The most familiar version of the Great Commission is depicted in the Gospel of Matthew 28:16-20:

> *Then the eleven disciples left for Galilee, going to the mountain where Jesus had told them to go. When they saw him, they worshiped him—but some of them doubted!*
>
> *Jesus came and told his disciples, "I have been given all authority in heaven and on earth. Therefore, go and make disciples of all the nations, baptizing them in the name of the Father and the Son and the Holy Spirit. Teach these new disciples to obey all the commands I have given you. And be sure of this: I am with you always, even to the end of the age."*

Some Christians believe the Great Commission ceased with the cessation of the gifts of the Holy Spirit proving that only the apostles were called to evangelization. They also say that nowhere in the Bible does it order new believers to evangelize. However, the majority of Christians who enjoy the mission of evangelization do not do it because they were ordered to do so by words in a book, but are prompted by the Holy Spirit who now lives in them. Evangelization is not a law, it is a privilege and a pleasure.

Guilt: extreme awareness of having done something wrong, sometimes accompanied by unforgiveness and self-degradation. Used by Satan to tempt people into moving progressively further from God.

Hades: a Greek word used to denote the state or place of the dead. All the dead alike went into this place before the Ascension of Christ. To "be buried," to "go down to the grave," and to "descend into Hades," are all equivalent expressions. This word is the usual rendering of the Hebrew word *sheol*, the common destination of the departed. This term is of comparatively rare occurrence in the Greek New Testament. It is contemplated as a kind of kingdom that could never overturn the foundation of Christ's Kingdom. (also see *Hell*)

Hallelujah: a word used to express thanksgiving and praise.

Heaven: primarily the region of the air and clouds, and of the planets and stars, but in Christianity it refers to the place of divine paradise above the visible heavens. It is commonly called "the third Heaven." People who accepted Jesus Christ as Savior dwell there with God, Jesus, and other individuals who were saved prior to their death. Some believe our deceased pets will also be there. We know little of the exact location and appearance of Heaven; however, the Scriptures tell us there is no sin or evil. (also see *New Jerusalem*)

Hell: the Hebrew word *Sheol* (occurring in the Old Testament 65 times) and the Greek *Hades*, usually translated "Hell," often signifies the place of deceased individuals who rejected Jesus Christ as Savior.

The term *Hell* is most commonly applied to the place of punishment in the unseen world and is usually represented in the Greek New Testament by the word *Gehenna*, *valley of Hinnom*. Other expressions are also used, to illustrate the dreadfulness of the suffering there. It is described as "outer darkness," "furnace of fire," "unquenchable fire," and "fire and brimstone."

The wretchedness of Hell will be accentuated because it lacks the love of God, and includes the presence of Satan. The degrees of suffering will be proportioned to the degrees of guiltiness. The fury of God will never cease to abide upon the unsaved.

A person can avoid this eternal Hell by accepting the finished work of Jesus Christ as truth. (also see *Hades*)

Heretic: one who believes false teaching.

Heresy: false teaching that is contradictory, or hostile, to the teachings of Christianity. An opinion or doctrine contrary to accepted church dogma.

Hermeneutics: the study of the methods of interpretation, specifically of the Bible.

Herod: the name of a number of Roman rulers in the Palestine region during Jesus' time.

Hierarchy: government by priests, as in the Roman Catholic Church.

Holiness: completely devoted to God in every aspect of life.

Holy: exalted or worthy of complete devotion as one perfect in goodness and righteousness.

Holy Ghost (Holy Spirit): the third person of the Trinity.

Holy Grail: the chalice used by Christ at the Last Supper.

Homily: from the Greek for "discourse." A homily is a sermon on a Biblical text; there is no distinction between a homily and sermon.

Hypostasis: that which forms the nature of something.

Icon: an image or representation. In the Eastern Church, it is an image of Christ, the Virgin Mary, or a saint.

Idolatry: the worship of a physical object as a god.

Immaculate conception: in the Roman Catholic Church, the miraculous conception by which the Virgin Mary conceived without original sin. It is further believed she lived a sinless life. This is not to be confused with the *virginal conception*. (also see *Virginal conception*)

Immersion: baptism by complete submersion in water.

Impute: to take something that belongs to someone and credit it to another's account.

Incarnate: in human form. Jesus was God incarnate.

Intercessor: one who intervenes on another's behalf, as Christ has done for us. We are also to intercede in prayer for others.

Jehovah: God's self-existent name, *I am who I am.*

Judgment, The Great White Throne: final judgment for those who have rejected Christ as Savior, and who are going to Hell regardless of their life's works or lack thereof. Remember, these may be very fine, moral people who have tried to work their way to Heaven rather than trusting in Jesus.

> *And I saw a great white throne and the one sitting on it. The earth and sky fled from his presence, but they found no place to hide. I saw the dead, both great and small, standing before God's throne. And the books were opened, including the Book of Life. And the dead were judged according to what they had done, as recorded in the books. The sea gave up its dead, and death and the grave gave up their dead. And all were judged according to their deeds. Then death and the grave were thrown into the lake of fire. This lake of fire is the second death. And anyone whose name was not found recorded in the Book of Life was thrown into the lake of fire.* Revelation 20:11-15

Not to be confused with the *Judgment Seat of Christ*. (also see *Judgment Seat of Christ*).

Judgment Seat of Christ (Christ's Judgment): this judgment is for those who have been saved by grace through faith, and whose names remain in the *Book of Life*.

If a person dies "as a believer" his or her name is retained in the Book of Life, but if he or she dies "as an unbeliever" his or her name is erased and they are considered unrighteous.

> *Erase their names from the Book of Life;*
> *Don't let them be counted among the righteous.*
> Psalm 69:28

This judgment is to decide what the believer's rewards, or lack thereof, will be in Heaven according to his or her works on earth. The judgment seat of Christ, therefore, involves believers giving an account of their lives to Christ. The judgment seat of Christ does not determine salvation – that was determined by our decision to accept or reject Christ's sacrifice on our behalf. At the judgment seat of Christ, believers are rewarded based on how faithfully they served Christ. Some of the things we might be judged on are how well we obeyed the Great Commission, how victorious we were over sin, and how well we controlled our tongues. The Bible speaks of believers receiving crowns for different things based on how faithfully they served Christ.

> *For we must all stand before Christ to be judged. We will each receive whatever we deserve for the good or evil we have done in this earthly body.*
> 2 Corinthians 5:10

Christ's judgment should not be confused with the *Great White Throne Judgment.* (also see *Book of Life* and *Judgment, The Great White Throne*)

Justification: what saves. When we are justified, it means that we are made righteous through grace because of the Blood of Christ. The Christian's righteousness is imputed by God because of his love for us. It is a gift and is not earned.

Kenosis: the theory that Jesus emptied himself of his divine nature during his incarnation (becoming a man). Although his form was in the likeness of men, Jesus did not cease to be God. However, during his earthly ministry, he did not display the magnificence of God, and he submitted himself to the authority of God the Father.

Kingdom of God: includes everything that is under God.

Kingdom of God (Kingdom of Heaven): there are several passages that show that the kingdom of God and the kingdom of Heaven are synonymous. Some futurists believe there are as many as three kingdoms of God, and possibly more.

King James Bible: the original Bible was written in Hebrew, Aramaic, and Greek. However, in January 1604, King James Charles Stuart of Scotland called the Hampton Court Conference in order to hear of things "pretended to be amiss" in the church. At this conference, Dr. John Reynolds, a Puritan, requested of the king a new translation of the Bible because those that were allowed during the reigns of Henry the VIII and Edward VI were corrupt.

In July of 1604, the king appointed 54 men to the translation committee. These men were the best linguists and scholars in the world. Much of their work on the King

James Bible formed the basis for our linguistic studies today. These men were not only world-class scholars, they were Christians who lived holy lives as deans and presidents of major universities such as Oxford, Cambridge, and Westminster.

In 1611, the Authorized King James Version of the Bible was published, and it has become the best-selling book ever. Of the more than 2,000 translations of the Bible, this is the most popular.

KJV: Abbreviation for the King James Version of the Bible.

Laity: the common people, as distinguished from the clergy. (also see *Laymen*)

Lamb of God: another name for Jesus Christ. (also see *Blood of the Lamb*)

Lamb's Book of Life: the specifics of the Lamb's Book of Life are debatable. Some scholars believe the names of all people were placed in this book in eternity past, but if a person dies being unsaved, their name is removed and they are sent to Hell. Other scholars believe a person's name is put into this book at the time he or she is saved and that their name remains there. (also see *Book of Life*)

Last Supper: the final meal of Jesus with his followers in Jerusalem the evening before his crucifixion on the orders of Pilate, around AD 33. During the meal Jesus is said to have expressed a desire to be remembered by breaking bread and sharing a cup of wine, inspiring the central ritual of Christianity variously called the Eucharist, Lord's Supper, or Holy Communion. (also see *Lord's Supper*)

Latin Vulgate: the Latin version of the Bible that was translated by Saint Jerome in the 4th century at the request of Pope Damascus. The Vulgate became the most commonly used version of the Bible by the Roman Catholic Church.

Law of Moses: the laws, beginning with the Ten Commandments, that God gave to the Israelites through Moses. It includes many rules of religious observance given in the first five books of the Old Testament. In Judaism, these books are called the *Torah*.

Laying on of hands: Christians place their hands on the head, or upper torso, of an individual to bestow blessings, including healings.

Layman: in Christianity, a person not of the clergy.

Leavened: bread that is made to rise or become soft using yeast or other agents. Leaven was a symbol of sin to the Jews. (also see *Unleavened*)

Levite: a descendant of the tribe of Levi. More particularly, an officer in the Jewish church, who was employed in manual service, as in bringing wood and other necessaries for the sacrifices. The Levites also sung and played musical instruments. They were subordinate to the priests, the descendants of Aaron, who were also of the family of Levi.

Liturgy: a system of rituals and ceremony, usually traditional, followed in church services and worship. An example would be a Catholic mass. (also see *Free worship*)

Logos: Greek, meaning "word" or "speaking." In Christianity, *logos* is the written word, such as the Bible, and not a direct revelation from God to you. This is the opposite of *rhema*. (also see *Rhema*)

Lordship salvation: the teaching that to be saved a person must not only trust Jesus as Savior, but also accept the Lord as his authority evidenced by good works. In other words, Jesus cannot be considered a person's savior without simultaneously being lord of that person's life, and good works are necessary to confirm salvation.

The opposing position is called *Free Grace theology*, which maintains that the Lordship salvation view is an indication of legalism therefore lacks graciousness. (also see *Galatianism*)

Lord's Prayer: the model for prayer that Jesus taught his disciples. This prayer serves only as an example of how one should pray, and is not a prayer to be used as a prayer *per se*. Jesus used it to show his disciples how an infinite variety of wants and requests can be compressed into a few humble petitions.

Lord's Supper: bread and wine representing the body and Blood of Christ, usually observed in church services. This is also known as *Communion* and *Eucharist*.

Lucifer: See *Satan*.

Lust: intense or unbridled sexual desire.

Mantra: the names of God, sacred words, or divine sounds invested with the power to protect, purify, and transform the individual who repeats them. A mantra received from an enlightened master is filled with the power of the master's attainment.

Martyr: a Christian who dies as a direct result of witnessing or working for Christ.

Mercy: not receiving the punishment deserved.

Metanoia: Greek word meaning "to change one's mind." This word is often translated into the word *repent* and incorrectly used as a command to stop sinning. (also see *Repent*)

Metaphor: a figure of speech in which a word or phrase that ordinarily designates one thing is used to designate another, thus making an implicit comparison.

Michael: an archangel who served as guardian over the heavenly battles related to Israel.

Minister: leader of a church.

Mission: a ministry commissioned by a religious organization to propagate its faith or carry on humanitarian work.

Monotheism: belief in one god.

Mount of Olives: a long ridge located on the east of Jerusalem, named after the olive trees that used to cover its slopes. It is holy to Jews, Christians, and Muslims; many religious traditions are tied to it.

At the foot of the mountain is the Garden of Gethsemane where Jesus stayed in Jerusalem, and it is where Jesus and his disciples retreated to pray after the Last Supper, the night before he was crucified. Gethsemane was also where the disciple Judas Iscariot betrayed Christ.

Major landmarks in this region are as follows:

- The Blessed Virgin Mary's tomb.

- In the Book of Zechariah, the Mount of Olives is identified as the place from which God will begin to redeem the dead at the end days. Therefore, many Jews want to be buried on the mountain, hence, beginning in Biblical times the mountain has been used as a cemetery for the Jews of Jerusalem.

- The Mosque of the Ascension covers the spot from which Muslims recall Jesus' ascension to Heaven.

- The Church of All Nations is at the foot of Mount of Olives. Its real name is "the Basilica of the Agony," but because the completion of the church's construction in 1924 was done through donations collected from all around the Catholic world, the name "Church of All Nations" became more. Here, according to Christian tradition, Christ prayed his last prayer before Judas revealed Jesus whereabouts to the Romans.

- The Church of Mary Magdalene is a Russian Orthodox church located on the slope of the Mount of Olives.

- Facing the Old City of Jerusalem, the sanctuary church of Dominus Flevit, which translates from Latin as "the Lord wept" was built to symbolize the tears of Christ. Here, according to the 19th chapter of Luke, Jesus, while walking toward the city, became overwhelmed by the beauty of the Second Temple and visualizing its future destruction he wept.

- Dominus Flevit is one of the newest churches in Jerusalem and during its construction archaeologists discovered artifacts dating back to the Canaanite period, as well, as tombs from both the Second Temple and Byzatine periods.

NASB: New American Standard Bible.

New Covenant: faith in the birth, death, and resurrection of Jesus Christ as Savior.

New Testament: the second part of the Bible that begins shortly before Jesus' birth and ends after his second coming.

NKJV: New King James Version of the Bible.

NLT: New Living Translation of the Bible.

Noah: the builder, navigator, and keeper of the Ark.

Non-Trinitarianism: the belief in the existence of the Father, Son, and Holy Spirit, but manifested in three separate persons. It is the opposite of *Trinitarianism*. (also see *Trinitarianism*)

Old Covenant: Jews observing laws to please God.

Old Testament: the first part of the entire Bible that begins with the creation of the world and ends at the New Testament.

Ordain: to decree.

Original sin: the first sin that Adam and Eve committed, which passed to all humans.

Orthodox: with a capital "O" it refers to Eastern Orthodox Christians, a division within the early Christian Church. When lowercase refers to the traditional and historical Christian belief that the Bible is the Word of God, written by men but inspired by the Holy Spirit. An orthodox Christian believes the original manuscripts are without error or contradiction, and that the Bible is the complete and sufficient revelation of God.

> *All Scripture is inspired by God and is useful to teach us what is true and to make us realize what is wrong in our lives. It corrects us when we are wrong and teaches us to do what is right. God uses it to prepare and equip his people to do every good work.* 2 Timothy 3:16-17

Papal infallibility: in the Roman Catholic Church, the dogma adopted by the Ecumenical Council in Rome in 1870 that the pope cannot, when speaking in his official character of supreme pontiff, err in defining a doctrine of Christian faith or rule of morals to be held by the Roman Catholic Church.

Parable: a brief story that illustrates a lesson. In Christianity, parables were used by Jesus to confuse unbelievers, but to make a point to those who have even simple faith. It is thought that unbelievers will not be able to understand the Bible and Jesus' parables unless they are *born again* and guided by the *Holy Spirit*. (also see *Born again* and *Holy Spirit*)

Parochial: in a parish or parishes.

Parochial school: a school supported and controlled by a church.

Passover: at midnight before the departure of the Israelites from Egypt, the Lord sent the Angel of Death throughout Egypt to kill the firstborn sons of all Egyptian families to show the distinction between the Egyptians' gods and the Israelites' God. Even the firstborn of every animal was killed. To keep the sons of the Israelites safe, Moses ordered each Israelite family to slaughter a pure white, innocent lamb, and to paint the blood over the doorway of the Israelite's house, which would cause the Angel of Death to pass over that home. Now, that historical event is celebrated within the Jewish faith in remembrance. Later, God gave an order that the Israelites must continue this tradition yearly. Today, the original Passover is a commemoration of life over death and the escape from bondage into freedom.

Christians observe a similar tradition by celebrating Easter, at which time Jesus is regarded as the lamb, but only once and for all. (also see *Blood of Christ* and *Blood of the Lamb*)

Pastor: leader of a church.

Patriarch: the paternal leader of a family or tribe.

Penance: to show repentance by undergoing imposed or voluntary punishment from confession to absolution. (also see *Absolution*)

Pentateuch: the first five books of Jewish and Christian Scriptures.

Pentecostal: a major denomination of Christianity.

Perseverance: the belief that a Christian cannot fall away from grace and will continue in good works until the end of his life.

Personal relationship with Jesus Christ: phrase used to describe the relationship one inherits after being born again. This intimate connection eliminates the need for intervention from church hierarchy. (also see *Born again*)

Pharisees: a prominent, sect of devout Jews during Christ's time, reputed to be experts in Jewish law and traditions. Their characteristic teachings included belief in oral as well as written law, resurrection of the human body, belief in the existence of a spirit world, immortality of the soul, predestination, as well as future rewards and punishments based upon works. They aggressively opposed Jesus' teachings. Jesus was very critical of their legalistic attitude, especially when it lacked kindness for mankind. The Pharisees were constantly trying to disprove Jesus, and plotted his death.

Philistines: The Philistines are prominent in the Old Testament as Israel's worst enemy, mentioned in the Old Testament more than two hundred times. The Philistines were a powerful people who inhabited the southern coast of Canaan; their territory is called Philistia in later contexts. This dominant people made recurrent invasions against the Hebrews, resulting in a continuous war. They maintained their independence until David subdued them, at which time the Philistines saw their powerful position deteriorate.

Polytheism: the belief in many gods.

Prayer warrior: one who is diligent in prayer.

Predestination: See *Unconditional election.*

Prodigal: reckless and wasteful.

Prodigal Son: Jesus' parable of the Prodigal Son is found in Luke 15:11-32. The Prodigal Son is a young man living on his father's estate, but who is dissatisfied with his uninteresting life. So he ventures into the world only to end up eating with pigs. The Prodigal Son represents those humans who reject God, and the father of the Prodigal Son represents God.

In telling the story, Jesus identifies himself with God and his forgiving attitude by welcoming his son home, imposing no punishment, and restoring the son's portion of the father's estate. The significance of this parable is to describe the graciousness of those who accept Jesus as Savior. Once lost, but now found. This parable summarizes Christianity.

Propitiation: a gesture of reconciliation to gain or regain the favor of someone or something. For the Christian, the propitiation for sin was the shed Blood of Jesus on the Cross.

Proselytize: the attempt to convert someone to a particular way of thinking or acting.

Purgatory: The definition of Purgatory in the Roman Catholic Encyclopedia is, "A place or condition of temporal punishment for those who, departing this life in God's grace, are not entirely free from venial faults, or have not fully paid the satisfaction due to their transgressions."

This sounds fair, except for one thing: Jesus Christ died for all of the sins of humankind on the Cross. He took all of the punishment we deserve. Stating that there is something we must do to pay for our transgressions is blasphemy. The belief in a place or condition in which a dead Christian must be cleaned-up is not Biblical. Claiming that a Christian must suffer for sins after death is contrary to everything the Bible says about salvation.

The concept of a place where the dead are imprisoned for cleansing dates to before Christ when many people would pray to the gods for those who had died. Not only is this continued today in Catholicism, but also in Mormonism, and Judaism.

Any religion that claims to be Christian, yet teaches cleansing following death, misunderstands the totality and finality of Christ's death. Furthermore, any Christian belief system that teaches that anything must be done either while here on earth or after one's death does not understand that Christ died for all people and all sins.

I ask you this: Which sins didn't Jesus die for? If we must atone, suffer, sacrifice, or tithe for forgiveness, then we are boldly stating that Jesus' death was not a perfect, complete, and sufficient sacrifice.

Rapture: at the time of the second coming of Jesus Christ, Christians will be raptured, or taken from the earth directly to Heaven, without dying first.

Reconciliation: the term used to describe what was accomplished when Christ died on the Cross, and the fact that his shed Blood satisfied God's judgment. Christ's Blood reconciled us.

Redemption: See *Salvation.*

Regeneration: the term used to identify the act of being born again and the internal change in which the Christian receives Spiritual life in addition to his or her physical (carnal) life.

Religion: from the Latin word *religare,* meaning "to tie or bind."

Repent: derived from the Greek word *metanoia,* meaning "to change one's mind." The word repent is often incorrectly used as a command to "stop sinning." (also see *Metanoia*)

Replacement theology (supersessionism): a theological doctrine that teaches that the Church has replaced Israel in God's plan. In other words, God has replaced Israel as his chosen people with the Christian Church, and has no future plans for Israel. (also see *Dispensationalism*)

Resurrection: Jesus Christ rising from being physically dead following his crucifixion.

Reverence: showing extreme respect and obedience.

Reverend: deserving of reverence. This is often used as the title of the leader of a church; however, many Christians believe that only God is worthy of this title.

Rhema: what God is saying to you personally. It is the opposite of *logos*, which is the written word and not a direct revelation from God to you. (also see *Logos*)

Righteousness: holy living based on God's standard of obedience.

Sabbatarian: one who favors a strict observance of the Sabbath.

Sabbath: derived from the Hebrew root *abat*, which means "to cease, rest." The term *sabbath* has evolved to refer to the seventh day of the week, named in the Ten Commandments as the day of rest, so observed by Jews and a few Christians on Saturday. The first day of the week, Sunday, is generally observed as the Sabbath by Christians.

Sabbath rest: a term used to describe "eternal" rest in Christ. This rest quiets a guilty conscience, stills troubling thoughts, and gives hope in desperation. In Christ, we find complete rest. Not to be confused with "resting" on a particular day of the week in observance with a religious act.

Sacrament: a ceremony that Christians believe brings God's blessing to those who partake in it. Generally, in Protestantism, these are baptism and communion. In Catholicism, the seven sacraments are baptism, communion, the Eucharist, matrimony, penance, holy orders, and extreme unction.

Sadducees: a prominent Jewish religious sect during the time of Christ. Their beliefs included acceptance of the law, rejection of oral tradition, denial of bodily resurrection, immortality of the soul, and existence of a spirit world. The Sadducees were a relatively small group, but they generally held the high priesthood. They actively denounced John the Baptist, Christ, and the Apostolic Church.

Saint: Biblically speaking, saints are the body of Christ; all Christians are considered saints.

Salt and Light: Jesus tells his disciples in Matthew 5 that they are to be the salt of the earth and the light of the world. Salt seasons food, and light points the way to the truth.

Salvation: the experience of being saved from eternal punishment in Hell by trusting in Jesus' finished work as payment for all sins – past, present, and future.

Sanctification: the growth process of the believer by lessening sinful behavior and living one's life by yielding to the guidance of the Holy Spirit. This process begins after a person has been justified, and is not instantaneous as is justification. It is a combination of the saved person's efforts with the counseling of the Holy Spirit. Sanctification is the result of a Christian becoming a *disciple* (follower) of Christ subsequent to being born Spiritually.

It is important to realize there are many disciples of Christ who have not accepted him as Savior, and thus have not been born Spiritually. Following the moral teachings of Jesus Christ is not the method for being born Spiritually. A person must actually agree that the death and resurrection of Jesus is the only means of receiving eternal life. Salvation is by faith and not by works.

Sanctification, or lack thereof, has no effect on justification. In other words, if a person fails to follow the guidance of the Holy Spirit and lives a life that lacks Christian deeds, that person continues to be justified.

Satan: from the Hebrew word meaning "the accuser." There are no verses or passages in the Bible that prove Lucifer was Satan. However, there are verses that make this presumption. In Christianity, Satan, the Devil, and Lucifer are known as a fallen angel that is evil and influences the thinking and actions of humans and has since the beginning of time.

Saved: is to receive eternal life in Heaven, thus avoiding the fires of Hell.

Savior: one who rescues another from harm, danger, or loss. In Christianity, Jesus is the Savior.

Scriptures: another name for the Bible, both Old and New Testaments.

Second Coming: Christ's first coming took place 2,000 years ago, and lasted 33 years. At that time, he promised to return. Views about the nature of this return vary among Christian denominations.

Secular: worldly; anything not spiritual in nature.

Seeker-sensitive church: a method of attracting people to a church using marketing techniques that appeal to the masses, even though the method may or may not be in conjunction with what is thought to be Scriptural.

Septuagint: Greece dominated the Mediterranean region in the centuries before Christ's birth, so Greek became the language of the entire region. The Jews of

Alexandria translated the Scriptures from the original Hebrew into Greek, called the Septuagint.

The Septuagint was a source of the Old Testament for early Christians during the first few centuries AD. Because many early Christians spoke and read Greek, they depended on the Septuagint for most of their understanding of the Old Testament. The New Testament writers relied on the Septuagint, as a majority of Old Testament quotes cited in the New Testament are quoted directly from the Septuagint. The Septuagint is still utilized today by a few denominations.

The Septuagint contains all 39 books of the canonized Old Testament, plus certain Apocryphal books. The term *Apocrypha* generally refers to the set of ancient Jewish writings written during the period between the last book in the Jewish scriptures, Malachi, and the arrival of Jesus Christ. The Apocryphal books include Judith, Tobit, Baruch, Sirach (or Ecclesiasticus), the Wisdom of Solomon, First and Second Maccabees, the two Books of Esdras, additions to the Book of Esther, additions to the Book of Daniel, and the Prayer of Manasseh.

The Apocryphal books were included in the Septuagint for historical reasons, but are not recognized by Protestant Christians or Orthodox Jews as being inspired by God. Most reformed scholars believe the New Testament writers never quoted from the Apocrypha, and that the Apocrypha was never considered part of the canonical Jewish scripture. However, the Roman Catholic Church and the Orthodox churches include the Apocrypha in their Bible, excluding the books of Esdras and the Prayer of Manasseh.

Sepulchre: a burial vault or tomb.

Sheol: See *Hades* and *Hell.*

Sin: an offense against religious or moral law. When it is something deliberate in action, such as murder or adultery, it is referred to as a *sin of commission.* If it is something we should have done but did not do, such as feeding a poor person, it is referred to as a *sin of omission.*

Sin unto death: the belief that God will take home early an individual who is saved because that person continues purposeful sinning.

Sola: Latin meaning "alone" or "only." (also see *Five Solas*)

Soteriology: theology dealing with the doctrine of salvation.

Soul: the inner person consisting of will, mind, and spirit.

Soul sleep: a belief embraced by a very few Christians who interpret the Scriptures to say that after a person dies, his or her soul sleeps until the resurrection. In the Bible portrayal of sleeping following one's death, it does not literally mean sleep, as we commonly understand sleep to be. The Bible is clear: At the moment of a Christian's death, his or her soul is present with the Lord for eternity. However, although our soul is in Heaven, our body will remain dormant until the resurrection, at which time it will be awakened and transformed into a new eternal body. Those who have rejected Jesus Christ as Savior receive eternal damnation.

Sovereign: supreme.

Speaking in tongues: In the early church, the ministers were given a special ability to vocalize a fluent speech-like utterance. The first occurrence was by the disciples on the day of Pentecost, as described in the book of Acts. It is believed by some that the disciples were not speaking human languages; they were speaking in unknown tongues. But God enabled those whose hearts were opened to understand what the disciples were saying. Recently, the Charismatic movement has brought speaking in tongues to the forefront, primarily by Pentecostalism. But there is considerable debate within Christianity as to its validity. It is claimed by a few to be one of God's special Spiritual gifts. However, this proclamation is one of the most controversial and vigorously disputed by many in Christianity. Opponents say speaking in tongues has no purpose and is gibberish, but proponents claim it is a necessary proof the indwelling of the Holy Spirit.

Spirit: the part of a human associated with the mind, will, and feelings.

Spiritual gifts: special gifts given to Christians for the purpose of furthering God's work and building up the Church. These gifts include wisdom, knowledge, faith, healing, miraculous powers, prophecy, Spiritual discernment, speaking in tongues, interpretation of tongues, and so forth. Many theologians believe these gifts exist today; however, many believe they ended with the death of the last apostle.

Synagogue: the building or place of assembly used by Jewish communities primarily for religious worship.

Syncretism: the reconciliation or union of conflicting beliefs.

Take up your cross: a phrase used to describe the act of giving up one's personal, worldly desires, and living for Jesus.

Talmud: the most significant collection of the Jewish oral traditions interpreting the Torah.

Temptation: as used in Christianity, temptation is a tool of the adversary to lure the Christian into sin. The first occurrence of temptation in the recorded history of man may be found in the first seven verses of the book of Genesis in the Holy Bible, where the serpent (Satan) successfully tempts the first woman (Eve) and the first man (Adam) to sin. The last occurrence of temptation in the recorded history of man may also be found in the Bible, where after the millennial kingdom of Christ upon earth Satan will successfully tempt the nations to rise up against Christ, only to have his rebellion crushed. Most scholars do not consider temptation a sin.

Ten Commandments: found in the Old Testament in the book of Exodus, chapter 20. They were given directly by God to the people of Israel at Mount Sinai after he had delivered them from slavery in Egypt.

Testament: a written document that serves as evidence of something.

Testimony: in Christianity, a testimony is considered a declaration of when, why, and how one trusted Jesus Christ as their Savior. (also see *Witnessing*)

Theistic evolution: belief that there is a God, who created the foundation of the world, but he allowed an evolutionary process to take over and life eventually emerged. Theistic evolutionists usually believe the Earth is billions of years old and that many creatures lived, died, and became extinct long before the entrance of mankind. This belief system conflicts with the Book of Genesis.

Theology: the study of religious faith, practice, and experience; used particularly to describe the study of God and of his relationship to the world.

Theophany: God in human form.

Thy will be done: when used in prayer, it is proclaiming that the one praying is willing to accept God's will – regardless of the outcome.

Tithing: in religion, the act of giving a *tithe* (meaning one-tenth) of one's income, as required by the law in the Old Testament Church. (also see *Free will offering*)

Topical Bible: a reference book that lists major Bible themes with corresponding chapters and verses.

Torah: in the narrowest sense, it is the first five books of the Bible, sometimes called the Pentateuch. In its broadest sense, it is the entire body of Jewish teachings.

Total depravity: See *Unconditional election.*

Transubstantiation: the belief that Christ's body and Blood are literally present in the Eucharist. This is primarily a Roman Catholic belief. (also see *Consubstantiation*)

Trine immersion: a form of baptism in which the candidate is immersed three consecutive times, in the name of the Father, the Son, and the Holy Ghost.

Trinitarianism: believes in the triune nature of God: God (the Father), Jesus Christ (the Son), and the Holy Spirit (the Counselor). It was adopted as the official belief of Christians, and it is still considered to be one of the fundamental foundations of Christianity.

Trinity: the triune nature of God: God (the Father), Jesus Christ (the Son), and the Holy Spirit (the Counselor) are one.

Triune nature of man:

1. Body – flesh and blood
2. Soul – who we are
3. Spirit – that which governs our body and soul following our regeneration- we are physically born Spiritually dead

Ubiquitous: existing or being everywhere, or at all places at the same time.

Unconditional election: a controversial Calvinistic belief in Christian theology, which states that because of humankind's sin, a person will never seek God by her or his own volition, so God chooses those whom he wants, although they may come kicking and screaming. However, because it is God's choice and not man's, God's grace is so irresistible that those whom he chooses cannot refuse. Calvinists believe God knew before he created the world who he would choose, meaning that a person's behavior has nothing to do with his or her salvation. Consequently, once a person is saved, she or he is always saved.

This Calvinistic position is in contrast to the Arminian doctrine of *conditional election,* which is the belief that God chooses only those who he forsees will have faith in Christ as their Savior. (also see *Conditional election*)

Unleavened: bread made without yeast or agents that will cause it to rise or become soft. Many believe that unleavened bread must be used to celebrate the Lord's Supper, but according to New Testament Scriptures, this is debatable. (also see *leavened*)

Unlimited atonement: the term used to state that Christ died for all people, whether or not they believe in him.

Venerate: to regard with respect or heartfelt deference.

Virginal conception: in Christianity, the virgin birth of Jesus.

Vulgate: a Latin version of the Scriptures, used as the standard for the services of the Roman Catholic Church.

White Throne Judgment: See *Judgment, The Great White Throne.*

Wineskins: usually made from goatskin, these were used as water containers and to ferment grape juice.

Witnessing: in Christianity, the act of sharing one's heartfelt faith in Christ, what he or she has personally done to change his or her life, what he or she has done to further Jesus' ministry. Christian witnessing is what spread the Gospel through the entire Roman Empire within a generation. The responsibility of Christian witnessing is still with us. 2 Corinthians 5:18 tells us that God has given us the task of reconciling the unsaved to him (winning the lost to Christ).

Works: behavior. In Christianity, it is used to describe the good works one does for God and mankind. Works are not a requirement for salvation.

Worship: act of revering a divine being or supernatural power, such as God.

WWJD: An acronym that represents the question *What Would Jesus Do?* Used to help a Christian make a decision based on how Jesus would probably handle a particular situation.

Yahweh: a name for the God of the Old Testament as transliterated from the Hebrew consonants YHWH.

Zion: a term that most often designates the land of Israel and its capital, Jerusalem.

Zionism: the national movement for the return of the Jewish people to their homeland and the resumption of Jewish sovereignty in the land of Israel. Jews of all persuasions, left and right, religious and secular, joined to form the Zionist movement and worked together toward these goals. Disagreements led to rifts. But ultimately, the common goal of a Jewish state in its ancient homeland was attained. Nathan Birnbaum coined the term Zionism in 1890.

Though generally agreed upon, there are many Jewish movements, groups, and organizations whose ideology regarding Zionism and the so-called State of Israel is that of the Torah – that any form of Zionism is heresy, and that the existence of the so-called State of Israel is illegitimate.

Index

NOTE: Because the theme of this book is primarily Christian salvation, words such as Christian, salvation, Jesus, and God are not included in the index because they appear on almost every page. Instead, we have chosen words that may be difficult for the reader to find without an index. The decision was made to omit many of the frequently used words to conserve space and paper.

Selected Scripture Index

Thank You

I want to take this opportunity to thank all of those people who demonstrated an interest in what I was doing and gave me encouragement, suggestions, advice, and prayers that were so needed and appreciated to complete this book. They are (in alphabetical order):

Barb Amburgery
Beth Held
Bill Ertle
D. Lynn Edgar-Smith
Dad and Mom
Darryl Swank
David Berkowitz
David Kirk
Donna Kemp
Dr. Harold Wilmington
Dr. Meg Miller
Elizabeth Smith
Jack Levine
Jane Medor
Jim Swank
Jody Ripple Snively
Joy Hawkey
Joyce Stone
Karen Silvestri
Kay Brauneller
Len and Faye Andersen
Linda Welch
Loveda Finley
Melissa Finley Nino
Nancy Latham
Richard Perks
Sandy Golden
Steve Brown
The late Norma Gerlach
The late Tami Finley
Thomas Finley

Tracy Pancione
Tyrone Page
Wendy Bernstein
Whitney Parks

I would like to give special thanks to Tom, Melissa, and Lynn who gave me extraordinary incentive to finish this project. You are the pride of my life.

I also want to especially thank those hundreds of people who I have talked with throughout the years who are under the false belief that *good people go to Heaven and that bad people go to Hell.* I pray this book will enlighten you regarding the purpose and truth of Jesus' death, burial, and resurrection. Jesus did for you what you cannot do for yourself.

If there are any individuals that I overlooked, I apologize. I am 65 years old and can't remember what I had for breakfast today, or if I even ate breakfast.

I WANT YOU!

Made in the USA
San Bernardino, CA
15 November 2013